KENYA

World Travel Guide

Author: **Marina Carle**
Translation: **Gila Walker**
Additional text: **Gila Walker** and **Penelope Poulton**
Editor: **Lisa Davidson-Petty**
Photo credits:
Hoa-Qui: De Wilde, pp. 124-125, 163; D. Huot, pp. 32, 136, 158; D. Lainé, pp. 74, 133; M. Orivel, pp. 15, 40-41, 79, 111; C. Pavard, pp. 63, 129, 187; Renaudeau, pp. 23, 98-99, 103; C. Vaisse, pp. 10, 28, 59.
Stock Image: C. Bouvier, p. 151; C. Cavignaux, p. 87; M. Gunther, pp. 54-55, 116-117, 155, 171; A. H., p. 95.

This edition published in Great Britain by **Bartholomew**, 12 Duncan Street, Edinburgh, EH9 1TA.

Bartholomew is a Division of HarperCollins*Publishers*.

This guide is adapted from *au Kenya*, published by Hachette Guides de voyage, 1989.

© Hachette Guides de voyage, Paris, 1991. First edition.
English translation © Hachette Guides de voyage, Paris, 1991.
Maps © Hachette Guides de voyage, Paris, 1991.

British Library Cataloguing in Publication Data
Carle, Marina
Kenya. — (Bartholomew world travel guide).
1. Kenya — Visitors' guides
I. Title
916.762044

ISBN 0-7028-1287-0

Printed in France by Aubin Imprimeur Ligugé, Poitiers
24/1285/6 — Collection 12 — Édition 92

·Bartholomew·

KENYA

World Travel Guide

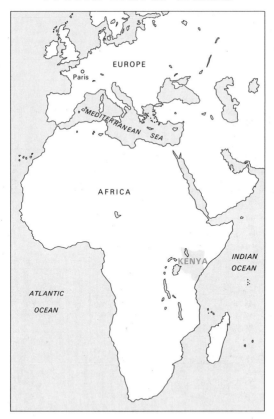

Bartholomew
A Division of HarperCollins*Publishers*

HOW TO USE YOUR GUIDE

- For background information, read the sections 'Planning Your Trip' p. 11, 'Practical Information' p. 15, 'Kenya in the Past' p. 33 and 'Kenya Today' p. 53 and 'The People of Kenya' p. 67.

- The rest of the guide is divided into chapters discussing either **cities** (Nairobi, Mombasa) or **regions** (Western Kenya, Eastern Kenya). Each chapter includes sections pointing out what to see and provides practical information about the particular area (accommodation, useful addresses, food, etc.).

- There are **maps** throughout the guide. To locate recommended sites on the city maps, refer to the map coordinates printed in blue in the text. Example: C3.

- Practical advice and information about people, places and events can be located quickly by referring to the 'Index' p. 201. For further information about Kenya, consult the 'Suggested reading' section at the back of the book.

SYMBOLS USED

Places of interest, monuments, museums

***	Exceptional
**	Very interesting
*	Interesting

Hotels classification

▲▲▲▲	Luxury hotel
▲▲▲	First-class hotel
▲▲	Moderately priced hotel
▲	Inexpensive hotel
①	Restaurant
②	Parking lot
③	Tennis courts
④	Swimming pool
⑤	Park

Restaurants classification

E	Expensive
R	Reasonable
I	Inexpensive

MAPS

▬ CONTENTS

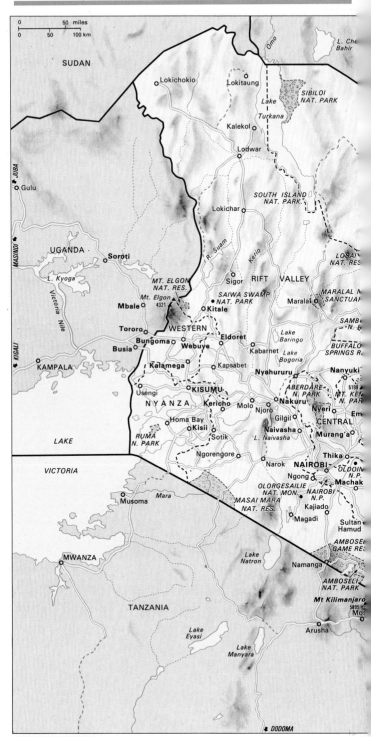

GENERAL MAP OF KENYA

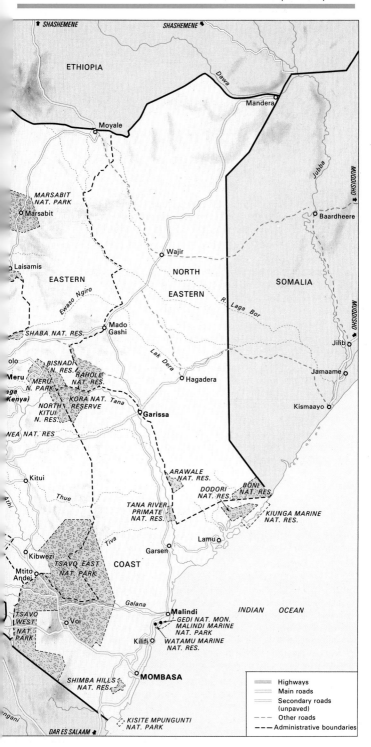

INTRODUCTION TO KENYA

More tourists come to Kenya each year than to any other African country. They are entranced, above all, by the beauty of its landscape and the abundant wildlife.

The safari (derived from the Swahili word for journey) has become practically synonymous with Kenya for adventure-seekers around the world. Though hunting safaris were the fashion earlier in the century, today conservation is in vogue; the result of the perfect shot on today's safari is no longer a dead animal but a beautiful photograph.

The country offers a kaleidoscope of memorable images. Parks are filled with innumerable species of animals, and heavenly beaches are shaded by coconut trees.

In Kenya, you can languish in the sun, swim in the warm, ocean water and plunge into a universe of coral reef and multi-coloured fish. All year round in Kenya's parks and reserves you can see an enormous variety of animal life, from the buffalo to the stealthy leopard.

During their periods of migration, thousands of animals invade the plains that stretch along the Tanzanian border. You can sometimes encounter wildlife outside the areas set aside to protect it, while within the reserves you can traverse long distances without seeing the slightest sign of life. The animals are free to roam where they please and they choose pastures and hunting areas that suit them; inside the parks they will avoid the roads and approaching cars whenever possible and they won't respect the limits if conditions outside suit them better. That's one reason you shouldn't limit your trip to just the Kenyan parks.

Traveling in Kenya also offers the opportunity to discover a multi-faceted society full of contrasting images: the silhouette of a Masai carrying a spear; a Kikuyu woman with an enormous load on her back, supported by a leather band to her forehead; the young woman in an air-conditioned office in the capital dictating to her secretary; the half-naked fisherman on Turkana Lake — Kenya offers all these images and more, of its people, wildlife and landscape.

Every region of the country is worth visiting. You can take the plane from Nairobi to many of the more popular sites. But by far the best way to travel is by land. You will need a bit of patience and endurance to reach certain parts of the country, but the rewards are worth the effort.

The gradual climb from Mombasa, at sea level, to Kikuyu country, at an altitude of 6000 ft/2000 m, can only be fully appreciated by car. Likewise, the dizzying effect of coming to the edge of a forest and discovering the vertiginous heights of the Rift Valley is an overwhelming experience that can be savoured only when on the ground.

Here the sculpted lush greenery of the tea plantations in the highlands gives way to the parched earth of the savannah that vibrates to the hooves of antelopes and zebra. Elsewhere the scattered dwarf plants of the sweltering plains cede to blossoming thickets, fragrant coffee, orange groves or giant, moss-covered trees.

If you study plants or birds, you will discover a wealth of species to observe. If you like sports, you can take advantage of a variety of activities ranging from fishing and mountain climbing to scuba diving and walking.

Kenya is a country of so many possibilities and such subtle variations that no one can expect to see it all in a single visit. It is better not to try. Take your time and choose well... Don't forget — you can always come back.

Kenya in brief

Location: Situated in East Africa, Kenya is bordered on the south-east by the Indian Ocean and on the east by Somalia; to the north lie Ethiopia and the Sudan; Uganda is to the west and Tanzania to the south.

Climate: Equatorial, though cooler at higher altitudes.

Land Area: 224,960 sq mi/582,646 sq km.

Coastal length: 232 mi/600 km.

Maximum altitude: 17,060 ft/5 200 m (Mount Kenya).

Capital: Nairobi (population 1,300,000); other important cities include Mombasa (300,000), Kisumu (150,000) and Nakuru (48,000).

Government: Independent member of the Commonwealth under a republican regime. The President (currently Daniel arap Moi) is elected by universal suffrage for a five-year term. The National Assembly is controlled by a single party: Kenya African National Union (KANU).

Population: 24 million (1989 estimate), including 80,000 Asians, 44,000 Europeans and 40,000 Arabs.

Official languages: English and Swahili.

Religions: 54% of Kenyans observe traditional African (animistic) rites, 37% are Christians (22% Catholic), 8% Moslems and 1% Hindus.

Principal resources: Agricultural production, in particular coffee, tea, corn and sorghum.

Monetary unit: Kenya shilling (Ksh).

PLANNING YOUR TRIP

WHEN TO GO

In general, the best time to visit Kenya is from September to March, although your decision will depend on the activities and regions that interest you. There are two rainy seasons: the 'long rains' from late March to mid-June and the 'short rains' from the end of October to early December; but Kenya's climate is mild enough to guarantee a pleasant trip whatever the season. January and February, the driest months, are ideal for mountain hiking or trout fishing. On the other hand, you might like to witness the exciting ruminant migrations, especially that of the wildebeest, which take place sometime between the end of June and the middle of September. The season for ocean fishing lasts from November to March when the gentle north-east monsoon is blowing.

In Lamu, the weather in October and November is pleasant, while elsewhere it is cooler and wetter. From July to October, temperatures in Nairobi can range from 68° F/20° C during the day to 14° F/−10° C at night.

Average temperatures (°F/°C)

		Jan	Mar	May	July	Sept	Nov
Mombasa	min	73/23	75/24	72/22	70/21	70/21	73/23
	max	90/32	90/32	84/29	82/28	84/29	88/31
Nairobi	min	55/13	57/14	59/15	54/12	55/13	57/14
	max	79/26	81/27	75/24	73/23	79/26	77/25

GETTING THERE

Plane

Kenya has two international airports: **Jomo Kenyatta** in Nairobi and **Moi** in Mombasa; most flights from Europe and the United States arrive in Nairobi. Regular scheduled flights link Kenya to major cities throughout the world (Air France, Alitalia, Aeroflot, British Airways, Egyptair, Iberia, Kenya Airways, KLM, Lufthansa, PanAm, and Swissair). Contact your local travel agent for up-to-date information about air travel to Kenya.

A multitude of organized trips and package tours are available for every possible taste, ranging from one week in Nairobi to extended safaris into Northern Kenya or a relaxing vacation at a beach resort. Travel agents can provide you with full documentation and details.

A young Samburu woman.

Jomo Kenyatta International Airport is 8.7 mi/14 km south-east of Nairobi along the Mombasa road. You can take a taxi to the city centre. Be sure to agree on a price with the driver before getting in: approximately Ksh 350 in 1989. Kenya Airways offers its passengers bus service to the airport for Ksh 40. Departures every hour until 8pm from the Kenya Airways Terminal, Koinäge St., Nairobi (☎ 29291 or 29271).

Before leaving Kenya, make sure you have $20 to pay the airport tax, in foreign currency; Kenya shillings are not accepted.

Car

Getting to Kenya by car is a difficult undertaking that requires both time and a sturdy four-wheel-drive vehicle. You can start your African trek from Algeria and pass through Niger, Nigeria, Cameroon, Central African Republic and the Sudan, or choose Egypt as your point of departure and reach Kenya via the Sudan.

Don't underestimate the problems you might encounter in many of the countries you'll pass through; besides the often unstable political conditions, your car and supplies can attract unwanted attention in regions afflicted by drought and famine.

Drivers' license and insurance

Your national driver's license is valid in Kenya for 90 days if you get it endorsed in Nairobi upon arrival at the airport. You can't do that, of course, if you enter Kenya by road. In that case, an international driving license will suffice.

To insure your car, you can get a temporary membership in Kenya's Automobile Association (AA). Membership entitles you to free repairs for minor breakdowns by the AA's repair vehicles or in one of their 50 or so garages throughout the country. Most car rental agencies offer AA membership. You will then also have access to the health services of Flying Doctor (see p. 13). For information, contact Automobile Association, Hurlingham Shopping Center, Box 40087, Hurlingham, Nairobi; ☎ 72 3195 (emergency service). There are also AA offices in Mombasa, Kisumu and Malindi.

▬ ENTRY FORMALITIES

Passport and visa

You must have a valid passport. A visa is also required for citizens from most countries, including Canada, Great Britain and the United States. Visas are issued for three-month periods and can be renewed in Kenya.

Vaccinations

No vaccinations are required; it is a good idea, however, to be vaccinated against yellow fever, polio, tetanus and diphtheria before you leave home. Kenya has relatively good sanitary and hospital facilities compared to other African countries; nevertheless it is better to take precautions.

Though cholera epidemics are rare, check with your local public health service before your departure. Remember that a ten-day interval is necessary between yellow fever and cholera vaccinations.

Malaria is endemic in Kenya, especially at lower altitudes. Anti-malaria medication should be started two to four weeks before you arrive in Kenya and kept up for one month after returning home.

Customs

You can bring into Kenya your personal belongings, cameras, unused film, one pair of binoculars, one typewriter, 200 cigarettes or 50 cigars, two bottles of wine or one bottle of liquor and one bottle of perfume. It is advisable to have receipts for all electrical and electronic equipment.

The only export restrictions concern protected wildlife and plants. Ivory, coral, shells, animal skin or fur, and bracelets made of elephant or giraffe skin are illegal items and will be confiscated by customs officials upon departure.

Because it is illegal to leave the country with Kenyan currency, you should change what you have before going through customs. Officials always ask departing passengers if they have any currency.

HEALTH

Insurance

You can become a temporary member of Flying Doctor, a philanthropic association with headquarters at Wilson Airport. In the event of illness or a serious accident, Flying Doctor will assure your immediate transport — free of charge — to the closest hospital or, if necessary, to Nairobi. The association also has a medical team capable of offering emergency treatment on the spot throughout the country, ☎ 33 6886 or 50 1280.

WHAT TO TAKE

If you're going on a safari, you will usually be allowed only a small piece of luggage. Bring along a cotton or jeans outfit (pants and jacket) and a hat and large scarf to protect you from the sun and dust on the back roads. Pack some warm woolen clothing for the evenings, when it can become chilly everywhere except along the coast.

Formal evening dress is required for dinner in many of Nairobi's top hotels.

For the mountains, a good pair of hiking boots is recommended and for the bush, sturdy walking shoes. Elsewhere, sandals suffice. Avoid walking barefoot: any cut, bite or sting can easily get infected in the dust and humidity. Along the coral reefs, your feet should be protected by rubber sandals, tennis shoes or flippers. To observe sea life, bring along your scuba equipment.

You will find it useful to have a sun-protection cream and sunglasses, preferably designed to keep the dust out of your eyes. Eye drops and an anti-indigestion remedy might also come in handy. Finally, don't forget to bring a supply of any medicine you take regularly.

MONEY

Currency

The monetary unit is the Kenya shilling (written as Ksh), which is divided into 100 cents. Notes are issued in denominations of Ksh 200, 100, 10 and 5. Coins of 1 Ksh, 50, 10 and 5 cents are available. The first two are made of nickel, the latter two of copper. The Kenya shilling is referred to as a bob (always in the singular; for example, 5 bob).

Prices are also indicated in Kenya pounds (K£): while the pound does not legally exist, it is the equivalent of Ksh 20. It is a good idea to change your money at the airport on arrival. This saves you long waits in town.

Credit Cards

American Express and Diners Club cards are accepted almost everywhere. The Barclaycard-Visa is also widely used. Since thefts are not uncommon, leave your cash and valuables in the hotel's safe-deposit boxes.

Budget

Your budget will, of course, depend on your style of living. In Nairobi, a room in a top-rate hotel can cost as much as Ksh 1200. The price of a night plus breakfast in one of Nairobi's more modest hotels averages Ksh 280 for a clean, single room with a shower and toilet. In Nairobi's restaurants the price range is just as wide. Count on spending between

Ksh 60 and Ksh 100 for a reasonable meal in a decent, if not luxurious, restaurant.

Places to stay in the game parks and in the less accessible regions of the country are costly. The 'tented camps' offer much more than simple tents. They include private bathrooms and lavatories and are often as expensive as the lodges. Outside the parks, lodging for one person in a tented camp can cost up to Ksh 2000.

Accommodation and restaurants in cities like Lamu are much cheaper. A double room in many 'lodgings' is about Ksh 90 a night (and some lodgings will allow tourists to sleep on the balcony or the roof for Ksh 50). A restaurant meal averages Ksh 30.

Transport costs also vary: buses are cheap, but airplane travel and car rental are expensive. The price of a one-way airplane ticket from Nairobi to Lamu is about Ksh 2000. You can rent a car for a week for about Ksh 2280 plus Ksh 4.50 per kilometre, or Ksh 6500 with unlimited mileage. A litre of superior gasoline costs Ksh 10. Renting a car can be an economical means of getting around if four people chip in. Camping, instead of staying at hotels, will cut costs even more.

▬ BEFORE YOU LEAVE: SOME USEFUL ADDRESSES

Australia

High Commission
POB 1990, Canberra ACT 2601, ☎ (062) 49 6911.

Canada

High Commission
Suite 600, Gillin Bldg., 141 Laurier Ave. W., Ottawa, Ontario K1P 5J3, ☎ (613) 563 1736.

Great Britain

High Commission
24-25 New Bond St., London W1Y 9HD, ☎ (71) 636 2371.

Tourist office
13 New Burlington St., London W1X 1FF, ☎ (71) 839 4477

United States

Embassy
2249 R St. N.W., Washington D.C. 20008, ☎ (202) 387 6101.

Consulates and tourist offices
60 E. 56th St., New York, NY 10022, ☎ (212) 486 1300; Suite 111-12, 9100 Wilshire Blvd., Dohen Plaza, Beverly Hills, CA 90212, ☎ (213) 274 6635.

PRACTICAL INFORMATION

▬ *ACCOMMODATION*

Kenya has an extensive system of accommodation, including luxury hotels, youth hostels, bed-and-breakfasts and campgrounds. Reservations are not necessary in the big cities where there are always vacancies. In the parks, be sure to book your lodge, *banda* or campsite in advance.

At Tsavo East, one of the lodges where animals can be observed around the pool.

Hotels

Nairobi has hotels in all categories, offering a wide range of amenities and prices. Many of the capital's hotels are not air conditioned since it is never very hot in the mountainous regions of the country. On the other hand, even the most inexpensive hotel has either a mosquito net around the bed or a screen at the window.

Lodges

There are lodges in each of Kenya's parks and reserves. Typically, the lodge has a central building with a dining room, sitting room, reception hall and shop, detached pavilions with rooms and a swimming pool. Because you'll be close to either a river or a pool you can observe the wildlife from your lodge. Prices usually include all meals; if you prefer to eat lunch in the park, the lodge will provide a picnic. Many lodges have gas pumps, reserved for their clientele, but they can be used in emergencies by other drivers.

Bandas

An alternative form of accommodation in parks is the *banda*; a bungalow with beds, shower and cooking facilities for up to four people. Eating and cooking utensils are supplied, but the bedding must be rented. A grocery store is on the premises. *Bandas* are found along the coast and in other places like Naro Moru, near Mount Kenya.

Boarding and Lodgings

These inexpensive establishments (often called B&Ls) offering bed and breakfast are found throughout the country. Some are clean and well-kept, but others can be really insalubrious.

Youth hostels

Similar to the B&Ls, youth hostels are often located in picturesque settings.

You can get information about the **Kenya Youth Hostels Association** (KYHA) from the Hon. Gen. Secretary, POB 48661, Nairobi, or the warden, Nairobi YH, ☎ 72 3012.

Campsites

Campsites are usually situated near a lodge. They offer neither sanitary facilities nor running water, but by paying the entrance fee to the lodge pool you can use the showers and toilets there. Since driving in the parks is forbidden after 6:30pm, campers cannot take advantage of dining facilities at the lodge after that hour. There are no groceries in camping areas.

Tips for campers

● Avoid setting up your tent under a tree: a variety of unwanted objects fall from trees, including pine needles, sticky sap and bird droppings. A lone tree can also attract lightning during a storm.

● Don't camp near a dried-up riverbed: it can fill up in no time.

● Before choosing a site for your tent, check the ground to make sure that there are no animal footprints and that you are not camped on an elephant track, for example.

● Never put on your shoes without first shaking them out to ensure there are no scorpions inside.

● Be aware that while mosquitos become less bothersome above 6600 ft/2000 m, the nights at that altitude can be extremely cold.

- Avoid leaving buckets of used water outside in dry regions where they can attract swarms of bees. If you are attacked by bees, jump into a lake or river; if there are none nearby, run into the nearest thicket. Get medical assistance immediately if you have been stung badly.
- Never bring a dog on a safari; dogs are choice lion food.
- Don't wander away from the circle of tents at night, when wild animals roam about; remember that nothing distinguishes the campsites from the surrounding bush.
- Don't leave refuse behind: either burn it or bury it.
- When you come to a village, ask *hodi?* meaning May I come in? before entering a house.
- If you want to camp in the Highlands, where the population is dense, always make sure you know whose land you're on, and ask permission.
- A camp fire will often attract a little group of people probably armed with *pangas* (a kind of machete). Don't be alarmed; they will simply be interested in knowing where you've come from and what your plans are. You can always ask them about the game in the vicinity and the state of the road ahead.
- If you can, procure a *panga* in Nairobi or any other large town. You will find it extremely useful when making a clearing for a campsite and for all kinds of tasks requiring more than just an ordinary knife. Other essential tools include a good jack, a spade, spare tyres (at least two) and, if you're heading for the desert, jerry cans of water and gas (petrol). As for lighter equipment, apart from a map, think of bringing binoculars, bandages, antiseptic cream, dried fruit and a flashilight with a supply of batteries.
- Don't underestimate the value of *kikois* (brightly coloured pieces of cotton material), which you can buy in the Nairobi market and in most big towns. They can be spread on the ground for picnics, used as wrap-around sleepwear, or scarves for protection against dust.
- You should not leave your vehicle unattended for too long. In town, you can always find someone to keep an eye on it while you're away (count on paying Ksh 10 for a few hours or at least Ksh 20 for a day). Wherever you are, make sure the windows are closed and the doors locked.
- In game parks and reserves you sign a document stating when you expect to leave. Officially, this is so that someone can be sent to look for you if you're having trouble. In Treetops Salient for instance, if you haven't signed out 36 hours after the time you said you would leave, a search party is sent.

▬▬ *BUSINESS HOURS*

Banks are open Monday to Friday 9am-2pm. Barclays Bank has a change counter at Jomo Kenyatta Airport near Nairobi open 24 hours a day and another at Moi Airport near Mombasa open 8am-8pm. Barclays Bank branch offices in Nairobi, Mombasa and Malindi are open Monday through Friday 9am-5pm.

Most offices are open Monday to Friday 8am-noon and 2-6pm. Administrative services are open on Saturday mornings. Travel agencies usually stay open a bit later in the evening every day except Sunday. Though the workday starts at 8am, if you don't have an early appointment you won't be received before 9am.

There are no generally accepted business hours for stores in Kenya. Some keep the same hours as offices while others close much later — for example in the lively district bounded by Moi Avenue, Racecourse Road and Ngara Road in Nairobi. In Lamu, some stores open only at nightfall. Souvenir shops are open daily 8am-8pm.

COURTESY

By all means, try to communicate in Swahili, even if you can only stammer a few words. Most Kenyans appreciate a foreigner's attempt to speak their principal language and will happily correct your pronunciation and enrich your vocabulary. Use the word *mama* when addressing a woman, *bwana* for a man and *mzee* (pronounced 'mim-zay'), a very respectful term, for an older man. An adolescent should be called *kijana* and a child, *toto*. Kenyans don't take kindly to being called blacks; they prefer being referred to as Africans. A useful term to express delight and appreciation is *mazuri sana,* meaning 'very good, indeed'. You'll find it relatively easy to express simple ideas in Swahili because verbs are rarely conjugated. To form a negative statement, you can simply add the word *hapana,* meaning 'no', to the simple verb.

On the other hand, avoid talking in Swahili in administrative offices, especially in the capital. Most officials and office workers pride themselves on their command of English, even if they are more comfortable speaking Swahili or their own tribal language. They may interpret your attempt to communicate in Swahili as an insult to their ability to speak English.

Do try to adjust your rhythm to the slow pace of life here. Showing impatience or losing your temper will get you nowhere; at best it will provoke laughter, and at worst you might hurt the feelings of the people you're dealing with.

As friendly and helpful as the Kenyans are, they generally hate to give information that might cause you discomfort and so they will often make things sound better than they really are. For instance, when you ask the way and how long it will take, you might be told that it's no distance at all and that you'll reach your destination in no time. Then, of course, you'll be surprised to find it taking much longer. It's a good idea to check directions and factual information with several sources. In Kenya there's a charming expression accompanied by a shrug of the shoulders and a look heavenward that explains all manner of mishaps: *Shauri ya Mungu,* literally, 'it's God's problem', indicating that there is nothing anyone can do about it.

Remember these rules of etiquette: When you hear the national anthem at the cinema or theatre, you should stand in silence, and it is forbidden to photograph the president, Daniel arap Moi, or the tomb of the former president, Jomo Kenyatta, in Nairobi. When photographing people you should generally ask permission and discuss a price beforehand. Furthermore, respect the dress rules of all religions; for examples, remove your shoes when you enter a mosque. Dress modestly in town. Finally, avoid nude bathing on the coast, however tempting.

When you go to the market or venture into a *duka* (small shop) where arts and crafts are sold but the prices are not indicated, you should bargain. Take your time and, like the vendor, bluff and laugh. Bargaining is generally considered to be a thoroughly enjoyable experience.

Finally, tipping should come as naturally as breathing. Keep a stock of shillings on hand to give to porters and waiters. If you go on safari don't forget your driver, ranger and guide.

CURRENCY EXCHANGE

When you arrive in Kenya, you have to fill out a currency declaration form. Keep it throughout your visit; when you change money, the exchange is recorded on this document. Customs officials will ask for the form when you leave the country. Sometimes they check it to make sure you haven't changed money illegally and are not exporting Kenyan currency. Only the banks and the big hotels are authorized to change foreign currency. The rate of exchange is better in the banks than in the hotels and better, in general, in Nairobi than in the rest of the country.

The National Bank of Kenya and the Kenya Commercial Bank (Kencom), Kenya's two largest banks, have branches in all the big cities. Barclays Bank and Standard Bank are also represented.

Traveler's checks, especially in US dollars, are accepted in numerous places in Kenya, though not in many of the smaller establishments. A commission is charged on all transactions usings traveler's checks. Always keep an updated record of the checks reference numbers: in case of theft, all reputable checks are covered for loss.

Keep a certain amount of shillings on you, and if possible apart from your bag. You can change them at the airport before your departure.

ELECTRICITY

Electricity is 230 or 240 volts, and some hotels have 110-volt outlets as well. Be sure to bring an adapter with you for small appliances like razors and hair dryers.

EMERGENCIES

The telephone number for emergencies is 999.

For hospital addresses and phone numbers, see '**Useful addresses**' for each city.

FOOD AND DRINK

Because of Kenya's temperate climate and its altitudes, ranging from sea level to 17,060 ft/5200 m, you will not only be able to enjoy tropical delicacies like mangoes, cashew nuts and guavas but also all sorts of other fruits and vegetables like strawberries, plums and asparagus. The choice of food, especially along the coast, is further enriched by the culinary influences left by the different peoples who once ruled the country, or had some other kind of cultural impact on daily life. The Portuguese brought peppers and sweet potatoes, the Arabs spices and dried fruits, the English their love of game meat and large breakfasts and the Indians *samosas, chapatis, pappadums* and curries. All these, combined with local specialities, make for delightful variety.

Meals

Most hotels and lodges follow the British custom. Breakfast consists of fruit, orange juice, cereal, eggs, toast and jam. Lunch is eaten between noon and 2pm, and dinner starts at 7pm. Meals in restaurants are usually well served and hearty. The main dish is often fish or seafood (freshwater trout, tilapia, Nile perch, kingfish with cassava and coconut, lobster, prawns, crab, etc.) though Kenya is also known for its quality lamb, beef and game meat (like rack of Thompson's gazelle or saddle of impala antelope).

It is customary to take a coffee break at 10am, accompanied by a *samosa* or *maandazi* (doughnut), and a tea break (around 5pm) with a choice of scones, bread and butter with jam, and sometimes bananas, sweet potatoes or *manioc*.

Specialities

Among the typically Kenyan specialities are *irio* (a puree of maize — sweet corn — beans, potatoes and spinach) and *sukuma wiki* (spinach, tomatoes and onions), both of which accompany meat. There is also *ebinyebwa* chicken (boiled chicken in a peanut sauce served with tomato, onion and pineapple) and *ngege* (freshwater fish in peanut sauce). Many Kenyan dishes include a peanut or coconut sauce (especially on the coast). *Simsim* is made of roasted sesame seeds and peanuts. Cow's blood cooked in sour milk is served with sweet potatoes or *ugali* (a sort of thick maize porridge). You may even come across grasshoppers fried in butter and served with *ugali* or *matoke* (plantain). These dishes may be offered in certain restaurants as daily specials or can be cooked on request.

Maize flour or cornmeal is an essential ingredient in preparing *ugali*, the country's staple food, as well as in *maandazis* and other kinds of bread. *Matoke* and sweet potatoes are other basic food. Sweet potatoes are sometimes mixed with manioc, coconut milk, carrot or grated cheese.

For pleasant culinary surprises you should try some of the food sold on the street or in little *hotelis* in country villages. Roasted maize cobs are found everywhere. In some areas you will see packets of spiced potato crisps with cashew nuts, an Indian speciality, or tasty Kenyan *mkate mayai*, minced meat mixed with egg and folded into a pancake.

A wide variety of fruit is available in Kenya. You can find mangoes, guavas, pawpaws, custard apples, granadillas (passion fruit), gooseberries, bananas, oranges, grapefruits and pineapples.

Drink

Tea is served everywhere at all times. Like coffee, it is included in the menu price shown in restaurants.

Passion fruit and other juices make interesting cocktails in most hotels and lodges, and when you are at the coast there's nothing better than a fresh lime drink to quench your thirst.

Wines are mostly imported and not always of the best quality (you pay a high price for a good one). Naivasha wines are beginning to make a name for themselves but are not as popular as the local beer, which is inexpensive and good. Tusker, Pilsner and Premium beers are the most popular brands.

Kenya Cane is a strong alcoholic drink made from sugar cane while Mount Kenya is a well-known coffee liqueur.

Generally speaking, tap water in the larger towns can be drunk. When it can't, you will be served boiled or bottled water. In most hotel rooms you'll find a carafe of drinking water.

HEALTH

Tap water in the big cities is usually safe to drink; elsewhere sterilize the water by boiling it or using purifying tablets. You can catch bilharzia (schistosomiasis) by drinking tainted water or by swimming, or even wading, in stagnant water. This disease is extremely difficult to cure. It is first carried by water snails and then develops into blood flukes (a kind of flatworm) in humans. Avoid eating raw, unwashed fruits and vegetables for the same reasons, and if you have digestive problems, keep away from spicy dishes. Don't brush your teeth with untreated water.

To protect yourself against malaria, start taking anti-malaria tablets two to three weeks before you arrive and continue for a month after your return home. If you come down with a fever, be sure to see your doctor.

Mosquitoes are found mainly on the coast but also can be particularly bothersome near the banks of rivers and lakes. Pick up an insect repellent and a disinfectant in any of the local pharmacies, or bring them with you.

In case of a medical emergency while on safari, Flying Doctor (see p. 13) of the African Medical Research Foundation (AMREF) assures patient transport to Nairobi via Wilson Airport.

LANGUAGE

More than 40 languages are spoken in Kenya. English and Swahili are the official languages, spoken by everyone who has gone to school, and many who have not. You will rarely find anyone who cannot speak either language.

Swahili is a Bantu tongue with borrowings from Arabic (and later from English). It was formed over centuries through contact between Arab, Persian and Asian merchants and the Bantu tribes (Giriama and Digo). The origin of the term 'Swahili' or 'kiswahili' is thought to be the Arabic word *sahel*, which means coast.

Under the guidance of the Omani Sultan Sayyid Said, the coastal people who had been living in Zanzibar since 1828, moved over time into the regions that later became Kenya. Carried by these settlers, Swahili became the generally understood language of the various tribal groups. Today Swahili is spoken by about 40 million people in Tanzania, Rwanda, Burundi, Somalia and Uganda, in parts of Zaire and on the Comoro Islands. A considerable amount of literature has been written in Swahili, which was originally transcribed in a variant of the Arabic alphabet. Since the beginning of this century, Swahili has also been written in Roman letters.

If you want to learn some Swahili, pick up a copy of *Teach Yourself Swahili* by D.V. Perrott (Hodder and Stoughton). For a basic tourist vocabulary, see p. 191.

MEDIA

There are two English-language dailies: the *Standard* and the *Daily Nation*. The Asian community has a newspaper in the Gujarati language. The Swahili newspaper, *Taifa Leo*, has a circulation of 50,000 copies and issues a magazine supplement, the *Taifa Weekly*.

The *Sunday Nation* and the *Weekly Review*, both English-language weeklies, appear on Sundays. For practical information, hotel listings, restaurants and entertainment information, pick up *Coastweek* (printed in English, German and Swahili) or *What's On*. The bi-monthly *Tourist's Kenya* provides a wealth of information for travelers, including hotels, restaurants, tour operators and entertainment. *Target and Lengo* is a Christian weekly published in English and Swahili.

Many of the specialized monthlies are in English: *Kenya Export, Auto News, East African Report, Farmer's Voice, Viva* are some examples. *Swara*, a bi-monthly put out by the East African Wildlife Society, is of great interest to anybody studying Kenyan wildlife.

The Voice of Kenya, the government-run radio station, broadcasts in English and Swahili, and the single national television station has programs in both languages from 5:30 to 10:30pm.

PHOTOGRAPHY

Kenya, with its stunning, varied landscapes filled with magnificent birds, animals and insects, lends itself perfectly to photography.

You can buy film easily in Nairobi and Mombasa, as well as in the large hotels and lodges elsewhere. Nevertheless, it is best to bring your own stock because film is expensive in East Africa. For most lighting conditions, ASA 64 or 100 film is sufficient, but you'd do well to have some rolls of ASA 160 or 200 film as well. The light available in a dense forest or narrow alleyway differs considerably from the brightness of the savannah. Ultraviolet or skylight filters protect lenses from dust and scratches. You will also need dust-proof wrappers for film and camera, a sunshade and a supply of batteries. Really serious photographers may want to carry two camera cases (24 × 36), complete with several lenses — including a telephoto, a zoom and a wide-angle lens — and a flash.

Most wildlife is best shot with a 135 or 150 mm telephoto lens. For monkeys, birds and other tree-dwellers, use a focal doublers (2X) attachment to magnify the focal length, or better still, a 300 mm lens. Keep in mind that doubler attachments necessitate opening up a stop. Be guided by your light meter.

Many Kenyans will absolutely refuse to have their pictures taken. Others are eager to be photographed, expecting to see their image immediately. To avoid disappointing them, warn them in advance if you don't have an instant camera. People often expect a small sum for being photographed; agree upon the figure beforehand. The Masai consider their cattle to be part of themselves and will not take kindly to their being photographed without permission.

Finally, it is completely forbidden to photograph (without permission) the president, the tomb of Jomo Kenyatta, the flag, members of the armed forces, their cars and barracks, or police officers.

Video buffs should note that Kenya has adopted the British colour broadcasting system, PAL; only videocassettes of that format can be watched on Kenyan video systems.

▬ POST OFFICE

Post offices are open Monday to Friday 8:30am-5:30pm.

If you are staying in Kenya for a while, have your mail sent to a hotel or a friend's post office box. Kenyan houses do not have numbers, and the mail service does not distribute door to door. Kenyans use post boxes or poste restante (General Delivery) at the post office to receive their mail. The poste restante system is not always reliable. Mail is filed by initials and errors do happen.

To send an international telegram, go to any post office or to a **Kenextel** (Kenya External Telecommunications Co., Ltd.) office. The Kenextel counter on Haile Selassie Ave., A3, (opposite the parcel post office) is open daily around the clock. You can, however, send a local telegram from any post office or train station.

Stamp collectors can go to the Kenya Stamp Bureau at the General Post Office, Kenyatta Ave., Nairobi, A3, which sells a complete collection of Kenya stamps and first-day envelopes.

▬ PUBLIC HOLIDAYS

The following dates are public holidays:
Jan 1: New Year's Day
March or April: Good Friday
               Easter Monday
May 1: Labour Day
June 1: Madaraka Day
October 20: Kenyatta Day
December 12: Independence Day
December 25-26: Christmas

The first day of Ramadan is also a public holiday. In 1991 Ramadan starts on March 18, and in 1992, March 8.

There are so many local festivals and religious ceremonies that it would be impossible to list them all.

▬ SAFARIS AND ORGANIZED TOURS

You can organize an excursion or safari through **UST** (Universal Safari Tours), Wabera St., POB 49312, Nairobi, A2, ☎ 33 6295, 33 8450 or 21 446, telex: 22 054, fax: 254 2 728440. Organized excursions are handled in the agency on the ground floor (entrance City Hall Way). On the 5th floor (entrance on Warbera St.) you'll find a staff ready to handle any arrangements you need, from renting a car to planning your whole stay, complete with reservations and vouchers.

Among Kenya's handcrafts: carved figurines in wood or soapstone, basketry and traditional clothing and jewelry.

Specialized tour operators include **Safari Camp Services** for the Lake Turkana region and **Flamingo Tours,** which organizes camel treks. For the addresses of operators in Nairobi, see p. 97; for Mombasa, see p. 170.

▬ SAFETY PRECAUTIONS

Theft is a problem in the larger cities of Kenya, as in major cities around the world. With common sense and caution, though, you should have no trouble at all. Place your valuables, including your return ticket, traveler's checks and their receipt of purchase, in the safety deposit box of your hotel. Don't leave anything valuable in your room.

It's a good idea to make a photocopy of your passport (with photo) in case of theft, though the original is necessary for all financial transactions.

Take along as little as possible when you are walking in the city, and hold onto your photographic equipment. At night, avoid walking around the city alone. Most tourists have supper in their hotels or nearby. If you want to listen to music or dance, stick to the nightclub or cabaret in your hotel or take a taxi.

Over the past few years Kenya has had a population explosion (the number of inhabitants has more than doubled since independence in 1963), which has created economic problems. Young people leaving school or university have a difficult time finding employment, and country people flock to the city in the hope of getting work. Once in town they see the *wa-benzi*, Kenya's elite, driving around in Mercedes. In these circumstances it's easy to see that anybody who seems to be better off could be a target for theft. If your bag is snatched in the street, shout 'thief!' or *mwivi!* but be ready to intervene once the crowd has caught the culprit; street justice has been known to result in hospital cases or worse. Don't be alarmed by this advice; just be careful.

▬ SHOPPING

You can buy a wide variety of souvenirs in Kenya. Most items are available at the same price in Nairobi as elsewhere in the country, and that means, happily, that you can leave the shopping until the end of your trip. The exceptions are sheepskin products, which should be bought in Nanyuki and Nakuru, while the best place for silver jewelry and fabrics is Lamu. Bargaining is standard practice everywhere except in fancy boutiques.

Animals

It is forbidden to sell any item made from wild animals. This restriction covers hides and trophies, snake and crocodile skins, elephant hair bracelets, ivory, horns and even sea shells.

You cannot possess any wild animal, bird, fish or reptile without a permit from the regional Wildlife Department. In Nairobi all animals sold legally are imported: the tortoises come from America, the canaries from Great Britain and the fish from Holland.

Jewelry

You can find some lovely and often fairly inexpensive jewelry: semi-precious stones (amethyst, malachite, topaz, agate; pendants, rings, bracelets and small boxes made of silver; Masai-style necklaces, headbands and bracelets made of tiny multicoloured beads; necklaces of large wooden, copper or amber beads.

Natural fibres

Natural fibres such as banana leaves, tree bark, sisal and the roots of certain plants are used to make costume jewelry, tableware, decorative wall hangings and more. Sisal mats are a speciality of Limuru, near the entrance to the Rift Valley.

In Mombasa you can get a good deal on a Persian rug from the crew of a dhow originating in Asia, but you run the risk of having to pay substantial taxes at customs upon departure.

Wood-carved items and furniture

You don't need a special permit to export antiques. In general, the export tax on merchandise costing less than £100/$170 is insignificant, but check with the salesman because the tax varies with the category of object.

Along the coastal strip from Mombasa to Lamu, you can find beautiful ancient and modern furniture, and lovely carved wooden combs or other small objects that are easy to transport.

Fabric

Cotton fabric can be bought in lengths that correspond to sizes of traditional clothing; a *kitenge* is a kind of sarong, a *kanga* is a patterned length of material worn as a skirt and a *kikoi* is a bright, single-colour or striped length of material often worn by fishermen and coastal tribesmen. Some fabrics are hand-printed using the batik method. You can also find oriental silk in shops selling Indian articles.

Miscellaneous

Baskets are ubiquitous and inexpensive: a *kikapu* is a plain, loosely woven, all-purpose basket; while the *kiondo* has a tighter weave and is generally coloured and patterned. It can be carried as a shoulder bag (some versions can be shut with a zip at the top).

Soapstone carvings from the Kisii area are sold in many markets and can be particularly appealing. They include vases, little pots, human and animal figures, chess sets and ashtrays.

▬ *SPORTS*

Temporary membership is accepted by many of Kenya's sports clubs.

Ballooning

In the Masai Mara National Reserve you can admire the scenery and wildlife from above (for Ksh 5000 per person). The departures are from the Governor's Camp, Serena, Keekorok, Kichwa Tembo and Sarova Mara lodges. Information and reservations at **International House,** Mama Ngina St., POB 48966, Nairobi, A3, ☎ 33 5474 or 33 4911 or through any travel agency (see pp. 97 and 170).

Fishing

You needn't obtain a fishing license in Nairobi to go trout fishing, but you do need a permit. Certain hotels, such as Naro Moru near Mount Kenya, will provide you with a temporary one- or two-day permit. If, however, you plan to do a lot of fishing, contact the Fisheries Department, Museum Hill (behind the Kenya National Museum), POB 58187, Nairobi, ☎ 74 2320 or 74 3579. It can furnish you with a list of all the river fishing camps and the people to see to obtain an authorization.

If you prefer lake fishing (mainly for Nile perch and tilapia), contact one of the fishing clubs of Kisumu or Naivasha or the Lake Turkana Lodge on the west bank of the lake.

The Indian Ocean abounds in marlin, shark, tuna, bonito, sailfish and more. Most of the hotels and lodges along the beach south of Mombasa (Shimoni, for example) and north to Malindi organize fishing expeditions. High season is between December and March.

Golf

Kenya has five 18-hole courses. Apart from the **Railway Course** in central Nairobi there are:

Karen Golf Club, POB 24816, Nairobi, ☎ 88 2801/2.

Muthaiga Golf Club, Kiambu Rd., POB 41651, Nairobi, ☎ 76 2414 or 76 7755.

Royal Nairobi Golf Club, POB 40221, Nairobi, ☎ 72 5769.

Sigona Golf Club, Naivasha Rd., Karuri, POB 10, Kikuyu, ☎ 32 431.

The annual golf open championship held in March at the Muthaiga Golf Club attracts large crowds.

Horseback riding

In certain regions horseback riding is widely practiced. Many hotels and lodges provide riding facilities.

Horse racing

Races usually take place on Sundays (first race at 2:15pm) at the racetrack on Ngong Road in Nairobi. For more information, consult the local newspaper or contact the **Jockey Club of Kenya,** Ngong Rd., POB 40373, Nairobi, ☎ 56 6108.

Mountaineering

The **Mountain Club of Kenya,** POB 45741, ☎ 50 1747 (after 8:30pm), at Wilson Airport just outside Nairobi: for a small annual fee, you can become a member, attend the weekly meetings on Tuesdays at 8:30pm, to meet the guides and participate in group outings.

Sailing

Sailing is possible from most of the hotels on the coastal strip. Lake Naivasha, Lake Baringo, Lake Victoria and the Nairobi Dam are all good places to sail. For information, contact the **Sailing Club,** Nairobi Dam, POB 49973, Nairobi, ☎ 50 1250.

Soccer and other field games

Soccer is extremely popular in Kenya, as it is in much of Africa. If you'd like to participate in a soccer match, register as a tempory member at the **Impala Club,** Ngong Rd., POB 41516, Nairobi, ☎ 56 5684. At the Impala and other clubs, you can play tennis, squash, rugby, hockey and cricket. The Ngong Road field is also a popular place for informal soccer and rugby matches.

Scuba diving

Certain beaches along the coast are unsuitable for scuba, particularly the sand beaches where the water is turbulent. In areas that have been designated as marine parks, the natural surroundings and animal life are protected. This is the case at Malindi, Watamu, Shimoni and Kisite Mpunguti (around Wasini Island). Nevertherless, you can spend your time under water simply observing the colourful variety of marine life around Manda Island near Lamu and farther north at Kiwaihu. For information contact the **Kenya Divers Association,** POB 95705, Mombasa, ☎ 47 1347.

Swimming

Many of the hotels and lodges have swimming pools. In the sea, if you are going out to a reef, be sure to wear rubber sandals or tennis shoes to avoid cuts on the corals. Lake swimming is sometimes advised against as you can catch bilharzia (schistosomiasis) from parasites that live in stagnant waters.

Tennis

Many hotels, especially those along the coast, have courts. In Nairobi, you can also play tennis (or participate in numerous other sports) at any of the following clubs:

Impala Club, Ngong Rd., POB 41516, ☎ 56 5684.
Nairobi Club, Ngong Rd., POB 30171, ☎ 72 5726 or 72 5331.
Nairobi Gymkhana, Forest Rd., POB 40895, ☎ 74 2804.
Parklands Sports Clubs, Ojijo Rd., POB 40116, ☎ 74 5164.

▬ *TELEPHONE*

The larger cities of Kenya are linked by automatic telephone lines and can be reached 24 hours a day. Other cities and towns are connected by a manual network divided into two categories: 'A', with continuous service; and 'B', with service only from 8am to 8pm.

No limit is placed on the length of a local call but rates are reduced by 50% weekdays between 6pm and 7am and between Saturday at 2pm and Monday at 7am.

Telephone booths are few and far between. You are most likely to find one in or near hotels or by post offices. You'll need a 1 Ksh coin to make a call.

For long-distance and international calls, it is best to go through the operator. To call people in the less accessible regions of the country, you will need their 'radiocall' number, where they can be reached at a specific time arranged in advance.

TIME

Kenya local time is GMT plus three hours. For example, when it is 6pm in Kenya, it is 3pm in London, 10am in New York and 7am in Los Angeles. That will vary when daylight-saving or summer time causes a one-hour difference.

TOURIST INFORMATION

In Nairobi, the offices of **African Tours and Hotels** and **Kenya Airways,** A2 *(open daily 8:30am-4:30pm)* are situated opposite the Hilton at the corner of Moi Avenue and Mama Ngina Street.

UST (Universal Safari Tours), on the corner of Wabera Street and City Hall Way, Cotts House, POB 49312, Nairobi, ☎ 33 6295, 33 8450 or 21 446, is another office offering extensive tourist information and organized tours.

In Mombasa, the information office, on Moi Avenue in Uhuru Gardens, is *open Monday to Friday 8am-noon and 2-4:30pm, Saturday 8am-noon.*

TRANSPORT

Boat

Kenya Railways operates boats on Lake Victoria along the Kavirondo gulf, with daily trips to Kendu Bay (same day return) and Homa Bay (return the following day). For information, ☎ 21 211, Nairobi *(Mon-Fri 8am-5pm, Sat 8am-7pm).*

Along the coast, you can sail on a dhow between Mombasa, Malindi and Lamu. The length of the trip depends on the strength of the wind.

Bus

Bus travel, the cheapest way of getting around, requires a good deal of patience. There are bus services practically everywhere, except in the parks. In certain places schedules are arranged specifically to meet the needs of the inhabitants of a small village. To permit the villagers of Marsabit to pick up supplies in the south, for exemple, a bus makes the round trip twice a week along a rough country road.

In Nairobi, KBS company, Gen. Waruingi St., POB 30563, ☎ 76 706, which leaves from the old East African Road Services station, usually sticks to schedule. Buy your ticket the day before departure. Private companies, servicing all the bigger towns and villages, leave from the Country Bus Station. The seats are comfortable, the prices are low (Ksh 150 to 200 from Nairobi to Mombasa) and the private buses stop less frequently than the public ones.

Whether traveling with a private or public company, you can never be sure what time you'll reach your destination. Buses are constantly stopping; passengers get off, peddlers get on to hawk their wares, the police frequently check to see if the bus is overloaded and will then force some passengers off (after interminable arguments), and almost all the buses need some repair.

In the smaller towns, don't buy your ticket in advance; several companies operate along the same routes and you never know which will leave first. When traveling, keep a close eye on your belongings.

Car rental

Driving is not the most economical means of transportation but it offers you the most freedom of movement. Gasoline costs about Ksh 10 a litre. You can choose from several driving options:

● Rental cars: according to the model, a car costs between Ksh 380 and Ksh 580 a day, plus Ksh 4.50 to Ksh 6.40 per kilometre (or between Ksh 6500 and Ksh 8400 per week with unlimited mileage). The latter

Buses operate throughout the country. They are cheap but require a good deal of patience.

includes a limited insurance plan covering car damage above Ksh 15,000. All-risk insurance costs extra (see p. 94 for agencies in Nairobi, p. 172 for Mombasa).

- Chauffeur-driven vehicles: you will pay a slightly higher rental charge plus Ksh 120 per day to the driver.
- Four-wheel-drive vehicles with camping equipment: they are available at UTC-Hertz and Habib's Cars Ltd (see p. 94).

Generally, with a credit card you'll pay half the estimated cost at the outset and the rest when you return the car. Avis, UTC-Hertz and Europcar offer the possibility of renting an ordinary car (not a four-wheel drive vehicle) in Nairobi and returning it in Mombasa or Malindi or vice versa. In 1988, Twiga Car Hire & Tours (see p. 94) began its newly opened firm with rock-bottom prices: Ksh 15,000 per month with unlimited mileage. You might check with Twiga to see if prices are still as low.

Hints for drivers in Kenya

- Driving is on the left. The speed limit is 34 mi/55 km per hour in town, 62 mi/100 km per hour outside of town and 16 mi/25 km per hour in the parks and reserves. To avoid bouncing through the roof of the car on the murram (dirt) roads and other roads in disrepair, it's best not to exceed 43.5 mi/70 km per hour.
- In Kenya, surfaced roads are called 'tarmac roads', unsurfaced or dirt ones 'murram roads'.
- All Kenyan roads are officially rated from A to F. The rating system corresponds to the amount of traffic (especially commercial) on a given route and not to the quality of the road.
- On paved roads be wary of truck drivers who don't leave you room to pass. You'll often find, surprisingly, that murram roads are better: they are wider and there's less traffic.
- Park roads are well maintained and have clearly marked directions; you'll need a four-wheel drive vehicle within the parks only during the rainy season. If you get caught in a storm during the dry season, put on your lights and drive slowly.
- In certain regions of Kenya a four-wheel drive vehicle is indispensable: in the mountainous zones of Mount Kenya and Mount Elgon, in the

highlands of Marsabit and Nyandarua (where the roads are closed during certain seasons) and in the north. In the Kerio Valley, once you leave the new road, you'll need a large, sturdy four-wheel drive vehicle with enough room for camping equipment, extra reserves of water and gasoline, at least two spare tyres, some tools and spare parts.

● Always take along a jerry can of gasoline; in remote areas service stations are few and far between. Also be sure to have plenty of water for yourself and for the car radiator, to prevent the engine over-heating.

● If your car breaks down, open the hood and leave a trail of branches over a distance of 33 yds/30 m leading up to your car. This is the local distress signal; it is customary to stop if you see others in difficulty.

● Local mechanics, be they professional or amateur, are usually extremely efficient and capable of inventing an imaginative solution to almost any problem.

● Picking up hitchhikers, if you use a little common sense, can be an enriching experience; your passenger will often turn out to be a good guide.

● Before setting out, be sure that you have a spare tyre and a toolbox, and that the driver has at least a rudimentary knowledge of car mechanics.

Matatu

Just about everywhere you'll see a variety of large vehicles — vans, minibuses, etc. — packed with passengers. These are known as *matatus* from the Swahili *tatu* meaning 'three', a term stemming from the colonial period, when this mode of transportation cost three shillings. At each stop the driver leans out to shout the destination and then whistles loudly to signal the departure.

Matatus are found in the city, on the main roads of the country and along some of the smaller roads linking the more remote villages. They do not provide service to the parks.

Plane

Without a doubt the best way to less accessible parts of the country is by air. Kenya has two international airports: **Jomo Kenyatta International Airport,** 7.5 mi/13 km south-east of Nairobi, and **Moi International Airport,** 7.5 mi/13 km west of Mombasa. Most of the larger cities have well-maintained runways. In addition, the country is linked by a network of smaller airstrips for monoplanes, twin-engine aircraft capable of holding up to 14 people, and even DC3s with 36-passenger capacity. Lodges have their own landing strips and generally provide car service from the strip to the lodge.

Kenya Airways (in Nairobi: Airways Terminal, Koinage St., A2, POB 19002, ☎ 29 291 or Jomo Kenyatta Airport, ☎ 82 2171; in Mombasa: Airways Terminal, Digo Rd., POB 99302, ☎ 21251) operates about 30 flights a week between Nairobi and Mombasa; a one-way ticket costs Ksh 920. Flights are also scheduled daily between Nairobi and Malindi.

Many private companies headquartered at Wilson Airport in the southern suburbs of Nairobi, link Lamu to Nairobi, Mombasa and Malindi:

Air Kenya Ltd., POB 30357, ☎ 501601, telex: 22939.

Africair, POB 45645, ☎ 50 1210, telex: 23061.

CMC Aviation Ltd., POB 44580, ☎ 50 1221.

Cooper Skybird Air Charters, POB 99222, Mombasa, ☎ 21443 (also offers flights to the parks and reserves); Malindi, ☎ 20860; Lamu, ☎ 3055.

Equator Airlines Ltd., POB 43356, Nairobi, ☎ 50 1399; POB 93934, Mombasa, ☎ 43 2355, flies between Wilson Airport and Lamu, but will land its 14-passenger planes in Mombasa and Malindi on request.

Pioneer, POB 43356, Nairobi, ☎ 50 1319; Mombasa, ☎ 43 2355; Malindi, ☎ 30585; Lamu, ☎ 139.

Rent a Plane, Ltd., POB 42730, Nairobi, ☎ 50 1431 or 50 0506.
Safari Air Services Ltd., POB 41951, Nairobi, ☎ 50 1211, telex: 22512.
Sunbird Aviation Ltd., POB 46247, Nairobi, ☎ 50 1421; POB 84700, Mombasa, ☎ 43 3220.

You can charter a plane from most airlines; this is expensive but could be worthwhile for group travel.

Rift Valley Peugeot

Rift Valley Peugeot (RVP) is a collective taxi service offering space for up to 8 passengers in a Peugeot 404 or 504, or up to 20 in a Mercedes minibus. Rates are about 20% higher than the bus fare but are considerably cheaper than car rental. The vehicles are comfortable and well maintained. The drivers are competent and they manage to arrive more or less on schedule.

RVP offers a daily taxi service to Eldoret, Kakemega, Kisii, Kisumu, Kitale, Malindi, Meru, Mombasa, Nairobi, Nakuru, Nyeri and Webuye.

RVP, bookings and freight, Duruma Rd., POB 48817, Nairobi, ☎ 26374 or 54 3597.

Mombasa Peugeot Services, POB 45274, Nairobi, ☎ 33 3176, offers the same services.

Taxis

Taxis in Kenya have no meters. In the big cities the red Mercedes taxis operated by Kenatco are the most reliable; rates are posted at the Kenatco agencies. For information contact **Archer's Cabs Ltd.,** Koinage St., POB 40097, Nairobi, ☎ 21935 or 20289.

For other taxis, be sure to negotiate the price before getting in.

Trains

Kenya Railways has replaced the defunct East African Railways Corporation, though you can still see the initials of the latter throughout the country. The railway network covers 1631 mi/2630 km. The main line runs from Mombasa to the Ugandan border, with branch lines from Voi to Taveta (on the Tanzanian border), Konza to Lake Magadi, Nairobi to Nanyuki, Nakuru and Gilgil to Nyahururu, and Nakuru to Eldoret and Malaba (on the Uganda border). The Nairobi station has become the central point of departure and arrival for all trains since the closure of the East African Railways.

Trains have three classes. Express trains have two-bed sleeping compartments, restaurant cars and bars. The third class is usually packed with all kinds of passengers (including chickens), the second class is less colourful and the first class is the most comfortable.

The bi-monthly *Tourist's Kenya* publishes the train schedules.

Departure from Nairobi:

● to Mombasa (daily): 5 and 7pm, arrival at 7:25 and 8am. The departure from Mombasa to Nairobi is also at 5 and 7pm. A one-way ticket in first class costs Ksh 594.

● to Kisumu (daily): 6pm, arrival at 8:05am. Departure from Kisumu to Nairobi at 6:30pm.

● to Malaba at the Uganda border via Eldoret: Tuesday, Friday and Sunday at 3pm, arrival at 8:30am.

● to Voi (halfway between Nairobi and Mombasa); Wednesday and Saturday at 5am, arrival at 9:50am.

The origins of the species

In 1871, Charles Darwin, to the general doubt of many of his contemporaries, put forward his theory of human evolution. In *The Descent of Man*, the controversial naturalist argued that humans had developed from a long chain of species that became more and more specialized through a process of natural selection. He thought, correctly, it turned out, that the origins of mankind probably lay in Africa. Fossil discoveries in this century have provided a great deal of evidence to support Darwin's once-ridiculed theory. They have permitted paleontologists to reconstruct the evolution and relationship of the successive forms of many species. A series of excavations by Mary and Louis Leakey and their son, Richard, in Kenya and Tanzania, as well as finds by other paleontologists in Ethiopia, have contributed greatly to our understanding of the origins of our own species.

Twenty million years ago, a new family of great apes emerged: the Ramapithecus. A fragment of Ramapithecus' jaw was first discovered in India. In 1961, a portion of a jaw and part of a backbone, uncovered by Louis Leakey in Fort Ternan, Kenya, was given the name Kenyapithecus. Later it was recognized as being 14 million years old and belonging to the Ramapithecus family, which lived during the Miocene era of the Tertiary Period, between 5 million and 20 million years ago.

The Ramapithecus spread throughout Asia and Europe. In Africa, climatic conditions resulted in the shrinking of the forests. The Ramapithecus took to the open savannah, changed its diet and adopted a semi-erect posture, depending increasingly on its hind limbs for walking.

During the Pliocene era, 3 million years ago, the genus Australopithecinae came into the world, it walked on two legs and used stone tools. Then, about 2 million years ago, the *Homo habilis* appeared.

En 1959, Mary Leakey discovered jaw fragments and fossil footprints dating from 4 million years ago in Olduvai Gorge, Tanzania. In Omo valley in Ethiopia, Don Johanson found a remarkably complete 3-million-year-old skeleton, commonly called Lucy, along with the remains of a group of about 30 even older specimens. Hélène Roche uncovered stone tools, 2.5 million years old, near the spot where Lucy died. They are considered to be the oldest in the world.

In 1972, on the banks of Lake Turkana, near the renowned excavation site of Koobi Fora, paleontologist Bernard Ngeneo discovered a fragment of a skull. Later, at the same spot, Richard Leakey's wife, Meavey, assembled 300 excavated fragments and reconstructed an almost complete skull — minus the jaw — of a 2 million years old *Homo habilis.*

From *Homo habilis* evolved the *Homo erectus.* Evidence of its presence has been found in the Rift Valley, from Tanzania to northern Kenya, and in Ethiopia. Several skulls belonging to the genus, some 1.5 million years old, were found at Koobi Fora. In 1984, west of Lake Turkana, Richard Leakey excavated the skeleton of a 12-year-old *Homo erectus* measuring 1.60 m; his size at that age suggest that, had he lived, he would have grown very large.

Excavations continue today on sites north of Lodwar under the supervision of Richard Leakey and his assistant Kamoi Kameo.

Our species — *Homo sapiens* — is thought to have evolved from *Homo erectus* 200,000 years ago. Fossil evidence of its presence in Africa has been discovered in Olorgesailie south of Nairobi, in Kariandusi, near Gilgil, and in the area around Lake Baringo. Bows and arrows, pottery and chiseled vases found near Elmenteita testify to the presence of a settlement during the 5th millenium. The Sahara was then already in the process of becoming a desert; a change that forced the hunter-gatherers to migrate in several directions. The origins of the Pygmies, the Bushmen, and the Dorobo of the central forests, can be traced to these ancient groups.

In the prehistoric sites of the Rift Valley, specimens of two distinct physical types have been found. At Gamble's Cave near Elmenteita, large people with narrow heads and prominent noses are reminiscent of the Somalis and Ethiopians. Smaller ones with round skulls and large faces, the remains of whom were found on a site near Bromehead, resemble the Bushmen and Dorobo.

KENYA IN THE PAST

EARLY COASTAL HISTORY

Scant contemporary writings have come down to us about the coastal region of Kenya before the 15th century, and none at all for the interior before the 19th century. The earliest written account of the coast is in *Periplus Maris Erythraei ('Periplus of the Erythraean Sea')*, from the 1st century AD. Its author, probably a Greek merchant living in Egypt, indicated that there was already a lively trade between Arabia and posts along the coast of present-day Somalia, Kenya and Tanzania.

Arab sailors, he wrote, traded ironwork, cloth, olive oil and other products for ivory, rhinoceros horn, cinnamon and slaves. 'The Arab captains and agents', the writer noted, 'are familiar with the inhabitants and both dwell and intermarry with them; they know all their villages and speak their languages'. These are undoubtedly the roots of the Swahili civilization that would blossom 10 centuries later.

The Greek astronomer and geographer Claudius Ptolemy provides us with the next source of information in his *Geography*, written around AD 150. The earliest existing version of the manuscript dates from AD 400. Though inaccurate in many respects, Ptolemy mentions several trading posts (now thought to be Lamu, Malindi and Mombasa) along the coast and even indicates the presence of the large lakes and the mountains of the interior.

The coastal area south of Somalia was then known to Arab traders as Azania or the Land of Zanj, meaning 'land of the blacks'. Arab and Chinese merchants sailed to the coast with the monsoon from the north-east and returned home with that from the south-west. Arab historians and geographers described the Zanj as worshiping nature, fearing the spirits of the dead and hunting elephants. Other than scattered references to the Land of Zanj by Arab or Chinese sailors, little additional written information or relics are found until the 9th century.

During the 9th and 10th centuries a significant increase in commercial activities took place along the coast, accompanied by an influx of Moslem settlers. You can still see the remains of an impressive coral seawall and some stone buildings dating from the 9th century on the island of Manda in the Lamu Archipelago.

Archaeological remains attest the importance of the ancient coastal town of Gedi.

By the beginning of the 10th century, we hear of Bantu-language speakers in the region. The Swahili language, a Bantu tongue with Arab influences, was probably developed during this century. It would become the first East African tongue to be transcribed, although, unfortunately, the oldest existing Swahili document dates only from 1728. A mosque, constructed in 1107, is evidence of the large Moslem population on Zanzibar, to the south-east.

By the 12th century, various written sources refer to Malindi, Kilwa (in Tanzania) and a town that is probably Mombasa. Archaeological remains from the 13th century testify to the importance of Gedi, nearby Kilepwa and Ungwana at the mouth of the Tana River.

At the end of the 15th century, on the eve of the Portuguese arrival, the coastal population was a mixture of Arabs and Africans. They spoke Swahili and were mainly Moslem.

Mombasa was a prosperous town with some 10,000 inhabitants. Malindi to the north was its main rival. There were thriving settlements on the islands of Pemba, Manda and Pate. The settlements were independent city-states with their own leaders from the Swahili-speaking population.

The interior was still virtually cut off from the coast, each region pursuing its own development. The events that drew the coast into the international arena did not affect the interior until three centuries later.

PORTUGUESE INVASION

The European chapter in the history of the coast opened with the passage of Vasco da Gama on his first voyage to India via the Cape of Good Hope. The great navigator had led a fleet of four ships out of Lisbon on July 8, 1497. He was accompanied by interpreters speaking Arabic and one versed in several Bantu dialects. He rounded the Cape of Good Hope on November 22 and arrived in Mombasa on April 7, 1498, and in Malindi one week later.

A text written by a coastal inhabitant describes the attitude of some of the Swahili population toward the foreigners: 'Those who knew the truth confirmed that they were corrupt and dishonest people who had come only to spy on the land in order to seize it.' The people of Malindi, though, welcomed the Portuguese, whom they saw as an eventual ally in the city's rivalry with Mombasa. 'The king and people of this place ever were and are friends of the king of Portugal,' wrote one Portuguese traveler.

The Portuguese then sailed across the Indian Ocean to their destination on the Indian coast, which they reached on May 20, 1498. In January of the following year, on the return trip, da Gama's greatly reduced crew again anchored at Malindi. There they set up a *padrão,* a stone pillar used as a mark of discovery and overlordship.

The Portuguese government immediately recognized the strategic importance of the East African coastal towns to their control of the trade route to the Spice Islands. Within a decade after da Gama's first trip, the Portuguese dominated the entire coast, their task made easier by rivalries between the towns. Rebellious Mombasa was sacked by the Portuguese in 1500, in 1505, and finally in 1528 (see pp. 167-168).

Clearly, however, the main interests for Portugal was the East Indies and the control of trade in the Indian Ocean. Along the African coast, the Portuguese settled only in the southern area (now Mozambique), where gold was found. Elsewhere, they avoided the burdens of direct rule, contenting themselves with a sort of absentee ownership.

In the late 16th century, threatened by Turkish expeditions, the Portuguese consolidated their hold on Mombasa with the construction of Fort Jesus (1593). Soon after, Portuguese traders settled in the vicinity, protected by the garrison at the fort, which never, in fact, exceeded one hundred men. Missionaries followed in their wake, but compared with the Moslems they had little influence on the inhabitants. Mombasa remained the main Portuguese base in East Africa for more than a century, until the fall of Fort Jesus to the Omanis in 1698.

THE RISE OF THE OMANIS

In the mid-17th century, Portuguese imperial power was declining. The Portuguese suffered losses to the Dutch and British in the East Indies and gradually lost control of the Indian Ocean. In 1622, the Persians took the port of Hormuz on the northern coast of the Indian Ocean. The Iman of Oman drove the Portuguese from Muscat in 1650.

Two years later, Oman attacked the Portuguese in Pate and Zanzibar. Over the next few decades, the Omanis made further incursions into Portuguese-controlled territory on the coast. In 1696, Sayf ibn Sultan laid siege to Fort Jesus.

The fort's fall, 33 months later marked the end of Portuguese control of the region, despite attempts over the next few decades to reconquer the fort. In 1729, after a short-lived victory, the Portuguese were finally expelled from coastal Africa north of the Ruvuma River (the current northern border of Mozambique).

The Omanis appointed their own governors to rule the coastal towns, each of which continued to act as independent city-states. In 1741, though, the Busaidi clan took over in Oman and the Mazrui governors of Mombasa opposed the new rule. The Mazruis stopped paying taxes to Oman and began extending their own power over other coastal towns.

Through most of the 18th century, and despite Busaidi efforts to overthrow the Mazruis, the Mombasa governors retained control over the coast all the way up to Pate and inland to Nyika. In Muscat, in 1806, Seyyid Said succeeded his father as ruler of Oman. After quelling opposition at home, he turned his attention to the African coast and soon gained control of Lamu, followed by Pate and Pemba.

A new era began with the signing of a trade treaty between Britain and Oman in 1798. At this time, the British were not present on the east coast of Africa and had no specific designs on the region. All this was to change because of two factors: Indian Ocean commerce and the slave trade. Little did either party suspect that the treaty would be the first step in a process that would lead to British colonization of a large area of East Africa within a century.

THE BRITISH CONNECTION

The purpose of the treaty was to safeguard the British route through the Persian Gulf to India and to prevent Omani trade with the French and Dutch. The next significant event came in 1807 with the abolition of the slave trade in British dependencies. Intent on using its diplomatic influence and military power to stop the trade, Britain signed a second agreement, the Moresby Treaty, with Seyyid Said of Oman in 1822.

The treaty outlawed the sale of slaves to Christian countries but allowed it between Moslem countries. Its significance for the future of Northeast Africa lay in that it implicitly recognized the claims of Seyyid Said over the whole coastal area north of Cape Delgado (at the mouth of the Ruvuma River on the northern border of present-day Mozambique). It also placed Britain in the role of protector of Omani rights.

The same year, strengthened by his alliance with Britain, Seyyid Said sent an expedition against the Mazruis. The Mazrui family asked the British to declare a protectorate over the region, and Britain found itself caught between the two clans. In 1824 a British naval force captain in Mombasa accepted the Mazrui proposal and raised the British flag. Two years later, however, his action was repudiated by the British government.

Said's personal power was considerably reinforced by this decision. He began an all-out campaign against the Mazruis the following year. Using Zanzibar as a base, by 1828 the Omani forces had taken over many of the areas under Mazrui control. By 1836 — after much struggle, diplomacy and fighting — Said had succeeded in uprooting the Mazruis.

THE GROWTH OF COMMERCE AND END OF THE SLAVE TRADE

During this period, the Omani sultan divided his time between Zanzibar and Muscat. He introduced clove cultivation on the island and was soon exporting the product. Under his leadership, Zanzibari merchants opened trade routes into the interior, traveling mostly along the path running south of Kenya from Zanzibar or Mombasa to Lake Tanganyika.

Ivory, copal, sesame, cowries, hides and coconut oil were exported, as were slaves, although less so after the Moresby Treaty. Said signed a series of friendship and commerce treaties between 1833 and 1844, opening all the ports in his dependencies to the Americans, the British and the French. His successor signed a further treaty with the Germans in 1859.

By 1840, trade was so prosperous that Said moved his capital from Muscat to Zanzibar. Continued British pressure to suppress the slave trade resulted in the signing of the Hamerton Treaty in 1845, prohibiting the export of slaves to Arab countries. Yet the treaties were insufficient to put an end to the lucrative but illegal trade.

The traffic picked up after Seyyid Said's death in 1856; in the 1860s an estimated 7000 slaves were still being sold each year on the Zanzibar market. In 1873, however, Sultan Bargash of Zanzibar signed another treaty with the British that effectively closed down the slave markets.

The next logical step was to stimulate substitute commerce. The source of commerce could come only from the interior, which remained hopelessly inaccessible. The white man knew nothing of the interior's peoples or their history; even today the past of inland Kenya — and much of Africa — remains a mystery.

THE DARK REGIONS OF THE INTERIOR

Nobody was writing down the things that happened in the interior before the 19th century, but we still know quite a bit about the way people there lived for the thousands of years before the arrival of a written language. We possess a wealth of sources — archaeological, linguistic and oral — allowing us to describe the movements of peoples, their political structures, the foods they ate, the tools they used and the beliefs they held.

If we find an archaeological relic of, say, a cutting tool made of stone in the Rift Valley, we garner information about people who were not yet familiar with the use of iron, although they possessed food-producing knowledge, and more. If we study linguistic similarities between tribes, we can learn that these people once communicated, even though they now might live at opposite sides of the continent; the specific choice of words borrowed from another language is particularly informative. Finally, we can learn about culture and prehistory by listening to the traditions and stories handed down from generation to generation in oral legends.

The problem is that we can look at these things in different ways and therefore interpret them differently. The rich and complex factors that shaped the history of these peoples through thousands of years is largely the realm of specialists — anthropologists, ethnologists, linguists and archaeologists. Without an insider's interpretation, this unwritten history recedes from the layman, who must perhaps be satisfied with accounts that are sketchy, necessarily simplistic and debatable.

That's why histories of Africa generally concentrate on the period after the European discovery of the 'dark continent'. Still, we simply cannot understand Kenya today without looking at the people and events that predated the European arrival on the scene.

A TRIBAL MELTING POT

Kenya lies in what linguists call the Fragmentation Belt, which stretches across Africa from Senegal to Kenya. Here the linguistic, and therefore the cultural, diversity and fragmentation are the greatest. It was in this area that the mobility of tribes in the past was the most notable.

Many people traveled through this land, interacting and influencing each other, before moving on through a harsh landscape that was not always conducive to settling down. Wherever they came to rest they absorbed, or were absorbed by, their predecessors.

With permanent water supplies a rarity, few settlements were capable of supporting large populations. Periodically, a small group would strike off in search of new sources of sustenance. The groups continued to be part of a tribe as long as they maintained a common language, system of beliefs and way of life.

Tribes were held together by a loose system of age sets (a group of men who went through the initiation ceremony at the same time) or clans and lineages. Kenya had no kingdoms like those found along the Nile to the north or in the area to the west and south of Lake Victoria.

The tribes that migrated to Kenya belong to three language families: Bantu, Nilotic and Cushitic (linguists group Africa's 2000 plus dialects into families on the basis of similarities in their grammar, vocabulary and tonal sounds). Of the important tribes in Kenya today, the Kikuyu, Embu and Meru speak Bantu languages of the Niger-Congo group. The Masai, Luo and Kalenjin are all Nilotic speakers (of the Nilo-Saharan group). The Cushitic language, a branch of Afroasiatic, is spoken today by the Somalis.

Cushites, it seems, lived in the grasslands of the Rift Valley and in the Central Highlands at the time of the birth of Christ. They originated to the north, in Ethiopia and Sudan. They hadn't as yet any knowledge of iron smelting. Their stone tools, though, were sophisticated and they were already food producers, supplementing their hunting activities with cattle raising.

Cattle herding, which began during the first millennium BC, represented a revolutionary advance over simple hunting and gathering. The milk from the herds provided the community with a permanent source of food.

The other revolutionary development of the period was iron smelting. Although the Cushites used Stone Age technology until the 12th century or so, the Bantu began to make tools and ornaments out of iron sometime in the first millennium.

The Bantu, then, were agriculturalists, tilling their land with iron tools. They had settled on the choicest, most fertile regions near Lake Victoria and in the Eastern Highlands. The Kikuyu, Meru, Embu and Kamba tribes are descendants of these people.

The Nilotic-speaking Kalenjin participated in the other great migration of that era. Moving into the areas of the western highlands where the Cushites lived, they both absorbed the Cushites and were influenced by them.

Ethnologists trace the organization by age sets accompanied by initiation rites (circumcision for adolescents), practiced by many Bantu — or Nilotic — speaking tribes, to the Cushites. The taboo on eating fish is also thought to be of Cushitic origin, and like the Cushites, the Kalenjin raised cattle, although they supplemented herding with farming.

There is evidence that a community of Bantu people moved to the coastal area north of the Tana River during this same period. Known as Shungwaya, the settlement is thought to have become an important centre of activity from the 12th to the 15th century; its name appears on European maps of Africa in the 16th century, when the Cushitic Galla probably invaded the region from the north.

THE PAST 400 YEARS: A SKETCH

At the end of the 16th century, the Nilotic-speaking Luo began to migrate from the areas west of Lake Victoria and from the Sudan. Essentially cattle raisers, they settled in the Kavirondo Gulf region north-east of Lake Victoria, pushing some Bantu communities to the north. They continued to spread and to gain influence over the next two centuries.

Undoubtedly the major event in the past thousand years, other than the arrival of the Europeans, was the territorial expansion of the Masai, Nilotic-speaking people including the Samburu. They came to Lake Turkana sometime in the 15th century and in the 17th century they began to move south. By the 1890s they dominated the Rift Valley from the Uasin Gishu plateau to Tanzania.

Their success was due to the tribes' militaristic structure; organized by age sets, the Masai gave particular importance to the warrior grade: the *moran*. Every male, from his teens to his thirties, was trained to defend the tribe and steal cattle. The Masai thus dominated a large region of central Kenya and made incursions along the coast despite their relatively small numbers.

Agricultural communities, in particular, were hard hit by the Masai raids. The Kalenjin were pushed to the edges of the grasslands. They sought shelter in the hills between Lake Victoria and the Rift Valley and eventually broke into isolated tribes. The present-day Keyu (Elgeyo), Suk (Pokot), Nandi, Kipsigis and Tatoga are all subtribes of the Kalenjin.

The Kikuyu and the groups living in the wooded highlands benefited from the natural protection of their environment. Other settlements built mud defense walls. But Masai relations with their neighbours, in particular with the Kikuyu, were not always warlike. Although the Masai periodically raided Kikuyu cattle, the two tribes also traded and intermarried.

The latter half of the 19th century was marked by intertribal wars. The Moslem Somalis arrived from the north, chasing the Galla and the Boran. In the west the Suk, the Nandi, and the Kipsigis attacked the other tribes in the Kavirondo region and then were threatened in turn by the Turkana. The Turkana had moved into the area around Lake Turkana in the 17th and 18th centuries.

Masai morans *or warriors*

In the 1880s the Masai suffered from a smallpox epidemic and lost their cattle to rinderpest and pleuropneumonia. They were further decimated by the civil war that followed the death of their *laibon* (respected ritual expert, or medicine man, though not the tribal chief).

By the time the Europeans divided up the region, Masai power was declining, while the Kikuyu and Luo populations were increasing and their influence growing. For complex reasons, the Masai would end up helping the British contain the resistance of the Kikuyu and other tribes. Only a generation before, the warlike Masai were the most feared tribesmen encountered by the European explorers and missionaries who had arrived on the continent with the intention of 'discovering and civilizing' it.

EXPLORERS AND MISSIONARIES: THE MOVE INTO THE INTERIOR

Late in the 18th century, overpopulation caused the Kamba to move from the Machako district to Kitui in the east. There they maintained close contacts with both the Bantu communities (the Kikuyu, Embu and Meru) and the coastal population, and they began trading with both groups.

In the early 1800s the Kamba tribe became the first to operate long-distance trade routes across the country. Until then, ivory and slaves had traveled slowly from inland to the coast, from village to village.

Later, Zanzibari caravans moved inland, but they still avoided Masai territory, preferring the southern routes through Tanzania. The Kamba managed to monopolize the trade route through Kenya for decades by exaggerating stories of Masai aggression. It wasn't until later, in the 1880s, that regular trade routes were operating in present-day Kenya as far west as Mount Kenya, on to the Winam gulf of Lake Victoria and north to Lake Turkana.

That was the extent of contact between the coast and the interior when the first European missionaries started to move west. In 1846, the German Ludwig Krapf and the Rev. J. Rebmann set up a mission station in the village of Rabai a few miles west of Mombasa. During the next five years, Rebmann and Krapf (who were later joined by their colleague, J. Erhardt) undertook several expeditions. On one of these, Rebmann spotted the snow-capped summit of Mount Kilimanjaro and met with the Chagga tribesmen on its slopes.

For years afterward, England's geographers scoffed at his discovery, convinced that snow in the region was impossible. On another journey, Krapf reached Kitui, met with Kamba tribesmen and saw Mount Kenya. In general, the tribespeople near the coast welcomed and aided the missionaries. Farther inland, however, the foreigners were subject to attacks by hostile tribes, particularly the Masai.

In 1858, John Speke became the first European explorer to reach Lake Victoria, which he correctly identified as the source of the Nile, long sought by explorers and geographers. His claim was challenged, causing heated debate in Europe. It wasn't until 1874 that the issue was settled, when Henry Morton Stanley circumnavigated the lake.

In 1882, Joseph Thomson, the Scottish explorer and naturalist, became the first European to traverse Masai country, where he managed to survive on his reputation as a *laibon*. He discovered Lake Baringo before arriving at Lake Victoria and exploring Mount Elgon. The book he wrote of his adventures, *Through Masai Land* (1885), stirred the imagination of the British public.

In the meantime missionary work was picking up, though Christianity was as yet making little headway. Slavery was legally abolished in the United States in 1808, but slaves were brought to the Americas as late as 1870. At this point, missionaries and anti-slavery humanists turned their attention from West to East Africa. They set up stations for freed slaves throughout East Africa, the most important of them being Frere Town near Mombasa established in 1875. Many of the first converts to Christianity were former slaves who then took the new religion back to their tribes. By 1885, approximately 300 missionaries were serving in East Africa.

THE DIVISION OF EAST AFRICA

Spurred by the reports of missionaries and explorers, Europeans began to scramble for a piece of what they called 'Dark Continent'. By 1885, hostilities were already brewing between the French, Italians, British, Germans and the Sultan of Zanzibar when Carl Peters obtained an imperial charter for his German East Africa Company. Diplomatic negotiations between Britain and Germany led to an agreement the following year that divided the region into 'spheres of influence'.

The 1886 Anglo-German agreement marks the formal beginning of the colonization of Africa. The British and Germans traced an artificial frontier that ignored existing boundaries: it ran in a straight line from just south of Mombasa in the southeast to the eastern shore of Lake Victoria and then bent south on the other side of Lake Victoria to the border of the Congo. To the north of this line, in the region that is today Kenya and Uganda, was the domain of the British; the German sector was to the south, in present-day Tanzania. The Sultan of Zanzibar retained control over the thin coastal strip from Cape Delgado in the south to the Tana River in the north.

A year later the British leased the coastal belt bordering their region from the Sultan of Zanzibar in exchange for customs duties. The Germans obtained a similar agreement for the strip adjoining their region. A British East Africa Company was set up in 1888, but both the German and British companies were soon replaced by each country's respective government.

For administrative reasons, Britain separated its 'sphere of influence' into two protectorates, divided along the east side of the Rift Valley. In 1902, the frontier was moved west to Mount Elgon, which now marks the present boundary between Uganda and Kenya.

THE ARRIVAL OF WHITE SETTLERS

In 1896, the British began building a railway from the coast to Lake Victoria. Progress was slow; the workers, many of them Indians, were beseiged by jiggers (mites), epidemics and wild animals. In June 1899, the railhead reached the Masai village of Nairobi.

The future capital became the central supply base. A few years later, inhabited by railway employees, it had one general merchandise store and a hotel made of wood and tin. Across the Rift Valley, the railway line dropped to the valley floor and then rose 9000 ft/2744 m to the Western Highlands. The rail builders arrived at Lake Victoria in 1903.

The cost of the railway was £7.9 million — more than double the £3 million initial estimate. The story of the line's construction and how two lions held its progress in check, terrorizing workers for 10 months, is recounted by the engineer, P.H. Patterson, in his fascinating book, *The Man-Eaters of Tsavo.*

To Sir Charles Eliot, commissioner of the East Africa Protectorate from 1901 to 1904, a white-settler economy seemed to be the quickest way to recover the costs of the railway and the administration. The solution seemed particularly attractive to him, given the vast, apparently uninhabited highlands with a mild climate suitable for farming.

To encourage settlers, the government took over all land considered uninhabited in 1901 and sold it at two rupees an acre under easy payment terms. The offer was tempting, but the risks were high and there were few buyers.

In 1902, there were a dozen European farms. The next year, there were nearly a hundred. By 1915, there were still only a thousand white farmers in Kenya; but they had in their hands 4.5 million acres/1.8 million hectares of the most fertile land. Most of it was situated in what became known as the 'white highlands', and it included territory the natives considered their own.

COFFEE, SISAL AND MORE

Neither Eliot nor the other Europeans who came to Kenya knew exactly what crops could grow in the fertile soil of the highlands. They experimented with a variety of activities: wheat and flax plantations ended for the most part in disaster, while the cattle on their ranches were often devastated by disease or raids from neighbouring tribes.

Many Europeans returned home bankrupt. Yet enough prospered to allow the protectorate to pay for itself by 1912. Sisal, used to make twine, and coffee were the chief crops responsible for this success.

The first attempts to plant Arabica coffee had been made by a Roman Catholic missionary in the Teita hills and by a Scottish missionary in Kibwezi in 1893. By 1900, St Austin's Mission near Nairobi was supplying locally grown coffee to settlers. The crop was first exported in 1907 and by the outbreak of World War I in 1914, revenue from coffee had soared from £270 to £18,000.

The economic viability of many of the farms and of the colony as a whole though, remained fragile for decades after. The major exports were subject to international price fluctuations and, hard hit by the slump of 1920, the economy again suffered from a drought in 1922.

Just as the settlers were beginning to see their ventures pay off, they were dealt another blow with the international stock market collapse of 1929. Prices for sisal plunged from £40 a ton to £12, while coffee dropped from £120 a ton to £70.

In 1935, however, the economy picked up when the pyrethrum flower was discovered to contain an insecticide, thus adding a new cash crop to Kenya's exports. The decision to opt for a settler economy was paying off for the Europeans, at least financially, but it had created a lot of native hostility.

THE ROOTS OF CONFLICT

Many farms were located on land deserted by the Kikuyu during the smallpox epidemic of the 1890s. The Europeans thought the seemingly uninhabited land was theirs for the taking. The Kikuyu, though, did not see matters in quite the same light;

in the tradition of the agricultural communities of the region, they considered the land as theirs to reclaim when needed. They soon saw that the foreigners had settled down permanently.

In many respects the conflict that was about to be acted out in Kenya was similar to those taking place in most of the other colonized countries of Africa. Yet there were two factors specific to Kenya that would shape the development of this conflict: the choice of a white-settler economy and the way the native societies were organized. These made for a three-way drama among the Africans, the settlers and the British government.

The absence of a central native authority had initially impeded opposition to colonial rule. Sporadic fighting had broken out, but it was easily overcome during a series of military expeditions between 1895 and 1908. Among the tribes that most actively resisted the British incursion were the Kikuyu, the Kamba and the Nandi. Several tribes, on the other hand, allied themselves with the foreigners, in particular the Somalis and the warlike Masai.

Armed opposition, though, was rare because neither the nomads nor the subsistence farmers possessed a centralized governing system capable of effectively organizing military resistance.

At the same time these 'stateless' societies prevented the British from establishing control through native chiefs, as they had done, for example, in Uganda. Likewise, the idea of fostering cash-crop farming by Africans seemed difficult to promote in Kenya; certainly such a policy would not yield the quick results of a white-settler economy.

The British attempted to appoint native tribunals. Their legislative authority, however, rarely corresponded to that of the elders and they were often ignored in favour of the traditional tribal system. The local district councils, set up in the 1920s, were no more successful.

Meanwhile, the white landowners were becoming increasingly influential and demanding, despite attempts by the British government to withstand their pressure. The seeds of contention had been sown with the taking of the land that the natives considered their own. The conflict grew over the decades, fed by issues of land and labour.

NATIVE RESERVES AND COMPULSORY LABOUR

In 1904, the colonial government and a Masai *laibon* named Lenana signed a treaty creating the first native reserve. Four more were set up in 1906 (for the Kikuyu, Kitui, Kikumbuliu and Ulu). The British saw the reserves as a concession and hoped they would satisfy native land claims. But the policy of confining tribes to reserves reflected a fundamental lack of understanding of tribal society and economy.

Frozen within the boundaries of a reserve, the traditional mobility of the tribes was blocked; even the agricultural communities had always moved like nomads when faced with the need for new fertile land to feed an ever-growing population. As often as not, the reserves ignored traditional tribal boundaries and long-time use of grazing land. What's more, they offered no security to the natives because the boundary descriptions were not immediately published by the government and because land could be taken away by unilateral government decision.

In the mid 1920s, though, in response to growing native discontent, the reserves were officially declared to belong to the African tribes in perpetuity. Later 2600 sq mi/8734 sq km were added to satisfy tribal claims.

The other major cause of conflict arose over the labour issue. The European settlers had expected to find a vast, easily available labour supply for their large farms. The natives, on the other hand, were accustomed to their subsistence economy and saw no need to work for the foreigners. While the settlers advocated some form of compulsory labour by the natives (with the support of the colonial government), British public opinion and the London government were against the idea.

Nevertheless, the Africans were soon obliged to work for wages to pay the taxes imposed on them. These taxes effectively forced the natives into the cash economy. By the mid 1920s, half of the Kikuyu and Luo men were wage earners on white farms. Before long they made their grievances heard on pay, taxes and other matters.

IN THE WAKE OF WORLD WAR I

During World War I many of the white settlers left their farms to join the armed forces. The German threat to Kenya was rapidly put down, and Britain was given a League of Nations mandate over Tanganyika, formerly German East Africa, now Tanzania, at the end of the war. To compensate for the loss of revenue from abandoned farms, land was offered to discharged soldiers at rock-bottom prices.

There were about 9000 settlers by 1920, when the East Africa Protectorate became Kenya Colony (named after the territory's highest mountain). The same year the coastal strip, on lease from the sultan of Zanzibar, became the Kenyan Protectorate, later to be incorporated into the colony.

In Britain, the idea of union of the three territories was making inroads. Initially scrapped because of local opposition (especially from Uganda and Tanganyika, both wary of eventual Kenyan control), the idea was fostered again in the 1930s. Many white settlers in Tanganyika and Kenya sought union at that time as a safeguard against the return of Tanganyika to German hands. Their fears grew with the British government's detached attitude toward the Italian conquest of Ethiopia in 1935.

Meanwhile the British government was faced with demands by Kenya's white settlers for 'responsible self-government'. Using the leverage they had gained during World War I, the settlers managed to obtain seats on the legislative and executive councils. While their influence was by no means negligible, the British government withstood pressure by settlers and began elaborating a policy protecting African interests.

The policy was first stated officially by the colonial secretary, the Duke of Devonshire, in a 1923 White Paper. Written in response to the growing conflict between European settlers and the Indian community over the issue of representation, the Devonshire White Paper rejected the idea of 'responsible self-government' and stressed the importance of African representation.

It was, in fact, official acknowledgment of a process that was already underway.

THE RISE OF AFRICAN NATIONALISM AND POLITICAL OPPOSITION

The 1920s marked the beginning of native political activism. In the forefront were young members of the Kikuyu tribe. It was they who had lost the most to the Europeans; it was their homeland (including Nairobi) that lay in the centre of the white farming region. It was also the Kikuyu who had the closest contacts with the settlers; they had lived with and worked for the white farmers and administrators and had learned the inner workings of the political process.

The first African political association was founded in 1921 by Harry Thuku. Like many of Kenya's future leaders, he was a Kikuyu and had attended a mission school. Missionary schools, it turned out, were great training grounds for Africa's politicians.

Thuku arrived in Nairobi in 1911 at the age of 16. There he was obliged to carry a *kipande* (metal identification tag) and to pay taxes on his already small wages as a telephone operator.

Africans who, like Thuku, were integrated into the cash economy were particularly hard hit during the slump. When the government, with the intention of helping the economy back on its feet, declared rupees no longer legal tender and replaced them by florins, the natives were left empty-handed. Further plans to reduce wages enraged the Africans.

Thuku and some of his fellow workers opted for political action on the British model and created the Young Kikuyu Association. Its members demanded political representation and spoke out against pay cuts and the ban on African's owning land and growing coffee. They also opposed the pressure by missionaries against certain tribal practices like female circumcision.

A political gathering organized by the group was violently repressed, and Thuku was arrested and sent into exile. The group disbanded in 1925, but many of its members formed the Kikuyu Central Association (KCA). Jomo Kenyatta, later the first president of Kenya, became the association's general secretary a few years later.

In an attempt to channel African demands into official networks, the colonial government set up district councils. These were alloted funds for road building and other community projects like schools, medical buildings and forestation. But although they exercised some local authority, the District Councils did not possess enough political power to satisfy the growing number of discontented Africans.

Political associations proliferated during the 1930s; many of them were created by specific tribes — the Luo, the Taita, and the Kamba, among others — and focused on tribal concerns. The Kenya African Union (KAU), formed in 1944, was the first intertribal coalition. Foremost among its demands was the return of the 'white highlands' to the natives. Jomo Kenyatta became KAU's president upon his return from England in 1946. He had been living there since 1930.

At the same time, to contain the rising tide of nationalism, the colonial government began granting the Africans political representation; in 1944 Eliud Mathu became the first black on the Legislative Council. Another African was added to the Legislative Council in 1946; there were four in 1948, and six in 1952 when one African joined the 12-member Executive Council. Reform was picking up speed, but the changes were too few, progress was still too slow, and it was coming too late.

MAU MAU UPRISING

Sometime during 1950, reports concerning the activities of a secret organization known as Mau Mau became more and more insistent. Essentially a Kikuyu movement, its members endorsed violent opposition to the British and pledged to drive the Europeans from Kenya.

In October 1952, the government declared a state of emergency and brought in military reinforcements. By 1956, the situation was once again under control, although the state of emergency was not officially lifted until 1960.

The bloody attacks of the Mau Mau on white farmers shocked the world, but it was the natives who suffered most. During the four years of heavy fighting, fewer than 100 whites were killed, including 63 members of the army. The Africans paid a much heavier price, losing more than 13,000 lives; about 4000 of them were killed by the Mau Mau for failing to support the revolt. By 1960, more than a million Kikuyu were confined by the British to designated villages.

In 1953, in the midst of the fighting, the Kenya African Union was banned after the arrest of several of its leaders, including Jomo Kenyatta. They were accused of inciting the revolt, though KAU leaders had never openly supported violence. Kenyatta was not released until 1961.

The Mau Mau revolt was, in fact, instrumental in the British government's commitment to transfer political power to the Africans. Constitutional changes conferring more political rights on the natives followed one after the other. In 1955, the civil service in Kenya was opened to Africans. At the same time, more local councils were established and their powers augmented.

The number of Africans on representative bodies gradually increased. For the first time, in 1957, the eight Africans on the Legislative Council were elected rather than appointed by the governor. Among them were Daniel arap Moi (the current president), Ronald Ngala, Tom Mboya and Oginga Odinga.

In 1959 the British government accepted the principle of returning the 'white highlands' to native ownership. The British began a program of land transfer in 1961, just two years before independence. The government bought approximately 1 million acres from European settlers and made them available to Africans on easy loan terms. The way was being paved for majority rule.

THE ROAD TO INDEPENDENCE

A constitutional conference was convened in London in 1960 with the stated purpose of setting up, as Colonial Secretary Ian Macleod put it, 'parliamentary institutions on the Westminster model' to form the basis of 'responsible self-government'. The principle of one-person, one-vote was accepted. The same year Africans obtained a majority on the Legislative Council and filled four of the 10 ministerial posts.

Two African parties were formed: the Kenya African National Union (KANU) and Kenya African Democratic Union (KADU). KANU was established by Tom Mboya and Oginga Odinga with Jomo Kenyatta, still in prison, as its president. It was composed mostly of the country's two dominant tribes, the Luo and Kikuyu, and it favoured a centralized government with extensive powers. KADU, headed by Ronald Ngala, represented many of the smaller tribes. Fearing the domination of the Kikuyu and Luo, it supported a federal constitution that would protect the rights of minority tribes.

An attempt to establish a coalition government failed. KANU won decisively, in the general elections held in May 1963 and Kenyatta became prime minister. The formal declaration of independence came on December 12, 1963.

British control of East Africa came to an end. Lasting 77 years, it left deep imprints on all of the region.

EAST AFRICAN COMMUNITY

With all three colonies on the verge of independence (Tanzania achieved independence in 1961, Uganda in 1962), the idea of some sort of economic union was revived. First proposed in the 1920s, union had been partially realized during World War II with the founding of a joint war council. Cooperation was extended in the post-war period with the establishment in 1947 of the East Africa High Commission, which administered certain common services.

In 1961, immediately before independence, the High Commission became the East African Common Services Organization, with a single currency, a common market and a unified system of customs and transportation.

The federation quickly proved unfeasible and in 1967 it was replaced by the East African Community, with each country issuing its own currency and providing more decentralized services. The gap continued to widen between the three colonies and even a minimal form of cooperation between Julius Nyerere's socialist Tanzania, Kenyatta's capitalist Kenya, and Idi Amin's militarist Uganda (after the coup d'état in 1971) seemed more and more impossible. The community was dissolved in 1977.

KENYATTA'S KENYA

Only a year after independence, Kenya became a republic, with Kenyatta as president. Widely popular at home and with a growing reputation abroad, Kenyatta was the chief designer of the road his country would follow even after his death in 1978.

Unlike the leaders in Uganda and Tanzania, Kenyatta opted for a mixed economy with a focus on private investment. He was largely responsible for managing a smooth transition from European to African rule.

Even before independence, Kenyatta had reassured the settlers that private property would be respected and had told European farmers that they were welcome to stay. 'We can all work together harmoniously,' he declared 'to make this country great, and to show other countries in the world that different racial groups can live and work together.'

By encouraging the white settlers to stay, Kenyatta knew he was tapping a valuable resource. These already established European farms would contribute greatly to the economic health of independent Kenya. More important for the future of his country, Kenyatta's acts and words generated widespread good-will.

The country has maintained friendly relations with the Western democracies. This policy and Kenya's political stability have been instrumental in attracting both foreign investments and tourists. But although they have contributed greatly to the steady economic expansion of the country, they have not been sufficient to overcome the tremendous financial problems that beset the nation.

The most formidable challenge facing Kenyatta after independence was to unite the many cultural and ethnic groups of Kenya. The country came into existence with borders drawn by the British and Germans. In their struggle to achieve independence, the Kenyans who lived within these artificial boundaries had, to a certain extent, drawn together. Now they were faced with the even harder task of building a nation.

Jomo Kenyatta found the perfect rallying cry to express this goal: *harambee*, meaning 'let us all pull together'. At mass meetings all over the country the *Mzee*, or 'old man', as he was affectionately and respectfully called, would invoke *harambee* (pronounced ha-ram-BAY), and the crowd would answer him in unison.

Under the *harambee* banner many things became possible: the creation of self-help projects, of hospitals, schools and more. But most of all, *harambee* meant national unity. That there has been no outbreak of tribal or racial violence since independence in a country of more than 70 tribes is no small accomplishment.

KENYAN-STYLE DEMOCRACY

Critics claim that the price paid for national unity has been the gradual suppression of political opposition. It is true that over the years a sort of benign dictatorship has taken shape in which open criticism is not tolerated.

It started only a year after independence, when the opposition party KADU was voluntarily dissolved. In 1966, Oginga Odinga, the Luo vice president, was ousted from the party for his criticism of conservative government policies concerning wealth distribution. He then formed the Kenya People's Union (KPU) with other KANU dissidents. The new party lost the general elections the same year; it was soon banned and its leaders, including Oginga Odinga, were arrested (he was released in 1978 along with other polical prisoners when Daniel arap Moi came to power). KPU was the last opposition party in Kenya, though the country did not formally become a one-party republic until 1982.

In 1969, the prominent Luo politician Tom Mboya was murdered, provoking a national scandal and demonstrations among the Luo tribe against Kenyatta. In 1975, Josiah Mwangi Kariuki, a popular Kikuyu politician, was also murdered. Kariuki had continually spoken out against the widening gap between the rich and the poor and against the power amassed by the privileged elite. The special police were implicated during the investigation that followed, but no action was taken.

Increasingly, politicians who took the government to task openly were arrested under the Preservation of Public Security Regulations. In 1977, professor Ngugi wa Thion'o, a writer, was detained after the publication of a novel considered too critical.

Kenyatta came under fire for the wealth and power amassed by his family. Yet he continued to benefit from widespread popularity and was constantly re-elected until his death in 1978. In a peaceful transfer of power — that is in itself fairly unusual in Africa — he was succeeded by his vice-president Daniel arap Moi (arap means 'son of').

Many doubted Moi's ability to quell tribal rivalry and unify Kenyans, but Moi, a member of the minority Tugen tribe (of the Kalenjin family), has proved himself to be an effective leader.

A brief period of liberalization flourished during the first few years of Moi's presidency. Moi released political prisoners and launched an anti-corruption campaign. An attempt to 'detribalize' politics resulted in some basically superficial changes, such as dropping the tribal reference in an association's name.

Soon, however, the cycle of protests and repression began again. In 1982, a coup d'état attempt by a part of the Kenya air force was put down by the army. In its aftermath, Moi became increasingly severe with opponents.

An almost comic story told by an American journalist demonstrates how intolerant government officials could be: a traveler crossing the border into Kenya was stopped by customs officers for transporting political posters said to insult the president; the posters featured a monkey and the French inscription 'Protège-Moi' ('protect me').

Moi also periodically shut down Nairobi University, which he described as 'a breeding ground for subversion'. In 1986 and 1987, dozens were imprisoned in a crackdown on an elusive opposition group known as Mwakenya.

The National Christian Council of Kenya (NCCK) and some US and UK groups have been increasingly critical of Kenya for political rights abuses. Many people, however, consider these violations to be minimal by African standards. They insist that most African countries are not strong enough to withstand tribal factions and self-interest groups using western-style democratic methods.

Be that as it may, foreign observers unanimously rank Kenya high among African countries for its economic development and political stability. Though much wealth remains in the hands of a few and the vast majority of Kenyans live in poverty, the growing middle class is becoming more important. Its members have a vested interest in political stability — as do the majority of Kenyans — and that bodes well for the future.

Chronology of historical events

1498	Vasco de Gama lands on the coast between Mombasa and Malindi.
1698	The Arabs force the Portuguese out of Kenya.
1840	The Imam of Oman, Said, transfers his capital from Mascate to Zanzibar (once a part of Kenya).
1888	British East Africa set up, encompassing all of Kenya except the coast, granted to Zanzibar but as a British Protectorate.
1890	Establishment of the borders between Kenya and Tanganyika.
1892	Railway started between Mombasa and Lake Victoria.
1902	Kenya's first constitution signed: 75% of Kenya is under British control, the outer regions remain the domain of the tribes.
1923	The Legislative Council is formed with 11 English, 5 Indians and 1 Arab (no African representation).
1922	Thuku, the founder of the Young Kikuyu Association (1921) is imprisoned, riots follow.
1924	Kikuyu Central Association (KCA) created with Jomo Kenyatta as secretary.
1930	Kenyatta leaves Kenya for England, following arrests of African leaders (returns to Kenya in 1946).
1940	KCA and other nationalist associations banned.
Late 40s.	Beginning of the Mau Mau rebellion.
1946	The Kenya African Union (KAU) is founded, with Kenyatta as president.
1952-60	State of emergency declared: Mau Mau is banned, all African nationalist organizations are again prohibited, Kenyatta and other leaders are arrested.
1961	Kenyatta released from prison.
1963	Colonial rule ends and Kenya becomes an independent nation with Kenyatta as Prime Minister.
1978	Kenyatta dies and arap Moi becomes President.

KENYA TODAY

Fifteen million years ago, under the strain of enormous volcanic eruptions, the earth's surface split apart in a giant arc from Mozambique to Syria. Lava flowed onto the floor of what was to become the Rift Valley. Petrified volcanic depositions formed escarpments on either side of a gigantic graben (or trough) — up to 50 mi/80 km wide. The parallel ridges of its abrupt, towering slopes resemble gargantuan steps.

A GIGANTIC SCISSION

In Kenya, this enormous north-south fissure leans slightly to the west. Lakes of all sizes cover the valley floor amid startlingly beautiful volcanic cones.

It is difficult to imagine anything disturbing the perfect stillness of the lakes apart from the thousands of birds that come to rest beside them. Here and there, though, intense volcanic activity still exists: steam escapes from the crevices of the rocks in a landscape that will not sustain the slightest vegetation.

On either side of this rift stretches a country of 224,960 sq mi/582,646 sq km. Kenya, which sits astride the equator, straddles both hemispheres and offers a wondrous diversity of landscapes. Its climate too, is complex.

Theoretically, there are two rainy seasons (the long and the short rains), but the rainy months are sometimes dry and the dry months sometimes humid. The region is, in fact, a composite of microclimates. The coolest months are July and August, but hot and cold weather coexist and the visitor can sometimes travel just a small distance (62 mi/100 km or so) to change climates.

A VARIED LANDSCAPE

Along the shore of the Indian Ocean, scattered patches of woodland dot the coastal plain. The terrain becomes increasingly dry toward the north until it merges into a sand desert along the Somalian and Ethiopian borders. The Marsabit massif and the Nyiro and Kulal mountains rise abruptly in the middle of this flat desert, their wooded slopes standing in sharp contrast to their surroundings.

The Galana River during the dry season draws numerous species to Tsavo East.

West from the coast, the land rises gradually. The hills overlooking the coastal plains are the first indication of this change in altitude.

Along the Tanzanian border, which extends in a practically straight line across 378 mi/608 km, lie the plains of Tsavo and Amboseli. Close to the border, they give way to the foothills that climb to the green slopes and snow-covered peak of Mount Kilimanjaro. Though almost all of the mountain is on the Tanzanian side, it dominates the whole area; you can see the summit from far away, unless clouds get in the way.

North of the border, the road from Mombasa to Nairobi traverses what seems to be a region of plains. No matter which way you look, the monotony of the extensive flatlands is broken only by the rolling hills along the northern horizon. That impression, however, is misleading; in fact, the land rises gradually from sea level to 5577 ft/1700 m at Nairobi — more than a mile in elevation.

The fertile valley north of the capital is wedged between the Nyandarua (Aberdare) range and Mount Kenya (17,057 ft/5199 m); the mountain's imposing bulk makes Mont

Blanc pale in comparison. To the north-east, before you reach the great plateaus of the north, you must pass through the undulating landscape of the Meru and Samburu foothills.

West of Nairobi, the earth continues its indiscernible ascent up to the edge of the Rift Valley; the escarpment there towers above the valley floor as high as 3281 ft/1000 m in certain places. The plateau to the north rises to a peak at Mount Elgon (14,147 ft/4312 m).

The highway to the west of the Rift Valley gently descends to the shores of Lake Victoria, which is shared by three nations — Kenya (with much the smallest part), Tanzania and Uganda.

You see diversity in landforms everywhere in this beautiful country. Even the vast regions of plains or plateaus are bounded or broken by hills, some wooded and some not. The variegated rocks, when they are not the subtle greys and blacks of lava, reflect changing hues all day long.

FROM DESERT TO ALPINE FLORA

An astounding diversity of vegetation corresponds to the diversity of Kenya's landscapes, accentuated by temperature variations at differing altitudes.

Typical savannah or grassland vegetation covers much of the lowlands. In areas that receive adequate rain, plants, flowers, trees and shrubs can become rich and varied. As the rainfall diminishes, the grasslands give way to a desert vegetation that is equally astonishing. Here stand the stark silhouettes of euphorbia, enormous cactus-like plants more than 6 ft/2 m high, and of acacia, which flare out like parasols, sometimes at ground level and sometimes high enough to remind you of pine trees.

The banks of the rivers or streams that flow through the savannah — like the Tana River from Mount Kenya to the Indian Ocean — are covered with lush forest galleries. Thriving here are palm trees, acacias, eucalyptus, and those spectacular baobabs with enormous trunks and twisted, often leafless, branches.

The coastal plain bristles with coconut palms, groves of mangoes and bananas and bougainvilleas. Along the coast, amid the sand-enclosed lagoons and estuaries are those exceptional mangroves; these aquatic forests are remarkable for the way the mangled roots of the trees rise into a labyrinth above the water.

At low tide, thickets of greenery appear to be propped up on stilts. Mangroves usually grow on marshy, muddy terrain in areas that are hard to reach without a boat. The only way through the thickets is to punt or row; the silence, broken by the slithering and creaking of hidden crocodiles or snakes, renders the atmosphere heavy and threatening.

The tropical forests of the interior are a colourful counterpoint to the aquatic ones. They vary in type and density according to the altitude. Fantastic plant life flourishes in this rich soil — with liana as large as young trunks, trunks as smooth as liana, and ferns so big they look like trees.

Evergreen trees dominate the forests above 6562 ft/2000 m; their trunks can reach a diameter of 9.8 ft/3 m. Moss, orchids and ferns wind around them and penetrate deep into their empty centres, dug out in their youth — hundreds of years ago — by elephants.

In certain regions, these conifers form an almost impenetrable thicket. Other woodlands are less dense — like the cedar forests that prosper in the drier terrain of the western slopes of Mount Kenya and Nyandarua (Aberdare).

Higher still, conifers give way to bamboo, 33 ft/10 m high, which form a virtually impassable enchanted forest obstructing access to the moors and glaciers beyond. Giant plants such as groundsel, ferns and lobelia flourish alongside dwarf plants with delicate leaves and fragrant flowers.

AN EXPLODING POPULATION

Undoubtedly, the single most important problem in Kenya is its explosive population growth rate. At 4.1% a year, it is one of the world's highest, with far-reaching repercussions on the country's social, political and economic future.

The population was estimated at 23.88 million in 1988. It had doubled in only 16 years, and if the fertility rate is maintained, it will double again by 2005. Even if the birthrate is brought down, there will be 35 million Kenyans in the year 2000. That means that in less than a generation there will be more than twice as many children needing schooling, youths looking for jobs and people to feed.

The reasons for this explosion are complex. Health improvements are a factor; since independence, life expectancy has risen (by 10 years) and the infant mortality rate has fallen (from 147, down to 80 per 1000 in the mid-1980s). Health conditions have of course progressed in other developing countries as well, but few of them match Kenya's growth rate.

Another important factor is social attitudes. Women in Kenya have an average of eight children; a survey in the mid-1980s showed that Kenyan women wanted almost as many children (precisely 7.2) as they were having.

When questioned, the women explained that having many children was seen as proof of their value; in a country where polygamy is still the rule, the ability to conceive gives a woman a better chance of holding on to her husband. These women also felt that the more children they had, the more chance that at least one of them would succeed in life; children thus provided their parents with a sort of insurance against poverty, in particular in old age.

Family planning programs — the first began in 1966 — have begun to reverse the birth trend only in the past two years. It is estimated that 17% of married women now use contraception, but the vast majority are among the wealthier the more educated.

The government is intent on setting up more extensive education and information services to curb births. If the growth rate is brought down to the target 3.7% (an average of 5.6 children), there will be 10% fewer Kenyans in 2000 than forecast — 34.8 instead of 38.5 million. This considerable difference would still require a significant expansion of the economy and large financial outlays to satisfy basic needs.

EDUCATED BUT JOBLESS

Kenya's population boom places a strain on the country's already fragile economy. A serious economic crisis awaits if something is not done quickly to both reduce the growth rate and to greatly expand opportunities for work.

According to World Bank estimates, merely to maintain the current, — already insufficient, — standards of education, health and housing, government spending would have to increase 7% a year. That is significantly more than the rate of economic expansion, which hovers around 5%.

Part of the problem is that fully 60% of Kenyans are below 18 years old, a condition that naturally places a heavy burden on the state's financial resources. Considering schooling a priority, the government devotes between 17% and 20% of its budget each year to education. The results have been impressive.

School enrollment between the ages of 6 and 17 has risen greatly (from 43% in 1970 to 78% in 1984). Primary school attendance is impressive: 89% of the 6- to 11-year-olds were in school in the mid-1980s. The figure, though, falls to 60% for teenagers (12 to 17). And only 1% of Kenyans go on to higher education. Girls are even more unlikely to finish secondary school than boys; many drop out because of pregnancy.

Adult illiteracy has decreased, although it is still quite high by Western standards. About six of every ten adults know how to read.

The differences between the sexes in literacy is significant : only 49% of the women are literate, compared to 70% of the men. Though statistics for separate age groups are not available, there is definitely more literacy among the young; as these young people grow to adulthood, the adult literacy rate will climb significantly.

The undeniable progress the country has made in the field of education is now being threatened. Government expenditure cannot keep pace. Parents already pay significant fees for their children's education (25% of primary school costs and almost 70% for secondary school). Increasing these fees could make education prohibitive to all but the wealthiest.

Even if the state budget could be raised, what hope would these graduates have of finding work in an increasingly tight job market? Each year hundreds of thousands of graduates leave school, but only 28,000 jobs are created. The ranks of the unemployed (estimated at 13% in 1988) swell, placing a further burden on the state's social budget. To accommodate job seekers, more than 6 million jobs will have to be created by the year 2000.

The educational focus today is increasingly on technical training for immediate job opportunities. Private businesses, which already employ more than half the country's wage earners, are expected to create most of the new jobs.

A Moslem school in Lama.

A PRECARIOUS DEMOGRAPHIC BALANCE

The growth in population also upsets Kenya's demographic balance. Only 15% of the land receives enough rain for farming and 75% of the inhabitants are already squeezed into those fertile regions. Around Lake Victoria, in the highlands and along the coast, density can reach 400 people per square kilometre.

The consequence of the population pressure is twofold: the land is expected to yield more to satisfy the needs of more and more people, but when these needs can't be met, people leave the countryside and flock to the city. This exodus is a serious problem. After independence, much of the farmland was divided into small, individual ownerships, at the beginning of the 1980s they numbered about 1.5 million, with plots averaging two acres.

It is easy to imagine the sequence of events when, upon the death of a father, the farm is divided among four sons into half-acre plots. Unable to feed, dress and educate their children, the men leave the tiny, unproductive farms to their wives and head to the city to seek work. Most of them end up there in the ranks of the unemployed.

THE URBAN INFLUX

In a country where almost 85% of the people live in the countryside, the above scenario is commonplace. It threatens to become even more so. Cities are growing at a rate of 7.4% a year, and the government estimates that there will be 9 million to 10 million city residents by the year 2000 — between 25% and 30% of the population. Six cities the size of Nairobi would be needed to accommodate them. In any case, large outlays of capital will be needed to create the necessary urban infrastructure of housing and transport.

Nairobi, in particular, is suffering from this trend. Less than a century has elapsed since the one-time Masai village became the main railway supply centre (see p. 43). From 1950 to 1980 Nairobi's population increased sixfold. Today, shantytowns are developing at an alarming rate around this sprawling urban centre.

According to a 1983 estimate, Nairobi already had more than a million residents and if the trend continued, 7 million people would live in the capital by 2050; that's 28 times the 250,000 inhabitants that Nairobi should ideally accommodate.

LAND: A PRECIOUS
AND RARE RESOURCE

The only possible way to counter the exodus is to make agriculture more profitable. Farming output will have to be increased but not at the risk of damaging the land through abusive cultivation. Careful planning is necessary to avoid depleting soil and destroying fragile ecosystems.

Certain practices have already provoked extensive deforestation and land degradation. Trees are cut down along the edge of the forests to clear new land for cultivation with no consideration for either the quality of the soil or the long-term effects on the environment. Likewise, the widespread use of wood as a fuel is shrinking the forests. Each year 38 million cubic metres of wood (the equivalent of a million tons of oil) is used as fuel.

Burning fields is another harmful and commonplace practice. Farmers use this technique as an expedient to get rid of weeds; herders use it to provoke the rapid sprouting of tender grass for their livestock and to eliminate the disease-carrying tsetse fly which ravages their herds.

All this activity has disastrous consequences on the environment. On the newly cleared slopes, rain carries off the topsoil and precious nutrients. The soil becomes degraded and dry. Scientists believe that climatic changes follow.

Environmentalists, researchers, bankers and government officials are aware of these risks. Several governmental bodies are trying to control the use of the country's valuable resources. The Department of Resources Survey and Remote Sensing has developed an early-warning system that should allow specialists to counter dangerous trends; the Rural Afforestation and Extension Services has contributed to the starting of more than a thousand tree nurseries.

The crucial problem is how to get farmers and herders to stop using techniques that have traditionally provided their very livelihood. These people, of course, cannot afford to think about the future economic health of the country as a whole. Feeding their families comes first.

Only practical alternatives that do not cut into farmers' income offer some hope of saving them from poverty and stemming their flight to the cities.

ENERGY

One fairly straightforward measure destined to protect the environment is to reduce dependence on wood by developing other sources of energy. What's more, wood and charcoal production methods are being refined to become more efficient.

Readily available materials such as burned grass and other agricultural waste products can be used to make ethyl alcohol. Similarly, the husks of coffee beans treated in a Nairobi factory are converted into carbon compounds.

Petroleum currently accounts for 86% of commercial energy. Its consumption must be reduced because it is a costly import that contributes significantly to the country's commercial deficit. Exploration incentives have been offered to foreign companies to look for oil. Unfortunately, the results so far have been discouraging.

Elsewhere, solar energy is being used, mainly on a small scale. Lodges use it to heat water, and there are projects underway to tap solar heat for the electrical energy in some villages.

The use of hydroelectric energy is being extended to rural areas. There are five major power stations on the Tana River. A vast hydroelectric station is under construction at Turkwel Gorge, in the Turkana district near Uganda. Built by Spie-Batignolles, a French construction company, the project has already resulted in the creation of a town and an airstrip.

Besides supplying hydroelectric power, the project should make possible the irrigation of 5000 hectares. Soon the whole region, once frequented only by gold prospectors and Turkana nomads, may be covered with farms.

RURAL DEVELOPMENT PROJECTS

Another irrigation project in the Nyanza district is expected to provide water for 3 million people. Satellite photographs were used to determine the most suitable location for the 750 water distribution points that will make up the network.

Meanwhile, agronomists and other specialists are weighing the risks and benefits of extending farms to marginal areas. The land susceptible to cultivation is not, however, infinite. Its limits have already been more or less reached, and the solution therefore lies in trying to increase the yield from existing farmland. One way is to use higher-quality fertilizers and insecticides and improved crop strains. Another is to encourage the cash-earning aspects of what have been largely subsistence activities but have high commercial potential, such as livestock raising and fishing. The marketing of produce is being helped by cooperatives and price adjustments. Many of these projects have been made possible in part by funding from international lending institutions like the World Bank.

In the vast regions of arid and semi-arid land that cover Kenya, 20% of the people draw their livelihood from livestock.

Several ongoing projects should increase the viability of these regions by encouraging commerce. Small-scale irrigation projects and drought-resistant fodder crops can go far to protect herds from harsh climatic conditions. An improved road network and the creation of marketing cooperatives will help livestock raisers transport fresh milk and meat to sales points around the country.

SELF-HELP ACTIVITIES

Many of the economic and social projects are carried out on the local level as part of the *harambee* system. *Harambee*, 'let us all pull together', is more than an abstract rallying cry or a slogan; it is the term used to designate self-help community-development programs.

There are 15,000 to 20,000 *harambee* projects, concerned with everything from the installation of water and energy systems to adult education. Almost 20% of all secondary schools, for example, are *harambee* institutes.

Financing comes from local contributions (Ksh 580 million were collected in 1987) and from the government, which also provides technical support. Each year the *harambee* system contributes an impressive 4% to 10% of government development expenditure. Furthermore, since the plans are locally inspired, they generally correspond more to the particular needs of each community than state-conceived ideas might. They also tend to galvanize a good deal of support among the people concerned.

The *harambee* system, moreover, serves a political function. Through the self-help groups, Kenyans have obtained some grass-roots influence on government policies and particularly on the development of social services like health and education. In return, the government can use the rural organizations to influence local events and to exchange ideas.

In 1985, aware of the necessity to decentralize its activities even more, the government adopted the District Focus on Rural Development. Forty two District Development Committees were set up to plan and operate local projects. The government allocates funds and retains control. Engineers and technicians help plan and carry out the locally initiated projects.

The rural development plan corresponded to demands by the International Monetary Fund and other lending institutions for Kenya to limit its budget deficits and its growing external debt. Under the new system, *harambee* projects have become increasingly viable, reaching an 85% rate of implementation.

AN ECONOMIC EVALUATION

Kenya is widely considered a model of economic progress in Africa. Its record is, in fact, rather mixed, but analysts think it is doing better than other African countries.

Its overall economic growth since independence is one of the highest in Africa. This accomplishment is all the more

Coffee is one of Kenya's key export crops, along with tea and sisal.

noteworthy since Kenya is not a rich country in terms of available resources: it has practically no petroleum or mineral deposits.

The gross domestic product (all the goods and services produced in the country) has, on the whole, been increasing at a healthy rate of about 5% a year (5.2% in 1988). Employment has been rising, too, with four times as many jobs today as there were at independence (up 3.7% in 1988).

Per capita income increased 10% between 1963 and 1988; the annual growth rate, however, has been declining over the past few years (5% in 1986 and 1987) as population pressure mounts. Real gross fixed investment rose 22% between 1984 and 1987 — the reflection of a buoyant economy.

AGRICULTURE: THE MOTOR OF THE ECONOMY

Food production is the mainstay of Kenya's economy. It still earns the most foreign exchange even though its share of the gross domestic product dropped from 72% in 1977 to 29% in 1988 as earnings from tourism and industry rose. Nevertheless, for many different reasons, food production is considered the key to the country's future.

One of every five workers earns a living in food production, and three of every four Kenyans subsist from agriculture and cattle-raising. The capacity of the country to survive its population explosion, to continue feeding its citizens and to stem the rural exodus, depends on the healthy development of these activities.

Kenya, in fact, lives off its own land. The country grows practically all the food it consumes: maize, sorghum, cassava, millet, bananas, potatoes. Cash crops include coffee, tea, sisal, pyrethrum (a natural insecticide), fruits, vegetables and flowers. Coffee is the leading export commodity, followed by tea. They account for some 35% of foreign cash earnings.

Unfortunately, revenues from coffee and tea are unstable, rising and falling with world prices. Making agricultural output more diverse is one way to insure against the uncontrollable variables — not only world prices but also Kenya's unpredictable and erratic rainfall.

Still, agriculture is a valuable foreign currency earner. Canned products, like pineapple and juices, are exported around the world, while flowers, beans, avocados and other fresh produce are sold in Europe.

The lack of cargo air space, though, has so far hindered the extension of this promising sector. Plans are underway to increase the volume of transports and to give priority to high-value foods such as mangoes, strawberries and beans.

The domestic market of the meat and dairy industries has been growing. A decontrol of the meat industry in 1987 resulted in an 18.7% rise in revenue the following year. Likewise, the breakup of marketing monopolies has stimulated the sale of dairy products.

TOURISM AND MANUFACTURING

After agriculture, tourism is Kenya's second most important foreign exchange earner. In 1988, 6.9 million tourists brought in revenues that contributed more than 25% of the gross domestic product. The average stay was 16 days. Tourism has been catching up with coffee and tea, and some statisticians think it has already surpassed them as the primary source of foreign exchange.

For this reason, the government has been giving priority to the promotion of tourism. It has made considerable efforts to improve the national parks and reserves, protect wildlife and the natural environment and fight against poachers (see pp. 83-86).

Manufacturing is also expanding and diversifying. It accounted for only 7% of the gross domestic product at independence, but it expanded by about 11% a year in the 1970s. It slowed to less then 6% in the 1980s. Nervertheless, by the end of the 1980s, one of every six workers held a job in industry, and they contributed 13% to the nation's economy.

As might be expected, one of the key manufacturing activities is the processing of agricultural products. The canning industry has been progressing significantly as have the enterprises that handle meat and dairy products. Kenya's precious resource, land, likewise provides the primary product used in the paper and textile industry. By recycling locally grown cotton, the latter has effectively reduced imports.

Kenya also has a petroleum-refining industry, but it suffers from the rising cost of imported crude oil. Other manufacturing industries include vehicles and pharmaceutical products. The fledgling pharmaceutical industry consists of 23 companies, five of which specialize in veterinary products. Export revenues from pharmaceuticals are growing each year.

SATISFYING LENDING PARTNERS

With a commercial deficit of almost 839 million in 1988, Kenya is largely dependent on international loans. The balance-of-trade deficit remains one of the country's major problems. To stimulate exports, the government has adopted a series of measures, including tax advantages and exempting export companies from paying import duties on essential equipment.

The nation, though, is growing in industrial strength. In fact, industrial supplies, machinery and capital equipment now account for most of Kenya's imports. Lending institutions, such as the International Monetary Fund and the World Bank are relatively forthcoming with loans because Kenya is considered to be reliable in paying them back.

Since independence the government has firmly supported a policy of mixed, public-private economy, with a focus on private investment. The private sector is increasingly becoming the principal force of economic development.

Protectionist policies designed to reduce imports of manufactured goods are being modified, a move that will expose Kenya's industry to international competition. The government is eliminating some of its monopolies and price control regulations as well. Flexible exchange rates, aligning farm prices with costs, and less complicated licensing policies are other measures aimed at boosting the economy.

These stringent policies are often the result of tough negotiations with international donors and lenders. In 1987, Kenya applied for the International Monetary Fund's Enhanced Structural Adjustment Facility — a long-term payment loan available to countries prepared for extensive structural modifications.

Among other steps, the IMF insisted that the government reduce its social services expenditure; in particular, it was decided to charge a user tax for education and health services. Participant fees are already significant, considering the income of most Kenyans, and raising them could lead to trouble. The controversial policies necessary for the economic health of the country could eventually produce unwanted political repercussions.

HORIZON 2000

In 1986, the state published a handbook entitled *Economic Management for Renewed Growth (The Sessional Paper),* which elaborated the strategy for development in the 1990s. It contains a list of goals that must be met if Kenya is to avoid an economic crisis engendered by its population explosion.

According to the handbook, agriculture retains the key role in the country's economy, but it must become more productive to provide food, bring in more export revenue, and supply more jobs. The targeted growth rate is 5% a year. The non-farm rural economy must be enlarged both to attract job seekers away from the cities and to stimulate the domestic market.

A more dynamic private sector, in particular small businesses, is essential, the handbook adds. Other targets include a reduction of the population growth rate to 3.7% per year and an expansion of the economy to 6% a year. The plan also calls for a 7.5% yearly increase in manufacturing.

These aims represent a formidable economic challenge that even optimists doubt can be met. Nervertheless, for more than a quarter of a century, since independence, Kenya has been a model of political and economic stability. Its record of fiscal and monetary responsibility and flexibility continue to inspire the confidence of lending institutions and the international community.

THE PEOPLE OF KENYA

Kenya's population of 24 million is composed of a rich variety of ethnic groups. There are 42 different tribes, the smaller of them, like the Mukogodo and El Molo, numbering less than a thousand, and the larger, like the Luo, Luhya and Kikuyu, totaling between 3 and 4 million each. Perhaps you won't be able to see the cultural differences between these people when you first arrive in such a cosmopolitan city as Nairobi. For many years, individual tribal traits have been ironed out not only in the capital, where most residents want to adapt to the international norms of contemporary city-dwellers, but also in the countryside. Traditional native garments have been mostly abandoned in favour of contemporary, Western-style clothing. By traveling around the country and especially by venturing into the remoter areas, however, you will get a much better idea of the diversity of the people and their customs. This variety is largely determined by the occupations of rural people; whether they are farmers or fishermen, herders or hunter-gatherers.

While the different ethnic groups still live in their traditional territories, Kenyan society is nonetheless marked by a mobility that is primarily due to economic pressure. People travel widely to look for work. They disperse and adapt, willingly speaking other tribal languages, as well as Swahili and very often English. The most ubiquitous are the Kikuyu, who can be found throughout the country running businesses or holding administrative posts. This countrywide mobility has brought about a breakdown of traditional values, and tribal practices are gradually disappearing. As a general rule, members of the older generation still adhere to their long-held beliefs and customs, but their juniors tend to be far less influenced by them.

The present population has evolved through a long history of mingling with immigrants from different parts of the African continent, intermarrying with some or retaining the customs of others who moved on. The different ethnic groups can be classified into three major categories — Bantu, Nilotic and Cushitic. There are also smaller groups of older origins, the hunter-gatherers, who have adopted elements from all three, and finally there are the relative newcomers, the Arabs, Asians and Europeans.

THE BANTU

The largest linguistic group in Kenya, the Bantu, spreads over the central, western and coastal parts of the country. Evidence of Bantu presence dates back about 2000 years, when successive Iron Age groups entering from the west and south-west met and mingled with earlier established peoples.

The Kikuyu

The most numerous and influential tribe of the central Bantu is the Kikuyu (4 million), based around three main towns north of Nairobi — Kiambu, Murang'a and Nyeri. You will probably have more contact with the Kikuyu than with any other tribe because they tend to dominate every domain, whether commercial, political, agricultural or touristic. According to tribal legend, they all belong to the extended *Mbari ya Moombi* (Moombi's family), the result of a union between Gikuyu, the first Kikuyu man, and his wife, Moombi, who was sent to him by Mogai (or Ngai), the Divider of the Universe. Gikuyu was granted rich farmland around Mount Kenya, Kere-Nyaga, which the Kikuyu have always held in great respect. They traditionally believe the mountain to be the resting place of Ngai when on earthly visits, and they face it when offering prayers during important events or when making ritual sacrifices. Gikuyu and Moombi settled near a grove of sacred fig trees and had nine daughters, the ancestors of today's nine major clans.

The early Kikuyu are believed to have encountered pygmy forest hunters known as the Gumba, who were gradually absorbed by the larger tribe. Through various transactions the Kikuyu acquired land from Ndorobo hunter-gatherers, which they cleared and cultivated. The work on the fields and around the homestead was traditionally divided between the sexes. Men cleared bush, cut down trees, built fences, tended stock and put up the framework for houses, while women cut and carried grass for thatching, plastered the walls with mud or dung, fetched water and firewood, and cooked. Both sexes were involved in planting, weeding and making beer. Children helped with the lighter tasks. At market, men sold livestock while women traded grains. Any extra wealth left over after supplying immediate family needs was invested in stock — cattle, sheep and goats — and a rich man was recognized by the size of his herds. The Kikuyu traded with the Kamba, their neighbours and fellow Bantu, as well as with the Nilotic Masai. Although there were frequent cattle raids between the Kikuyu and the Masai, intermarriage was common.

Apart from the family group or *mbari,* traditional Kikuyu tribal organization extended to the clan or *moherega,* a group of larger units that shared the same ancestors and had a common name. The people were further united through a system of *riika* or age-grading, whereby boys and girls were bound by ties of loyalty to others who were initiated into full membership of the community at the same time. With the initiation of each new generation — a rite of passage from childhood to adulthood through circumcision and clitoridectomy — a new 'age-set' was formed. For an adolescent the build-up to the initiation ceremony was an intense time of learning. Both boys and girls

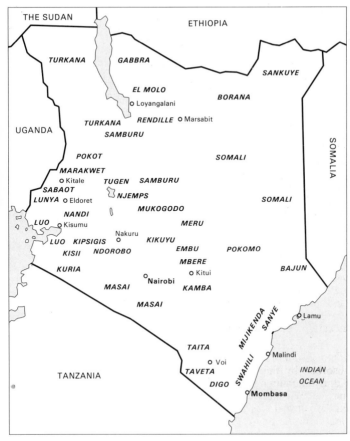

MAP OF TRIBES IN KENYA

were instructed in the laws and customs of the tribe, how to behave toward parents and elders, how to conduct sexual matters, what tribal duties to fulfill and so on. Apart from the physical operation itself, initiation consisted of ceremonies with elders, invocations of ancestral spirits, appeals to *Ngai,* purification rites, feasting and dancing. Marriage was not regarded as a simple affair either, but included family visits with presents of beer and payment of a dowry insurance in installments. It was considered bad luck to pay it all at once.

A man's status in society was closely related to the size of his family, for the more wives and children he had, the better equipped he was to conduct tribal matters; he would have gained precious experience in the management of a large group. Before attaining the status of elder, he passed through various warrior grades and their rituals of admittance. A woman was expected to marry and have children. On becoming a wife, she shared the social status of her husband. The system of government was democratic and egalitarian, with no position inherited; personal merit was the decisive factor. Age was extremely important; the respect due to a person was largely in accordance with his or her years.

In the tribal judicial system, a minor dispute was dealt with by the family council, but anything more serious, like land transaction, stock theft, debt or a problem over the dowry, was taken before a public court or an assembly of elders. This body exacted fines, meted out punishment and enforced compensation to the injured party. As far as religion is concerned, the Kikuyu traditionally regarded Ngai as God, the creator and giver of all things. They also had a reverential attitude towards nature, the provider of their livelihood as farmers. Finally, in keeping with a desire to preserve a sense of tribal continuity, they communed with ancestral spirits. Around 1929, because missionary teachings disagreed with certain tribal beliefs and practices, especially clitoridectomy and polygamy, some Kikuyu converts broke away from the church to form their own sects, taking what was relevant from Christian doctrine and adapting it to their own religious needs. It was not unusual to find sons baptized with names like Solomon or Jacob — important men from the Old Testament who had all been polygamous! Today, as with many other tribes, Kikuyu men and women may be Protestants, Catholics, or of no particular religion, some adhering to traditional beliefs, others not.

Contemporary Kikuyu lands are intensely cultivated small farms producing coffee, tea, pyrethrum, bananas and flowers. Livestock is also raised. You pass through this country on the way up from Nairobi to Mount Kenya, an area characterized by rich red soil on steep hillsides and busy trading centres like Karatina, where *matatus* come and go with great speed, hoots and shouts, loaded to the brim with people and produce. The Kikuyu own and manage much land elsewhere in Kenya, including the majority of former European properties in the old white highlands.

The Kamba

These central Bantu, the fourth group in Kenya, live in an area of plains and plateaus east of Nairobi, much drier than the Kikuyu highlands. Their main towns are Machakos and Kitui. Believed to have migrated from settlements farther south in the Kilimanjaro region of what is now Tanzania, they crossed into present-day Kenya and eventually settled in Ukambani (their present lands) in the 18th century. The Kamba developed into talented traders, partly through necessity after famines and droughts had diminished their lands and livestock. Ivory was an important commodity that they exchanged for goods from the coast like calico, beads and shells. They were skilled hunters, one of their traditional weapons being an iron arrow tipped with poison from a special bark. They traded with the Kisii, Samburu and Taita but even more so with the Kikuyu, who provided them with food in return for arrows, poison, brass chains, ivory armlets and snuff containers.

Life changed with the arrival of the British who came to build the Kenya-Uganda railway. They chose Machakos as the site of a British East Africa Company station and then enlisted many Kamba in the armed forces that invaded German East

Africa during World War I. The Kamba troops saw the popularity of locally carved wooden sculptures in Tanganyika and, once demobilized, began carving, and selling, their own sculptures. Today they are well-known for their handicrafts, which apart from the woodcarvings include woven baskets, stools, bows and arrows, bracelets and pottery. The Kamba cultivate their land and to a lesser extent rear livestock. However, the region is subject to drought and there is considerable deforestation. Of the Kamba who move away from their rural homes to seek employment in towns, many join the army and police forces or become security guards. One of the traditional features of Kamba society is their extraordinary acrobatic dance — now rarely performed or at least not the real thing, much tribal dancing put on for tourists not being necessariliy authentic. Interestingly, it has been noted that the dances of herdsmen like the Masai and Samburu include much higher jumps than those of the farmers, who tend to bend toward the ground and make trampling or digging movements.

The Meru, Embu, Mbere and Tharaka

In many ways these four tribes resemble the Kikuyu. The most numerous are the Meru, who live in the area around the town of the same name on the north-eastern shoulder of Mount Kenya. Oral tradition maintains that their ancestors were enslaved by a people who set them complicated tasks, one of which was to find a spear that could touch both earth and sky. Because they failed to do so, they decided to escape and were led to safety by a young man with the aid of a magic stick. Meru ancestors are in fact believed to have moved inland from the coast, which was under Arab control at the time. During their journey they came into contact with Nilotic and Cushitic peoples from whom they adopted practices like circumcision and the ban on eating fish (neither of which were in force on the coast). Once in the forested Mount Kenya area they gradually cleared land for cultivation. Apart from animal husbandry and bee-keeping, the Meru today cultivate terraced hillsides with maize, coffee, market vegetables and *miraa,* a stimulant much appreciated by truck drivers who chew it to keep awake on long hauls to the coast.

The Embu live south-east of Mount Kenya and lead a primarily agricultural life. According to tribal legend, they are the descendents of Mwene-Ndega, who lived with his wife, Nthara, in a sacred grove that bore his name. The Embu believe their ancestors came from the north. Disputes were settled by the supreme authority, a council of elders known as *Kiama kia Ngome.* From the early days of a hunting and gathering economy the Embu gradually began to clear land and cultivate crops like millet, sorghum, cassava and yams. Toward the end of the 19th century coastal traders introduced maize into the region, and it became the staple foodstuff.

The Mbere live on lower ground south of the Embu, with whom they have much in common. According to oral tradition, their territory once stretched much farther south, but there they warred with the Masai who despoiled them of their women and cattle and forced them to retreat to their present lands. Today the Mbere herd cattle and goats on the plains, keep bees and, where there is sufficient water, usually in the higher areas, grow tobacco, cotton and bananas.

The last of the central Bantu, the Tharaka, live east of the Meru and Embu in the Tana Valley. Their livelihood is mainly derived from cattle and goats, although there is some cultivation. The Tharaka were once renowned for witchcraft and the traditional adornment of feathers and wild animal skins for men and cowrie shells for married women.

The Luhya

Kenya's western Bantu people consist of the Luhya (the second largest group in Kenya), the Kisii and the Kuria. The hilly, densely populated Luhya lands are north of Lake Victoria around Kakamega and Bungoma, where you see clusters of family huts standing among *shambas* or fields. Because the area is rich and well-watered, people support themselves with mixed agriculture, predominantly maize, cassava, cotton, sugar cane and tobacco. Cattle, sheep and goats are endowed with more than mere economic importance; they are valued in social customs like dowry and for their part in rituals. Traditions and rituals vary according to the group. Male circumcision is generally practiced, although some groups circumcise only the eldest son, others not at all. Traditional crafts include basketry, woodwork and pottery. Finally, the Luhya are avid soccer enthusiasts; their team is one of Kenya's strongest.

The Kisii and Kuria

Separated from the Luhya by the Luo and a long arm of Lake Victoria are the Kisii, also known as the Gusii. The ancestors of the Kisii migrated from Uganda into Kenya near the foothills of Mount Elgon and then gradually moved south to Lake Victoria, from where they were pushed south again by the arrival of the Luo. During this transitory period they had conflicts with the Masai and the Kipsigis, who were especially interested in stealing their cattle. In the 18th century they eventually reached a thickly forested highland area, their present home, which they began to clear and cultivate. They now occupy one of the most densely populated areas in Kenya, the cool fertile highlands around the town of Kisii, where they grow abundant supplies of bananas, other fruits and vegetables, as well as cash crops like tea and pyrethrum. Their huts have a distinctive roof thatching composed of neat ridges. Kisii lands, like most tea-growing areas, have afternoon storms often accompanied by violent lightning that strikes and occasionally kills. Kisii stone carvings are sold throughout Kenya, so if you don't manage to venture as far as Tabaka where the stone is quarried, you will have a chance to see the Kisii, smooth, softly coloured soapstone figures, chessboards, candlesticks and vases elsewhere. Less well-known Kisii handicrafts are the attractive wooden stools embedded with patterns of coloured beads.

The Kuria are a smaller group living in the south-western corner of the country. Their territory is one of rolling savannah lands on the border with Tanzania. The border in fact cuts right through their lands leaving part of the tribe in one country, part in the other, a fairly common feature of the arbitrary frontiers drawn by colonial governments. Before settling in the area the Kuria moved south from around Mount Elgon. They had contact with the Luo and the Masai and possibly because of a history of frequent raids from the latter, they now live in stockaded enclosures, their livestock firmly protected.

The Taita and Taveta

The last of the Bantu groups comprises people on or near the coast, from warmer, friendlier climes. These include the Taita, the Taveta, the Pokomo, the Mijikenda and the Arab-influenced Bajun, Swahili and Shirazi. Wundanyi is the main town of the Taita Hills, which rise out of savannah plains west of Voi. The Taita themselves have put the slopes to profitable agricultural use with the help of a locally devised irrigation system. Many years ago, before the creation of Tsavo Park, they traded ivory and rhino horn. Like the majority of coastal Bantu groups, the Taita claim to have originated in Shungwaga, an area thought to be somewhere in southern Somalia. From there, upon the arrival of the marauding Galla peoples in the 17th century, they fled to the south.

The Taveta are a much smaller community on the Tanzania border directly west of the Taita Hills, where their family plots of land touch on large sisal plantations. They share linguistic affinities with the Taita but do not believe they have the same historic origins. Apart from cultivation and livestock rearing, their economy is based on fishing in two picturesque lakes, Chala and Jipe.

The Pokomo and Mijikenda

The Pokomo and related riverine peoples live in eastern Kenya, along the lower reaches of the Tana River. Their territory stretches from south of Garissa down beyond Garsen toward the coast. Like the Taita and Mijikenda, the Pokomo tell of ancestors from Shungwaya. Today their small villages are clusters of distinctive habitations, either mounds of neatly ridged thatch touching the ground or huts on stilts built to withstand the Tana when it floods. Their livelihood depends almost entirely on the river. They fish from it in dugout canoes and grow bananas on the banks, rice in the adjoining lowlands and maize wherever possible. The colourful floor mats they weave from the doum palm make their way into markets along the coast.

South of the Pokomo, in the hinterland stretching from the Galana River to the Tanzania border, live a much larger group, the Mijikenda, who also say they settled here after the legendary migration from Shungwaya. Related tribes of this group originally lived aroud a *kaya,* a fortified hilltop centre for religious and political gatherings. In the 19th century, though, as the population grew and Galla attacks subsided, the people moved down from these sites and dispersed into scattered settlements. The *kaya* remains are still considered sacred constructions by the elders, who revere ancestral spirits supposedly living in them.

The Bajun, Swahili and Shirazi

The Bajun live in the Lamu archipelago and other islands off the northern Kenya coast. They speak Swahili dialects (such as Kiamu on Lamu Island), show a strong Arab influence and are Muslims. Apart from fishing and boat-building, they grow coconuts, various fruits and mangroves, which are cut into poles and heaved aboard dhows for export. Tourism is becoming

increasingly important in the form of boat expeditions to the islands. The Bajun are renowned woodcarvers, as you can see from the beautifully ornate doors in Lamu — many of which have been bought up and exported by foreigners. They are also skilled leather workers known especially on Pate Island for their Siyu sandals.

The Swahili and Shirazi live on the coastal strip and, like the Bajun, are Swahili-speaking Muslims. The maritime trade route between Arabia and the East African coast has been plied by dhows for centuries, propelled by the monsoon winds. With the arrival of the Arabs on the coast, a long history of mingling and intermarriage began between the local Bantu and the Arab newcomers. From this contact the Swahili language and culture emerged. Swahili (or, more correctly, Kiswahili) is basically a Bantu language coloured by words adopted from Arabic, Asian tongues, Portuguese and English. The Shirazi claim to be descendants of immigrants from Shiraz in Persia, who established ruling dynasties in coastal towns like Malindi and Mombasa. These aristocratic origins have little value today, however, and there is no real distinction between the Shirazi and the Swahili.

THE NILOTES

Ancestors of today's Kalenjin group entered from the north about two thousand years ago. They mingled with and eventually absorbed the local Southern Cushitic peoples, adopting some of their practices. This first wave of Nilotes eventually settled in the Western Highlands; they were followed many years later by others who now occupy the western plains, and others still, now one large tribe, who live around the shores of Lake Victoria.

The Kipsigi

The term Kalenjin is a relatively recent one denoting a group of people who speak a common language, Kalenjin, or variations of it. These include the Kipsigi, Nandi, Tugen, Elgeyo, Marakwet and Pokot. The largest Kalenjin tribe is the Kipsigi; they live in the cool highlands and the formerly forested areas of a broad region around Kericho, where they grow tea, pyrethrum and maize on family farmlands. They are also skilled cattle raisers. Because of economic and demographic pressure, their cattle raising has been curtailed since the days when they could send their herds to graze in grasslands much farther north, guarded by a warrior-set of young men.

The Kipsigi have a rich culture of folklore, mythology and ritual, which, as is the case for most tribes, is less and less important to the younger generation. The supreme social event of the tribe was initiation through circumcision and clitoridectomy, an occasion anticipated by children from an early age, marking the time when they would finally be admitted into adulthood as full members of the tribe. Minor rites during childhood included the piercing and enlarging of earlobes by inserting ever larger

A Masai woman. Once a powerful tribe of livestock-raisers, the Masai now number only 250,000.

plugs of wood. You tend to see older men and women (from other tribes, too) with impressively elongated earlobes, some adorned with beads, others 'wound' round the rest of the ear. Another childhood practice was the extraction of two or four lower front teeth, the gaps serving as a type of insurance in the case of lockjaw, providing a space through which food could pass. The period of initiation into adulthood known as *tumda* could last as long as nine months. The initiates lived for that time in a fairly isolated patch of forest where food would be brought by their families and left to be collected after dark. The *mutiriots* or selected elders who acted as mentors to the initiates gave them a kind of intensive course in tribal matters, covering everything a person worthy of the Kipsigi tribe ought to know. This included the history of the tribe, behaviour toward elders and the priorities of the tribe. Today the *tumda* instruction has been lost. The boys are still circumcised, an operation that now takes place in a hospital during school holidays. The boys then return to school to learn English, mathematics and the official history of their country.

The Nandi

The Nandi live north of the Kipsigi in fertile highlands around Kapsabet. Formerly livestock-raisers, they now cultivate *shambas* (fields), although livestock, especially cattle, are still highly valued. In the past, relations with outsiders were particularly hostile. Nandi warriors were long feared by neighbouring tribes against whom the Nandis waged war and led livestock raids. The Masai in particular suffered frequent attacks, but the Kipsigi were left in peace. The British met with strong resistance when they attempted to take over Nandi territory, a process that ended in 1905 and required five military campaigns. Today Nandi prowess is of a different nature; it has been converted into the speed and stamina of cross-country runners who often win world championships.

The Tugen, Elgeyo, Marakwet and Pokot

The area inhabited by the Tugen, Elgeyo and Marakwet is one of the loveliest in Kenya. It includes the Kerio Valley and its forested escarpments. Tugen territory covers the eastern part of the valley and the adjoining hills above the Kerio River. Kabarnet is the administrative centre, the hometown of President Moi. The social structure of the tribe is similar to that of the Nandi. In the past the Tugen exchanged goods with passing trade caravans, which they often later ambushed under the protective cover of dense forest. Similarly, they increased their flocks and herds through frequent raiding. Today they are a peaceful people, cultivating wherever the rainfall permits and raising cattle, sheep and goats. Their environment, however beautiful, is not an easy one. It is subject to erosion has extremes of rainfall, high in the hills and very low in the valley.

Opposite the Tugen live the Elgeyo, spreading over a dramatic sweep of land stretching down the escarpment from around Tambach in the west to the bottom of the Kerio Valley. On the highest ground the Elgeyo raise cattle and grow wheat, lower down they cultivate maize, beans and coffee, and on the less hospitable valley floor they rear goats. In spite of the dense population and the need to clear more land, stretches of forest still stand with their huge cedar and podo trees, a luxuriant contrast to the thorn and scrub below.

Sharing this environment of extremes are the Marakwet, who live north of the Elgeyo, most of them along the Kerio valley floor but some in the fertile Cherangani Hills to the west. They, too, keep cattle in the hills and goats in the valley. Cultivation consists mostly of maize and bananas, aided by an ingenious system of irrigation.

The last of the Kalenjin, the Pokot (also known as the Suk), speak a special dialect and in many ways resemble the Nilotes of the plains, probably as a result of their proximity. Kalenjin live north of the Marakwet, some cultivating the northern slopes of the Cherangani Hills, but most of them tend livestock on the plains beyond. They have distinctive ways of adorning themselves with weights of bead necklaces, elaborate armlets and wide coils of metal earrings for the women.

The Turkana

The Nilotic Turkana, who, like the Masai and Samburu, are a plains people, inhabit the vast desert corner of Western Kenya between Uganda and Lake Turkana. They migrated into Kenya from Uganda about two centuries ago, bringing with them a small breed of cattle that was not suited to the new territory. This deficiency they were soon to rectify by embarking on a lasting campaign that consists of acquiring more resistant stock from their neighbours. They have a reputation for belligerence and have frequently raided the Samburu, pushing them ever farther south and east. They keep goats, sheep and cattle, as well as camels, which are important for their milk, not as beasts of burden. A camel can produce about four times as much milk as a cow. Donkeys are used to transport possessions when a family moves. Although women have traditionally planted millet along streams, cultivation has not been a Turkana pursuit. Today, however, government projects are encouraging them to change from their almost total reliance on stock and to settle along the Turkwel and other rivers, where irrigation is being developed. Other groups are also being tempted to Lake Turkana to earn their livings from fishing.

The Masai and Samburu

The name Masai is derived from the language Maa, which is also spoken by the Samburu, the Njemps and some tribes in Tanzania. Present Masai lands stretch west and south of Nairobi over the Narok and Kajiado districts to the Tanzania border. They were once vast but with the arrival of the Europeans in the 19th century the Masai had to give up much of their territory. Earlier, their migration southward into Kenya from an area beyond Lake Turkana less than a thousand years ago took them into the Kerio Valley and over pasturelands both east and west. They enjoyed considerable respect as a mighty warrior force and enlarged their herds through successive raids. They also fought among themselves. Then the 19th century brought a series of calamities such as cholera and smallpox as well as rinderpest, which killed off many of their cattle.

As livestock-raisers, the Masai first and foremost hold their cattle in the highest esteem. They believe that *Enkai* (the sky of God) made them a gift of all cattle and consequently the pursuit of animal husbandry is essentially a noble one. Traditionally, they look with disdain upon anyone who cultivates the earth. The Masai also herd sheep and goats. Their diet is chiefly milk, sometimes mixed with blood from the jugular vein of a cow or bullock, and meat on ceremonial occasions. Today, however, many also eat *ugali,* the staple maize porridge, and buy vegetables from neighbouring farmers. Family groups who share grazing for their herds live in an enclosure known as an *enkang,* but young warriors are traditionally billeted in a separate *manyatta.* Men pass through four 'age-grades', in a lifetime, the first two as warriors, the second two as elders. On reaching maturity, youths attain the *moran* status through circumcision and so begin their service as warriors. In the past, they would remain junior warriors for 15 years, but this period is shorter now. The *eunoto* ceremony (when their long hair is shaved by their mothers) gives them senior warrior status and they are allowed to marry. With time, they become junior and then senior elders. As with many other Kenya people, warriors are engaged in protecting the assets of the tribe, but there is no corresponding period of duty for girls. They are initiated into womanhood and married almost immediately to husbands who may be much older. They are, however, permitted to have affairs with their husbands' peers. Ceremony and celebration are important features of Masai life, and the *oloiboni,* or 'ritual leader', commands special respect.

Today the Masai, numbering about 250,000, are under considerable pressure to reduce their herds, mainly because of the scarcity of land in Kenya. Their pastures are coveted, and they are encouraged to settle. For some years now there have been wheat-growing projects in the fertile Mau highlands, and on lower ground a more permanent form of ranching has been set up. To encourage the Masai to adapt to changes in Kenya, the government has been curtailing their tribal practices, going so far as to ban one of their major ceremonies. Many Masai who leave the rural life find employment in tourism or become security guards in towns.

The Samburu, originally part of the southward Masai migration into Kenya, now live south of Lake Turkana in semi-desert country. Maralal is the main town. They herd cattle, sheep, goats and, for some time now, camels, because they can withstand the increasingly dry environment. Not all Samburu territory, though, is arid. In certain scenic ranges of hills, pastures are richer and, what's more, some Samburu have turned to planting maize, vegetables and wheat.

The Luo

The Nilotic Luo, the third largest group in Kenya, live in the west around Lake Victoria. Kisumu is the main town. They are an enterprising people who have played a large part in shaping modern Kenya. Their first appearance in the country dates back to the 16th and 17th centuries, when they left their homeland in southern Sudan and migrated south in groups, acquiring cattle on the way and crowding out the Bantu from the lake shore where

Samburu warriors.

they eventually settled. At first they raised livestock, but limited land and considerable population pressure forced them to change their lifestyle and become farmers and fishermen. Despite these activities, the Luo are strongly attached to their cattle, which are a symbol of wealth and serve to bind social events like marriage. In the past each warrior had his own ox, which went with him into battle. The status of an influential man, a *ruoth,* was partly determined by the number of cattle he owned. As for ritual, an important part of traditional life, the Luo are one of the few tribes in Kenya that do not perform circumcision or clitoridectomy. Over the past few decades they have adapted quickly to change, many leaving their family lands to enter business, politics and other professions.

THE CUSHITES

This group is generally divided into Southern and Eastern Cushitic peoples. The early Southern group has died out. The Eastern Cushites were later arrivals who are divided into those who speak a language known as Sam (the Somali and Rendille) and those who speak Galla or Oromo (the Borana, Gabbra, Sakuye and Orma). These groups first entered Kenya from southern Ethiopia and now occupy the greater part of Kenya's vast north-eastern desert.

The Somali

The Somali are an independent, assertive people, physically and culturally distinct from other Kenyans. Because their lives are governed by the pasture needs of their stock, their frequent moves require light, portable houses. These the women erect while the men build stock enclosures and protective fences around the settlements. Over the years the name Somali has been associated with *shifta* bandits, groups of marauders crossing the border from Somalia into Kenya to attack and raid. They were especially active in the 1960s. More notorious still are the poachers, often armed with automatic weapons, who have massacred many elephants for the ivory trade. They return to Somalia with the tusks, or they ship them from the coast of Kenya. Since the Kenya government has embarked upon a strong policy for the eradication of the trade, there have been fewer attacks.

The Rendille

The Rendille are a peaceful tribe with grazing lands that stretch from south east of Lake Turkana to the Marsabit region. The southernmost clans have intermarried with the Samburu, and some have taken to raising cattle. The others, like the Somali, have a primarily camel-centred economy. Rendille clan groups move as many as five times a year, the male camels transporting their homes and household effects. Men are usually over 30 when they marry, but most women become wives in their teens immediately after clitoridectomy. The Rendille women adorn themselves with beads and thick leather necklaces. On the birth of her first son, a woman fashions her hair into a plaited cox, which is not removed until the death of either the husband or the son.

The Borana, Gabbra, Sakuye and Orma

Borana territory stretches from around Moyale on the Ethiopian border through Marsabit to Garba Tula. Ancestors of the Borana lived in the Ethiopian highlands before moving south as a result of political persecution. On arrival in the less fertile environment they began to raise livestock, mostly cattle. Because of increasingly poor grazing and the loss of their stock during *shifta* raids, the Borana have gradually been forced to take up camel herding, an occupation they traditionally considered inferior.

The Gabbra, fellow Galla who may once have been a sub-group of the Borana, live to the west of them in the Chalbi Desert and the area north of it to the Ethiopian border. They resemble the Borana, with regard to social organization, religious beliefs and dress. Their economy, however, depends almost exclusively on camels, as opposed to cattle, although like most pastoralists they keep some sheep and goats. The Gabbra move their settlements with the dry season, loading their camels with small children (adults rarely ride) and the family belongings. You may notice guardsmen armed with rifles instead of the more prevalent warrior's spear of other ethnic groups; they need these weapons to discourage the frequent raids common in the north.

The Sakuye are the smallest of the Galla group and live well east of Marsabit. They raise camels and goats but tend to be less nomadic than the Gabbra or Borana. They have often been victims of *shifta* raids.

The final group of the Galla people, the Orma, live a good way south of their linguistic relatives in more fertile country along the Tana River and the adjoining bushland. Garsen is the administrative centre. Their lifestyle is nomadic, and the organization of their clans is fairly similar to that of the Borana. They herd cattle and, to a much lesser extent, camels. Temporary Orma houses, grassy mounds of thatch over a frame of poles, belie the skilled craftsmanship of their inhabitants. Women weave fibre from the doum palm into a variety of mats and baskets; the men carve fine wooden stools, ladles and cups.

HUNTER-GATHERERS AND OTHER SMALL GROUPS

These are the people whose lifestyles suggest that their ancestors were present in Kenya before the Bantu, Nilotic and Eastern Cushitic groups moved in. Kenya's early inhabitants depended solely on hunting and gathering, not farming or raising livestock. Today's hunter-gatherers may well be the descendants of these groups, although in some cases origins are difficult to determine.

The Dahalo, Boni and Sanye

These three groups live on the coastal hinterland. The oldest of them, the Dahalo of the lower Tana River, are believed to have been present before the arrival of the Southern Cushites. Their language is punctuated by clicks, a characteristic also of early groups in southern Africa and Tanzania. The Boni were later arrivals who share a common language, Sam, with the Somali and Rendille. They have moved from forest into small villages in the Lamu hinterland, where they hunt with bows and arrows and also cultivate small plots. The Sanye live farther south, many intermingling with the Mijikenda, with whom they have age-old trade links. Their livelihood depended to a large extent on the elephants they hunted for meat. Today they can no longer hunt elephants, but can pursue only smaller animals outside game reserves. They've had to change their lifestyle as a result.

The Mukogodo, Ndorobo and Okiek

These people from the upland areas of Central and Western Kenya once roamed freely through the highlands, hunting forest animals, gathering herbs and plants and tending to their bees. Their material requisites were beehives, honey containers, spears, bows and arrows. Today their hunter-gathering pursuits continue on a reduced scale because they, too, have had to adapt to a rapidly growing population that has restricted their former hunting grounds and cleared vast portions of their forests. Many of them speak Kalenjin, others Masai dialects. They keep bees and may hunt a little, but have increasingly settled down to herd and cultivate.

The El-Molo

The El-Molo are fishermen who live in a harsh volcanic environment in the north on the eastern shore of Lake Turkana, near Loiyangalani. Nobody knows where they came from, although oral tradition claims they were hunters and fishermen who migrated from the north, possibly from the Omo delta just beyond Lake Turkana. The small tribe lives in a cluster of huts made of doum-palm leaves, reeds and grass.

They eat mostly fish, supplemented occasionally by hippopotamus and crocodile. They fish with harpoons, nets or baskets and spread the catch out on the shore to dry. Their rather frail-looking fishing craft, made from doum-palm logs, are gradually being replaced by more modern boats.

THE FOREIGN COMMUNITY

The Asians

While an Arab influence can be felt in the architecture, dress, customs and religion of the coast, the Arabs themselves do not have a high profile, mainly because they have long mingled with the local inhabitants. The Asians (approximately 80,000) are a different matter. You see them in Nairobi, Kisumu and Mombasa, where they own shops and run businesses. Many have become Kenya citizens since independence and continue to play a significant part in the country's economy, investing in industry and in services. The term Asian covers a number of Indian and other groups who may be Hindus, Muslims, Sikhs, Roman Catholic Goans or Ismaili followers of the Aga Khan. The Aga Khan has funded schools, hospitals, clinics and development programs. Their mosques and temples make for delightful architectural surprises in the larger towns.

The Europeans

The *wazungu* (Swahili for Europeans) number about 44,000. Fewer than 4000 are the descendants of settlers and others who came to Kenya at the turn of the century from England, South Africa and various European countries. Many are Kenya citizens. The others are less-permanent residents, many of them sent to Kenya on two-year contracts by European and American multinational firms. Others work for the United Nations, some are teachers and still others are involved in agricultural and veterinary development projects funded by foreign aid. Finally, the coast's tourist industry has attracted foreign interest in the form of luxury hotels, those in the vicinity of Mombasa largely managed by Germans, those in Malindi by Italians.

WILDLIFE: A NATIONAL TREASURE

Some countries have oil, minerals, gold or diamonds. Kenya has its wildlife. It is one of the country's most valuable assets, but it is neither unlimited nor inexhaustible; the government understands that it must be nurtured and protected if it is to survive.

Conservation, though, is not an easy task. It requires enormous sums, and Kenya, like many other developing countries cannot foot the bill alone. What's more, if an end is to be put to the killing of elephants and rhinoceroses, international cooperation is needed to stop the trade in illegal ivory and horns.

Conservation is, moreover, a delicate balancing act. Over-protected species can endanger micro-environments. The space and food requirements of animals must be carefully weighed against the needs of farmers for land and the damage that herbivores can do to crops and carnivores to livestock. Achieving a satisfactory balance is an ongoing challenge and requires careful planning. In July 1989 the governmment appointed Richard Leakey, the well-known archaeologist and former director of The National Museums of Kenya, as head of the Department of Wildlife Conservation.

PARKS AND RESERVES

A national park is a zone, managed and financed by the government, in which all wildlife is protected. A national reserve has the same purpose and rules but the financing is regional. Set aside for the purpose of protecting a threatened species, both areas are left untouched. The terms 'park' and 'reserve' are interchangeable in everyday conversation.

As population grows in certain areas and the fertile regions under cultivation expand, wildlife retreats increasingly into the reserves and parks that have been set aside.

Parks and reserves are guarded by rangers of the Ministry of Tourism and Wildlife. The Department of Wildlife Conservation is a division of the ministry but has almost complete autonomy. The management of national monuments and historical sites, once called national parks, is the responsibility of the National Museums of Kenya.

British foresight is largely responsible for wildlife preservation; in 1900 the Northern Reserve was created to protect
the fauna and flora of the Marsabit mountain.

Many parks were established after World War II: Nairobi
and Mount Kenya in 1947, Amboseli and Masai Mara in 1948,
Aberdare in 1950, and so on up to the founding of the last two,
Hell's Gate in 1984 and Lake Nakuru in 1988.

Today more than 10% of the country is set aside for the
preservation of nature. Of the nation's parks the most popular is
Amboseli (148,700 visitors in 1987), followed by Lake Nakuru
(127,900) Nairobi, Masai Mara, Tsavo West and Tsavo East.

CONFLICTS WITH TRIBES

The will to preserve wildlife is deeply anchored in Kenya:
reserves such as Tana River have been established specifically to
protect two threatened species of monkey, even at the cost of
holding back agricultural expansion in the region. A country with
such a high population growth has to consider carefully any
plans to limit development of land suitable for agriculture
and livestock.

Planners, of course, try to use the desert for wildlife reserves.
But even in deserts, setting up a park can create difficulties for
the people who live there. For some communities, hunting is the
main food source; for others hunting is linked to important rites.

In the east, there are certain small tribes, such as the Boni
and the Sanyes, who still subsist from hunting and gathering. The
Sanyes used to live in the plains of Tsavo, and not understanding
why hunting became illegal in 1977, many of them became
poachers.

One of the traditional rites involved in the initiation of the
Masai *morans* was the single-handed combat with a lion.
Although this custom has generally been abandoned, the Masai
continue to wear a *motonyik,* a headdress made of 30 or 50 birds
shot with bow and arrow by the person wearing it. The Samburu
have the same custom.

According to one estimate, this practive could lead to killing
2.4 million birds over 20 years. As a result, it has recently
been prohibited.

THE FIGHT AGAINST POACHERS

Undoubtedly the major problem for wildlife is poaching.
Elephants are massacred for their ivory and rhinoceroses for their
horns. Rhinoceros horn sells for US $2500 a kilo; it is used for
medicinal preparations in Asia. The money earned from the sale
of a single horn provides the poacher with a living for a full year.

Prices for ivory skyrocketed as the commodity became rare
after the hunting was banned. Poachers are estimated to export
50 tons of ivory each year.

Increasingly, poachers are professionals using military tactics. In 1988 the game warden's headquarters in Meru National Park was attacked by a team of poachers using heavy artillery. They killed the five white rhinoceroses protected in the park and made off with their horns before reinforcements arrived. Poachers were also responsible for the violent death of Joy Adamson, in 1980, and her former husband, George, in August 1989. Five tourists were killed by poachers in 1989.

The government's reaction has been firm. In a highly publicized act, President Moi set fire to a 15 ft-/4.6 m-pile of ivory with an estimated value of US $3 million. The destruction of the ivory confiscated from poachers symbolized the government's determination to fight.

Armed anti-poacher squads have been created to patrol the parks. They are well trained and have orders to shoot on sight. The problem is that round-the-clock surveillance of Kenya's enormous park and reserve network is virtually impossible. Tsavo National Park, for example, is the size of Massachussets. Putting an effective halt to poaching through park surveillance is simply too costly. The only real solution is to stop the trade on the international level.

ACHIEVING AN ECOLOGICAL BALANCE

No less important than efforts to halt poaching are the attempts to raise threatened species in captivity and then reintroduce them into the wild. Private ranches, such as Solio, Brooke Bond and Lewa Downs, have nurtured certain endangered species. The animals are then introduced into the well-protected parks such as Lake Nakuru (completely closed in), Tsavo, Nairobi and Aberdare. These animals are solitary and must be placed in the same region if they are to have a chance of meeting during breeding season.

At the same time, environmentalists know that too much protection of wildlife can produce unwanted results. For example, elephants have caused the destruction of young trees in some places. If the 18,000 or so remaining elephants continue to reproduce at their present rate, they will in turn threaten the balance of vegetation in the country.

Richard Leakey, as director of wildlife conservation, has emphasized a global approach. The hunting ban — while necessary — changed the age-old ecological equilibrium between the people of the region and their environment. Today, new solutions must be found to renew the ecological balance.

Another controversial matter is the effect of tourists on the animals. The increasing number of tourists in certain parks and reserves interferes with the daily life of animals, particularly their reproductive cycles. The vehicles wear away the fragile ground, in particular in Amboseli Park.

Some people say that the busiest parks, such as Masai Mara or Amboseli, should be temporarily closed. The economic importance of tourists is so great, however, it is unlikely such drastic action will be taken. Nevertheless, some measures must be adopted if the very resource that attracts tourists is to survive.

VISITING THE NATIONAL PARKS AND RESERVES

You can contribute to the preservation of wildlife by following certain guidelines: don't buy objects made from animals; avoid driving near a lioness that has just given birth; and opt for trips off the beaten track to some of the less-popular parks.

To prepare for your visit to the parks and reserves, read a field guide to wildlife and bring it with you to help identify the different species. There are, for example, about 1035 different kinds of birds in Kenya.

You might also take a trip to your local zoo where you can see many of the animals native to Kenya (giraffes, gazelles, leopards and more). This kind of advance preparation will help you identify animals such as an impala or a Rothschild's giraffe. To better appreciate the rich variety of each species, pay attention to details of its external appearance: the position of horns, ears, spots and stripes.

▬ PRACTICAL INFORMATION

Accommodation

It is advisable to reserve ahead either in a Nairobi agency (see pp. 97-98) or through the represented hotel chain (see pp. 90-93).

Lodges

The lodges in the parks and reserves are usually very comfortable. Each lodge does its best to attract the animals to a distance observable, with binoculars at least, by installing drinking pools and hanging pieces of meat from trees.

In Mount Kenya and Nyandarua parks the lodges are situated in the trees or on pile foundations. They are specifically designed to attract the animals right up to their walls. Floodlights are left on all night so that the guests can watch the nocturnal activities. Whenever a particularly interesting animal is sighted, a bell will ring in the rooms of the guests who have asked to be informed.

Tented camps

Some parks have tented camps. They tend to be less luxurious and therefore less expensive than the lodges, but not always. Those that offer the same amenities as the lodges charge the same prices.

Entry fees

The cost to enter a park is usually fixed at Ksh 200 per person for non-residents, Ksh 15 for residents and Ksh 30 for the car (April 1990). It is advisable to have a four-wheel-drive vehicule capable of going anywhere, even after heavy rains. At Masai Mara, only four-wheel-drives are authorized.

Guides

Being accompanied by a specialist is an absolute necessity; you won't see much of anything without one. The ideal guide is a ranger, but since guiding is not their official job, they are not always available. Always buy a map of the park; the ranger will point out the spots where certain animals were last seen or the areas frequented by others.

If you can't find a ranger, you can seek information from the drivers of organized safaris. Many of them have visited the parks often and know the wildlife habits. They can usually indicate the best places to go and might even accompany you.

Baboons can be playful thieves and nasty biters.

Rules and suggestions

Parks and reserves have a certain number of rules mostly designed for your own safety :
- No driving is allowed after 6:30pm.
- The speed limit is 15 mi/25 km per hour. For your own sake, you won't want to drive faster. The roads are full of bumps and holes that are not always obvious. In addition, if you drive slowly you'll have a better chance of spotting the animals.
- Don't get out of the car except in those areas where the warning signs tell you specifically that you may do so safely.
- Feeding animals is prohibited.
- Never approach a lion, even if it seems to be sleeping. Some visitors have done so and never returned to tell the tale. If you get out of your car to film or photograph an animal, you might provoke fear and then aggression, especially if the animal is protecting its young.

• If your vehicle breaks down, stay where you are until help comes. The rangers always note the license plate numbers at the entrance to the park and check the departing cars. If you're stuck, they will know about it.

• If you absolutely must get out of the car and you encounter an animal, stay calm and don't move. Or, you can take shelter in a tree.

• Some animals, the elephant, for example, can become aggressive even toward a car, particularly in forested regions. A young elephant suddenly finds itself on the open road in front of a car and the frightened mother charges the vehicle. Get out of the way as quickly as possible.

• Baboons and vervet monkeys can inflict nasty bites. Don't open your car windows to get a better look at them, and certainly don't try to feed them. Most monkeys are thieves and will open or make off with anything they can get their paws on, so make sure your tent and the windows at the lodge are tightly closed.

• Finally, always check that your tank is full before starting out. There are gas stations at the entrances to the parks and in certain lodges.

NAIROBI

Nairobi plunges the visitor into a surprising world. Its climate doesn't correspond to the image of an equatorial city nor does its appearance correspond to that of an African capital. The weather, especially in the morning, is much cooler than you might expect. Because of Nairobi's high altitude of 5512 ft/1680 m, the average annual temperature is 64° F/18° C. At midday it can become very hot, but nights are often quite chilly. The architecture is also surprising. The modern tower of the Kenyatta Conference Centre is a reminder that Nairobi is a modern city.

Nairobi was part of Masai land when the British arrived. Its name comes from a small river that the Masai called Enairobe, meaning 'Cold Water'. The modern capital was born with the construction of the railway. Untamed nature reigns, even today, in much of the area around the city, particularly in the savanna near the airport and in the nearby national park.

At the entrance to the city, the road from the airport becomes a splendid, garden-lined avenue, shaded by beautiful, flowering trees. It follows almost the same route as the railway line into the heart of the European district.

Despite the international-style skyscrapers that are increasingly dominating the city centre, Nairobi retains an old British charm, evident in the Parliament building, with its clock tower modeled after Big Ben, the old Law Courts building, the manicured parks, and the houses and gardens in the residential suburbs of Muthaiga, Westlands and Hurlingham.

Although you might be disappointed at first if you're looking for the exotic, Nairobi has a way of growing on you. Due to its central position, the capital is an ideal base for your trip. Here you can catch up on all your shopping and business needs. It is also the perfect place to wind down between journeys into the countryside: the rhythm is calm, there are few traffic jams, you can walk just about anywhere and the weather is refreshing.

Finally, Nairobi is a cosmopolitan city with a rich variety of people. You'll encounter Europeans, Africans and Indians, dressed in Western attire or, very rarely, colourful traditional costumes. All you need to do is wander around the city to get a sense of the character and architecture of each district.

NAIROBI IN THE PAST

Situated on the marshy plateau that separated Kikuyu and Masai land, the area that is now the Kenyan capital was used as a watering hole by cattle herders from both tribes in 1896. The Enairobe River descended here from the Ngong hills. For the same reason, Sergeant Ellis chose this site in 1898 as the main materials depot for the building of the railway. The engineer P.H. Patterson in his book *The Man-Eaters of Tsavo* stressed the problem of finding sufficient water for hundreds of workers. Due to its abundant supply of water and despite the difficulty of building on swampy terrain, the area remained the central colonial railway settlement.

The land was drained, and by 1906 engineers had already constructed a city comprising several districts: an Indian bazaar, African villages, a business quarter, military barracks and residential villas. Despite the city's spectacular development and the construction of many high-rise buildings, its basic structure has changed little. In 1907, Nairobi was declared the country's capital.

▬ *PRACTICAL INFORMATION*

Map coordinates refer to the map p. 91.

When to go

The high season extends from mid-December to April when the weather is dry and sunny but not too hot. Average temperatures range from 68° F/20° C during the day to 14° F/−10° C at night. July and August evenings in Nairobi, as in all high-altitude regions of the country, are particularly chilly.

Accommodation

Hotels

Nairobi has numerous hotels in every category. A selected list of the capital's better hotels, with their approximate cost, appears in *Tourist's Kenya* and *What's On*, available at news stands and hotels throughout the city.

In the centre

▲▲▲▲ **Hilton International Nairobi,** Watalii St. off Ngina St., A2, POB 30624, ☎ 334000, tlx: 22252. 344 rooms. ① Conference hall, sauna. All the luxury of the Hilton chain in this 19-floor tower. Upon arrival, you will find a basket of fruit in your room. Travel agencies, boutiques, and airline offices on the ground floor.

▲▲▲▲ **Hotel County,** corner of Uhuru Highway and Haile Selassie Ave., A3, POB 41924, ☎ 26190 or 28647. 45 rooms. ① ③ ④ In quiet surroundings, the County attracts business travelers and a large clientele with a conference hall and travel and car-rental agencies. A temporary membership card gives the holder access to golf, tennis, the swimming pool and restaurant of one of the clubs of Nairobi.

▲▲▲▲ **Hotel Inter-Continental Nairobi,** City Hall Way, Uhuru Highway, A3, POB 30353, ☎ 335550, tlx: 22631. 440 rooms. ① ④ Situated in a peaceful area near Parliament and the beautiful gardens of Uhuru Park. Boutiques and a hunting-trophy gallery.

▲▲▲▲ **Nairobi Safari Club,** Koinange St., University Way, A2, POB 43564, ☎ 330621, tlx: 25391. 159 rooms. ① ④ Sauna and gym. Visitors must become members of the club to stay in this luxury

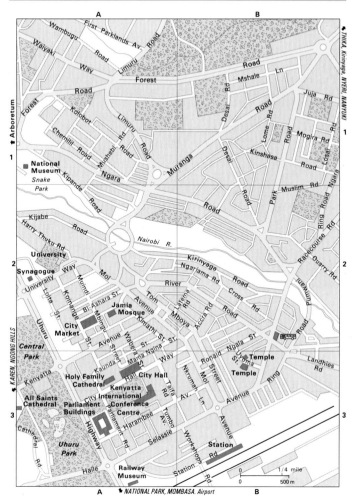

NAIROBI

hotel run by the Intercontinental chain. Phone in advance for conditions of membership.

▲▲▲▲ **New Stanley Hotel,** corner of Kenyatta Ave. and Kimathi St., A2, POB 30680, ☎ 333233, tlx: 22223. 212 rooms. ① ④ Shops, gym, solarium. First-rate grill room with a changing menu (smorgasbord on Friday and an African buffet on Wednesday). A lively café-restaurant, the Thorn Tree, located on a terrace at street level; it is one of the capital's favourite meeting places where you can find a safari partner by consulting the notice board on the central pillar. The popular disco is open nightly. Small buses travel daily to the Outspan Hotel at Nyeri (see p. 156).

▲▲▲ **Six-Eighty Hotel,** corner of Muindi Mbingu St., Kenyatta Ave., A2, POB 43436, ☎ 332680, tlx: 22513. 340 rooms. ① A favourite for group tours. Good Japanese restaurant. No air-conditioning.

▲▲ **Hotel Ambassadeur,** corner of Moi and Luthuli Aves., B2, POB 30399, ☎ 336803. 70 rooms. ① Centrally located, the Ambassadeur is decorated in Swahili style and caters both to groups and to business travelers (typists and typewriters are available). Two discotheques are open every night except Monday.

▲▲ **Meridian Court,** Muranga Rd., AB1, POB 30278, ☎ 33 3916 or 33 3751. 80 rooms, 28 suites. ① ④ Boutiques, conference hall. Excellent Indian restaurant, the Khyber Pass.

▲▲ **Oakwood,** Kimathi St., A2, POB 40683, ☎ 20592. 23 rooms. ① A charming and very comfortable small hotel opposite the New Stanley.

▲ **Hotel Gloria,** Tom Mboya St., B2-3, POB 32087, ☎ 28916. 24 rooms. Small, clean hotel in popular residential neighbourhood right near the city centre.

Near the centre

▲▲▲▲ **Nairobi Serena Hotel,** Nyerere Rd., Kenyatta Ave., A3, POB 46302, ☎ 725111. 191 rooms. ① ④ ⑤ A large, modern building surrounded by beautiful trees that shade superb gardens. A favourite for group tours, the Serena offers a wide range of amenities, including a beauty parlour, pharmacy, sauna and gym.

▲▲▲▲ **Norfolk Hotel,** Harry Thuku Rd., A2, POB 40064, ☎ 335422. 124 rooms. ① ④ Constructed in the style of a British country inn, the Norfolk is in a quiet neighbourhood near the university and not far from the city centre and the National Museum. The cooking is good, particularly Wednesday's lunchtime African specialities. You can eat anytime in the afternoon at the Delamare on the hotel's terrace, a combination of bar, tea room and coffee-snack shop.

▲▲▲ **Panafric Hotel,** Valley Rd. at the end of Kenyatta Ave., A3, POB 30486, ☎ 720822. 128 rooms. ① ④ Ultra-modern architecture and decor in peaceful district near city centre. Frequented by government officials. Hearty buffet lunch. Avoid walking in this area alone late at night.

▲▲ **Fairview Hotel,** Bishops Rd., A3, POB 40842, ☎ 723210, tlx: 25584, fax: (254-2) 72 1320. ① ⑤ A stylish hotel in a grey stone building behind the Panafric. Apartments with two double bedrooms, a living room, kitchenette and bathroom can be rented.

West of the centre

▲▲ **Grosvenor Hotel,** Ralph Bunche Rd., off map, POB 41038, ☎ 722080/-1. 50 rooms. ① ④ ⑤ A colonial-style hotel in the residential district of Hurlingham. The excellent Japanese restaurant, Shogun, is open daily.

▲▲ **Heron Court Apartment Hotel,** Milimani Rd., off map, POB 41848, ☎ 720740. ① ④ ⑤ Sauna, gym, hairdresser. At the western end of Kenyatta Ave. You can rent a furnished apartment in a modern building by the day, week or month.

▲▲ **Milimani,** Milimani Rd., off map, POB 30715, ☎ 720760/-3, tlx 22613. 150 rooms. ① ④ Bar, discotheque. The cubic, concrete silhouette of this hotel stands out on the top of a hill in the Hurlingham district.

▲▲ **Silver Springs,** Valley Rd., off map, POB 61362, ☎ 722451 or 722454. 80 rooms. ① ④ Discotheque.

▲ **Hurlingham Hotel,** Argwings Kodhek Rd., off map, POB 43158, ☎ 723001 or 721920. 10 rooms. The Hurlingham has been run by the same British family for several decades. In a quiet and hospitable family atmosphere, guests can eat made-to-order Kenyan dishes.

North of the centre

▲▲ **Boulevard Hotel,** College Rd., between Uhuru Hwy. and Nairobi River, A2, POB 42831, ☎ 27567. 70 rooms. ① ④ ⑤ Conveniently located near the gardens of Ainsworth Hill, the museum and the casino. Good restaurant.

▲▲ **Jacaranda Hotel,** Waiyaki Way, Westlands, A2, off map, POB 14287, ☎ 742272, tlx 23295. 125 rooms. ① ④ Bar, boutique. A recently renovated hotel now under the direction of the Block Hotel chain, situated in the Westlands suburb. A shuttle operates between the hotel and the centre twice a day.

▲▲ **New Mayfair B & B,** Parklands, off map, POB 43817, ☎ 742731. 106 rooms. ① ④ ⑤ Sauna, discotheque. Gardens are filled with lovely tropical plants.

▲ **Chiromo B & B,** Chiromo Rd, A2, off map, POB 44677, ☎ 742921. 37 rooms. ① A French-run hotel with four restaurants, including one of Nairobi's finest Swiss restaurants. Its discotheque, Le Chalet, also has a good reputation.

▲ **Hotel Com'fy,** Keiyo Rd., off map, POB 20320, ☎ 742730 or 743969. ① A small, hospitable hotel 1.2 mi/2 km north of the city centre.

Environs of Nairobi

▲▲▲▲ **Masai Lodge,** for reservations: POB 48559, ☎ 334411. ① At the edge of Nairobi National Park, the lodge overlooks Python Pool, where animals and birds come to drink. Walking or horse-back riding tours of the park are organized from here. Considered a private club, visitors must pay an entry fee.

▲▲▲ **Safari Park Hotel and Country Club,** POB 45422, ☎ 802673 or 802838. Managed by the Signet Hotels & Lodges chain, this hotel is situated 6.2 mi/12 km north-east of Nairobi on the Thika road. 118 rooms. ① ③ ④ ⑤ Bar, casino, horse rental. The low buildings are spread out in 37 ac/15 ha of gardens and decorated in Swahili style. Solicitous staff and impeccable service. Minibus to city centre.

▲▲▲ **Westwood Park Hotel,** Karen, in the Ngong forest south-west of Nairobi, POB 45664, ☎ 21855. 54 rooms. ① ③ ④ ⑤ Bar, miniature golf, horses. Daily bus service to the city centre. Camp-grounds are nearby.

Campsites

There are campsites in the gardens of the Westwood Park Hotel and at the Rowallan camp, near Jamhuri Park, run by the Kenyan Boy Scouts. Both sites are guarded around the clock. There are also campsites available in all the reserves and parks as well as along the coast and in Nairobi.

Youth hostels

See p. 16.
Youth Hostel, Race Course Rd., POB 27354, ☎ 29768.

Getting around Nairobi

On foot

Walking is the best way to get around the centre of the city. The distances are short and the streets are well marked. Driving is on the left, so Americans, Canadians and others not used to that rule should be very careful to look first to the right when crossing a street.

Bus

The public bus transport system in Nairobi is extensive. Kenya Bus Services (KBS) goes to all areas of the city, as well as to the suburbs and the two airports. The cost is only Ksh 6. Buses do not run frequently, however, and they can be jammed during rush hour. For information on bus routes, ask at the station on the corner of City Hall Way and Moi Avenue, B2.

Car rental

All major international rental companies have offices in Nairobi, and there are many local agencies, too. If you reserve a car before you leave for Kenya, you can avoid having to pay a costly deposit.

Avis, Union Tower, Moi Ave., A2, POB 49795, ☎ 336794 or 334317. Avis also has offices at the Hilton (☎ 29576 or 29577) and Serena (☎ 725111) hotels and at the Jomo Kenyatta International Airport (☎ 822186). You rent a car in Nairobi and leave it in Mombasa.

Central Rent-a-Car, Fedha Towers, Standard St., A2, POB 49439, ☎ 22888 or 322296.

Coast Car Hire, New Stanley Hotel, Standard St., A2, POB 56707, ☎ 25255 or 21845. Agency also organizes air and road safaris.

Habib's Cars, Agip House, Haile Selassie Ave., B3, POB 48095, ☎ 20463 or 20985. All types of vehicles, including caravans with camping material.

Hertz-UTC, Muindi Mbingu St., A2, POB 42196, ☎ 331960. Desks also at Jomo Kenyatta and Moi International Airports.

Interrent, IPS Bldg, Kimathi St., A2, POB 30984, ☎ 726423.

Rasul's Car Hire & Tours, POB 18172, ☎ 558234 or 541355. Relatively unknown, Rasul's offers tourist vehicles and four-wheel drives at rock-bottom prices. Write well in advance to make sure that your car will be waiting for you at the airport, and check the vehicle carefully before driving off.

Twiga Car Hire and Tours, Kimanthi St., A2, POB 14365, ☎ 337330 or 337388. Some of the lowest prices in town.

Taxis

The yellow-striped vehicles with metres are the only officially licensed taxis. They can be found in front of the train and bus stations and on Moi Avenue near the Ambassadeur Hotel. You will discover, however, that most taxis have no metres. Be sure to negotiate the price before getting in; it will be about Ksh 50 for an average trip in the city.

Food

Hotels offer international style and Indian cuisines, usually served as a buffet. Some hotels will prepare African dishes on request; in others, specific days of the week are set aside for African meals. You can find a hot meal at the Norfolk Hotel at any time of the afternoon; the Wimpy has cafeteria-style service; Jax and African Heritage are open non-stop from 8am to 9pm.

Asian

Akasaka, Six-Eighty Hotel, Kenyatta Ave., A2-3, POB 47153, ☎ 20299. Japanese cuisine. Open daily. E.

Curry Pot, Moi Ave, A2, POB 44516, ☎ 331666 or 28684. Fine curries and a lively atmosphere. R.

Hong Kong, Koinange St., A2, POB 48255, ☎ 28612. The best Chinese restaurant in Nairobi. Closed Mon. E.

Khyber Pass, Meridian Court Hotel, Muranga Rd., A2, POB 30278, ☎ 333916. Excellent Indo-Pakistani cuisine. E.

Minar, Banda St., A2, POB 41869, ☎ 29999. Good restaurant serving Indian specialities. A complete meal costs about Ksh100. I.

New Three Bells, Utalii House, Utalii St., B2, POB 72607, ☎ 20628 or 23464. Popular and inexpensive restaurant. Try the excellent chicken *masala* and *tandoori* chicken. Open daily. I.

Shogun, Grosvenor Hotel, off map, POB 62628, ☎ 720563. Nairobi's top Japanese restaurant. Open daily. E.

Stavros, Post Bank House (opposite market), Market St., A2, POB 50449, ☎ 728157. Inexpensive Asian restaurant offering some international dishes. I.

Tin Tin, Kenyatta Conference Centre, A3, POB 58077, ☎ 29093. Top-quality Chinese cuisine. R.

A young Nairobi woman.

International

Alan Bobbe's Bistro, Caltex House, Koinange St., A2, POB 44991, ☎ 21252 or 24945. Known for its excellent fish and seafood platters. Reservations are recommended in the evening. Meals cost about Ksh300. Closed Sun. E.

Amboseli Grill, Hilton Hotel, Mama Ngina St., A2, POB 30624, ☎ 33 4000. Good food, although tourist-oriented. R.

Arturo's Restaurant and Bar, Moi Ave, A2, POB 47231, ☎ 26940. Hospitable Italian restaurant. Closed Sun. R.

Bacchus Club, Standard St., A2, POB 20106, ☎ 33 3233. You'll need to join the club to eat in this elegant and expensive restaurant; call for conditions. Dinner dress recommended. Closed Sun. E.

Carnivore, Langata Rd., off map, POB 56685, ☎ 50 1775 or 501709. Excellent grill in a restaurant outside the city centre on the road to Karen. Open daily. E.

Château, Inter-Continental, City Hall Hwy., A3, POB 30667, ☎ 335550 or 337074. Dining by the hotel pool. Live music at weekends. E.

Delamere Coffee Shop, Norfolk Hotel, Harry Thuku Rd., A2, POB 40064, ☎ 335422 or 24201. A popular and lively meeting place on the terrace of the Norfolk Hotel. Hot meals available at any hour of the afternoon. Kenyan dishes on Wednesday. R.

Dolphin, Meridian Court Hotel, Murang'a Rd., A2, POB 30278, ☎ 333916 or 333751. On the 7th floor around the pool, with a lovely view of Mount Kenya and the Ngong Hills. R.

Foresta Magnetica, Corner House, Kimathi St., A2, ☎ 728009 or 23662. Dinner accompanied by jazz pianist. Closed Sun. E.

Horseman, Langata Rd., Karen, off map, POB 24360, ☎ 882033 or 882782. Far from the city centre, in a lovely old house near the Karen Blixen Museum. E.

Hurlingham, Hurlingham Hotel, off map, POB 43158, ☎ 723001 or 721920. Excellent family cooking in hospitable and intimate atmosphere. R.

Jax, Kimathi St., opposite the New Stanley, A2, POB 72207, ☎ 28365 or 29175. Simple but delicious cafeteria-style fare on 1st floor overlooking the patio. Good salads. I.

Joli Jardin (formerly 'Jardin de Paris '), Maison de France, corner of Loita and Monrovia Sts., A2, ☎ 336263. Top-quality French cooking in lively atmosphere. E.

Lobster Pot, Cabral St., A2, POB 45774, ☎ 331189 or 20491. Specializes in fish and seafood. Open daily. R-E.

Mandy's, Koinange St., A2, ☎ 20193. Pizzas and hamburgers. I.

Marino's, NHC House, Aga Khan Walk across from City Hall Way, A3, POB 72549, ☎ 336210. Nairobi's finest Italian restaurant. Closed Sun. E.

Mayur, Supreme Hotel, opposite Nation House, A2, POB 42945, ☎ 25241. Vegetarian restaurant. Closed Tues. R.

Tamarind, National Bank House, A3, POB 744930 ☎ 338959 or 20473. Seafood specialities. Open daily. E.

Thorn Tree, New Stanley, Standard St., A2, POB 30680, ☎ 333233 or 28830. Extremely popular and lively café-restaurant where you can eat any time of the day. Some Indian dishes. I.

Toona Tree, at the casino on Museum Hill, A1, POB 45827, ☎ 742663 or 742637. Delicious food. R.

Kenyan

African Heritage Café, Banda St., A2, POB 72157, ☎ 28045. Good African food and some Indian dishes served in cafeteria-style buffet. I.

Night life

Casinos
Tourists are required to present foreign (non-Kenyan) currency in exchange for their chips. The stakes are generally low.

Casino de Paradise, Safari Park Hotel and Country Club, 6 mi/10 km north-east of Nairobi on the Thika road, POB 45422, ☎ 802673 or 802838.

International Casino, Chiromo Rd., opposite the museum, A1, POB 45827, ☎ 742600.

Cinemas
Almost all the major hits are shown at the Nairobi cinemas. There are always Indian and usually one or two Kung Fu films playing as well. Be sure to stand when the Kenya National Anthem is played to avoid attracting unfavourable attention.

Fox Drive-In, Thika Rd., off map, POB 40067, ☎ 802293.

Kenya Cinema, Moi Ave., A2, POB 44067, ☎ 27822.

Nairobi Cinema, Uchimi House, off Aga Khan Walk, A3, POB 30678, ☎ 26603.

20th Century Fox, Mama Ngina St., A2, ☎ 27957.

Discotheques

The city centre empties out after 6:30pm. If you'd like to go dancing, try the **Tamango,** Kimathi St., A2, near the hotels in the centre. The **Carnivore,** Langata Rd., off map, POB 56685, ☎ 501775, a bit farther away, is especially lively on Wednesday, Friday and Sunday evenings. The **Visions Discotheque,** Kimathi St, A2, POB 40591, ☎ 332331 or 340398, prepares a midnight meal for its guests *(open Tues-Sun from 9 pm)*. You can dance and dine at the **Bacchus Club,** Wabera St., A2, POB 20106, ☎ 333233. The fabulous singer Zembi often performs here during her trips home from London, where she teaches music.

Theatre

The **Professional Centre Theatre,** Parliament Rd., between Harambee Ave. and Haile Selassie Ave., A3, POB 72643, ☎ 336146, offers an international repertory performed by several theatre companies in a lovely setting.

The **Kenya National Theatre,** Harry Thuku Rd., opposite the Norfolk Hotel in the University building, A2, POB 43031, ☎ 20536, presents all kinds of plays, including productions by amateur groups. It is also a centre for dance performances and concerts.

Organized Tours

Nairobi's numerous travel agencies (there are over 500 tour operators) organize safaris, camping trips and specialized tours on horseback, by camel, by air, etc. While travel agencies also offer tours of the capital and its surroundings, you can do just as well on your own. On the other hand, to visit Nairobi National Park, unless you have rented a car, you will have to go through a travel agency as there's no transport inside the park.

Across Africa Safaris, Bruce House, Standard St., A2, POB 49420, ☎ 332744 or 23013, fax: 332419, tlx: 22501.

African Tours and Hotels, Utalii House, Uhuru Highway, A3, POB 30471, ☎ 336848 or 23285, fax: 336961, tlx: 22033.

Big Five Tours and Safaris, Phœnix House, Kenyatta Ave., A2, POB 10367, ☎ 29803 or 23319.

Bunson Travel, Pan Africa House, Kaunda St., A3, POB 45456 ☎ 21992.

Flamingo Tours, Hilton Hotel, Harambee Plaza, entrance City Hall Way, A3, POB 44899, ☎ 27927 or 28098, fax: 333262 or 331360.

Gametrackers, Finance House, corner of Banda and Loita Sts., A2, POB 62042, ☎ 338927 or 22703.

Ivory Safaris Tours, Mama Ngina St., A3, POB 74609, ☎ 26623 or 26808.

Jet Travel, HFCK Bldg., Banda St., A2, POB 58805, ☎ 23144 or 23333.

Kimbla Kenya, Koinange St., A2, POB 40089, ☎ 337892.

Nilestar Safari Centre, Hilton Hotel, City Hall Way, A3, POB 42291, ☎ 337392 or 24885.

Rhino Safaris, Hilton Hotel, City Hall Way, A3, POB 48023, ☎ 28102 or 25419.

Safari Camp Services, corner of Koinange and Moktar Daddah Sts., A2, POB 44801, ☎ 28936 or 330130. This agency specializes in camping safaris and is reputed for its weekly 'Turkana Bus', a huge truck that transports campers north to Lake Turkana.

The centre of Nairobi.

Safaris Unlimited, Jubilee Insurance Exchange Bldg., Kaunda St., A3, POB 20138, ☎ 332132 or 726209. Offers among other options, a five-day horseback trip through Masai Mara.

Tropical Ice, Jubilee Insurance Exchange Bldg., entrance Mama Ngina St., A3, POB 57341, ☎ 23649. Hiking and mountain climbing.

United Touring Company, Kaunda St., A3, POB 42196, ☎ 331960 or 728922. Desks also at: Jomo Kenyatta Airport, ☎ 822339; Inter-Continental Hotel, A3, ☎ 331960; Nairobi Safari Club, A2, ☎ 330621; New Stanley Hotel, A2, ☎ 331960; Norfolk Hotel, A2, ☎ 335422; Jacaranda Hotel, ☎ 742272.

Universal Safari Tours, Cotts House, corner of Wabera St. and City Hall Way, A3, POB 49312, ☎ 21446 or 22522.

Shopping

Luxury boutiques and sometimes shopping plazas can be found in all of the big hotels.

You can purchase silk fabric and semi-precious stones at Indian shops on Koinange Street and Market Avenue.

The department stores in the city centre include **Uchumi,** on the corner of Muindi Street and Aga Khan Walk, A3, and **Woolworths,** on Kimathi Street opposite the New Stanley Hotel, A2.

Nairobi has some wonderful markets that should not be missed. On **Market Street,** A2, artisans sell basketware, figurines of banana leaves and more. There are new shops and stalls at the **Sarit Centre,** in Westlands, others in Hurlingham or along Chiromo Road.

Finally, you'll need a taxi to get to the **Kamukunzi** second-hand clothing market. Also known as Machakos Airport, the market runs the length of Puwani Road. The most picturesque spot is where the river crosses the market south of Digo Road: there, countless *kangas* (rectangles of colourful cloth) are stretched out on wooden frames.

Bookshops

Text Book Centre, Kijabe St., A2, POB 47540, ☎ 33 0342. This is Nairobi's best bookstore. Stop in before going on a safari.

Two other stores offering a good choice of books on Kenya are the **Nation Bookshop,** by the entrance to the New Stanley Hotel, A2, Kimathi St., POB 14107, ☎ 33 3507, and **Prestige Book Sellers & Stationers,** Prudential Assurance Bldg., on Mama Ngina Street near the 20th Century cinema, A3, POB 45425, ☎ 23515.

In Westlands, you can go to the **Sarit Centre Bookstore,** off map, POB 44309, ☎ 74 7405 or 74 7406, a branch of the Text Book Centre.

Camping equipment

You can buy just about anything you'll need for camping. The following is a selective listing of some of the better Nairobi camping stores.

Ahamed Bros, Enterprise Rd., A3, POB 40254, ☎ 55 5919 or 55 8986. Here you can rent good-quality camping material and safari clothing.

Atul's, Biashara St., between Koinange St. and Moi Ave., A2, POB 43202, ☎ 28064. Rents tents and camping equipment.

Low and Bonar, Addis-Ababa Rd., in the industrial zone south-east of Haile Selassie St., B3, POB 42759, ☎ 55 7355. This store offers a wide selection of material, especially suited to safaris and mountain hikes, from 8-person tents to chemical lavatories. Few rental possibilities.

Safari Crafts, Muindi Mbingu St., A2, POB 10228, ☎ 24868. Specializes in professional camping and mountain-climbing equipment (jerry cans, ropes, winches, etc.).

Yellow Bird, Hilton Hotel, Mama Ngina St., A2, POB 30624, ☎ 33 4000. Stylish and sophisticated safari outfits, hats and shoes.

Handcraft and curio shops

Most of Nairobi's handcraft shops are in the area between Koinange Street, City Hall Way, University Way and Government Road and more particularly on Kenyatta Avenue, A2-3. Don't miss **African Heritage,** Kenyatta Ave., A2, POB 17871, ☎ 33 3157, where you'll find a large variety of items — fabrics, dresses, cushions, tableware, sculptures, jewelry, carpets and books.

Batiks & Jewellery Ltd., Uhuru Highway, A2, POB 40793, ☎ 22727; City Hall Way, A3, POB 30529, ☎ 72 9995. Rings and semi-precious stones at reasonable prices.

The Collector's Den, Simba St. (behind the Hilton Hotel), A2, POB 22291, ☎ 26990. Figurines made out of banana leaves.

Gallery Watatu, Standard St., A2, POB 41855, ☎ 28737 or 33 5480. Engravings, fabrics, batiks. Photographic enlargements.

Panorama, Moi Ave., near University Way, A2, POB 10886, ☎ 22269. Lovely amethyst necklaces, wooden combs. Reasonable prices.

Rowland Ward, City House, Standard St., A3, POB 40991, ☎ 25509. Fantasy jewelry, fabrics, basketware and woodwork.

The Spin and Weave Shop, Kimathi St., A2, POB 40683, ☎ 33 2170. Dyed fabrics, clothes, quality hand-woven carpets.

Treasures and Crafts, Kaunda St., A3, POB 30529, ☎ 28356 or 33 7981. Gems and semi-precious stones. Fairly expensive.

Photography

Most photo shops are in the city centre in Westlands. **Studio-One,** Moi Ave., A2, POB 11275, ☎ 24144, does laboratory work. Another recommended shop is **Supercolor,** in the Westlands shopping centre.

Sports

For information about golfing, horse racing, tennis, squash and other sports, see p. 25.

Useful addresses

Airlines

Air Canada, Hamilton House, Kaunda St., A3, POB 42479, ☎ 719146.

Air France, Fedha Tower, Muindi Mbingu St., A2, POB 30159, ☎ 726265; Hilton Hotel, Mama Ngina St., A2, POB 30159, ☎ 728910.

Air India, Jeevan Bharati Bldg., Harambee Ave., A3, POB 43006, ☎ 334788.

Alitalia, Hilton Hotel, Mama Ngina St., A2, POB 72651, ☎ 72651.

British Airways, International Life House, Mama Ngina St., A3, POB 45050, ☎ 334362.

Japan Airlines, International Life House, Mama Ngina St., A3, POB 42430, ☎ 20591.

Kenya Airways, Airways Terminal, Koinange St., A2, POB 19002, ☎ 29291.

Pan Am, Hilton Hotel, Mama Ngina St., A2, POB 30544, ☎ 23581.

TWA, Rehema House, Standard St., A2, POB 30493, ☎ 24036.

The following domestic airlines have offices at Wilson Airport, Langata Road off map (bus 14). See also p. 29.

Aero Club of East Africa, POB 40813, ☎ 501772.

Africair, POB 45646, ☎ 501210.

CMC Aviation, POB 44580, ☎ 501221.

Pioneer, POB 43356, ☎ 501319.

Safari Air Services Ltd, POB 41951, ☎ 501211/-2/-3.

Sunbird Aviation Ltd., POB 46247, ☎ 501421.

Banks

American Express, c/o Express Kenya, Silver Spears Tours, Bruce House Standard St., A3, POB 40433, ☎ 334722.

Barclay's Bank of Kenya, main office: Bank House, Moi Ave., A2, POB 30120, ☎ 332230 or 337485. Offices: Moi Ave.,A2, ☎ 332230; Kenyatta Ave., A2, ☎ 20523; Haile Selassie Ave., A3, ☎ 21806; Harambee Ave.,A3, ☎ 333132; Jomo Kenyatta Airport, ☎ 822395.

Commercial Bank of Africa, main office: Wabera St., A2, POB 30437, ☎ 28881. Branch office: Hilton Hotel, A2, ☎ 28881.

Kenya Commercial Bank, main office: Kencom House, A2, POB 48400, ☎ 339441. Branch offices: Moi Ave., A2, ☎ 336681; Kenyatta Ave., A3, ☎ 333465; Tom Mboya St.,A2, ☎ 335089.

National Bank of Kenya, main office: Harambee Ave., A3, POB 72866, ☎ 339690 or 339699. Branch offices: Kenyatta Ave.,A2, ☎ 340880; Moi Ave.,A2, ☎ 331780; Jomo Kenyatta Airport, ☎ 822260.

Standard Bank, main office: Stanbank House, Moi Ave., A2, POB 30003, ☎ 330200. Branch offices: Harambee Ave.,A3, ☎ 24857; Kimanthi Ave.,A2, ☎ 23295; Kenyatta Ave., A2, ☎ 331832.

Car repair

Rift Valley Peugeot, Duruma Rd., B2, POB 48817, ☎ 26374 or 543597.

Embassies

Australia, 3rd floor, Development House, Moi Ave., B3, POB 30360, ☎ 334666 or 334672. *Open Mon-Fri 9am-noon.*

Canada, 6th floor, Comcraft House, Haile Selassie Ave., A3, POB 30481, ☎ 334033 or 334036. *Open Mon-Thurs 7:30-11am; Fri 7:30-11am (Canadian citizens only).*

Great Britain, 3rd floor, Bruce House, Standard St., A3, POB 30465,
☎ 335944 or 335960. *Open Mon-Fri 8:30-11:30am, 1:30-3:30pm.*

Ireland, 4th floor, Maendeleo House, Monrovia St., A2, POB 30659,
☎ 26771 or 26772. *Open Mon-Fri 8:30am-12:30pm, 2-4:30pm.*

United States, USA Embassy Bldg., Moi Ave., B3, POB 30137,
☎ 334141 or 334150. *Open Mon-Fri 8:30am-3:00pm.*

Emergencies

Aga Khan Hospital, Parklands Ave., off map, POB 30270, ☎ 742531.
Private hospital. Accepts American Express card.

Gertrude's Gardens Children's Hospital, Muthaiga Rd., off map, POB
42325, ☎ 763474.

Mater Misericordia, South 'B' Dunga Rd., off map, POB 30325,
☎ 556666 or 556524.

Nairobi Accident and Police, ☎ 22222 (24 hours a day).

Nairobi Hospital, Argwings Kodhek Rd., off map, POB 30026,
☎ 722160. State hospital. Accepts American Express card.

St John Ambulance Brigade, ☎ 24066 (24 hours a day).

GETTING TO KNOW NAIROBI

Map coordinates refer to the map p. 91.

The business district

Nairobi stands on the western edge of the immense Athi plateau. The
city's skyline is dominated by the Kenyatta Conference Centre. Heading
to the city from the airport along Uhuru Highway, you'll pass **Uhuru and
Central Parks**,** A2-3. You can take a walk amid the parks' thick wooded
areas and spacious lawns bordered with multi-coloured bougainvilleas or
you can go canoeing on the Uhuru Park lake. Uhuru Park is a lovely place
to spend an afternoon, but don't venture in after dark; the park never
closes and has a reputation for late-night muggings.

Opposite the park, at the corner of Harambee Avenue and Parliament
Road is the **Parliament Building,** A1. Its clock tower was once the highest
construction in the capital. Today, the Kenyatta Conference Centre, a
little farther east, completely overshadows the Parliament. On a clear day
you have a good view of Nairobi from the top of the Parliament Building
tower. Note the shields in the hall representing the various tribes of
Kenya; admire the beautiful tapestry in the Commonwealth Parliamentary
Association Room.

Continuing along Harambee Avenue toward the conference centre, you'll
pass the **Kenyatta Memorial,** A3, where the revered Jomo Kenyatta,
Kenya's first president, lies buried. It is forbidden to visit or photograph
the tomb, which is guarded by armed officers.

North of Harambee Avenue, you can visit the **Kenyatta Conference
Centre**,** A3. The first few floors of the square structure that supports
the centre are bordered by flowering terraces. You can enjoy a
spectacular **panorama** from The Studio restaurant on the 27th and
28th floors (open very irregularly).

Harambee Avenue is a quiet artery that encompasses the highest circles
of the Kenyan 'establishment', including the Office of the President, the
Ministry of Foreign Affairs and the Treasury. Numerous banks and the
offices of EC representatives line the avenue from Uhuru Highway to
Moi Avenue.

Over the last dozen years, the area between Taifa Road and Moi Avenue
has undergone a complete transformation. Many modern buildings and
shops have gone up, interspersed with gardens, parking areas and
narrow lanes enlivened by foliage.

To enter this bustling area, take **Aga Khan Walk,** B3, opposite the
National Bank. On one side is the Uchumi Department Store, on the other

The Jamia Mosque.

the Re-insurance Plaza, with an interior patio surrounded by two floors of cafés, bakeries, shops and offices. It's a favourite lunchtime spot for nearby office workers. The relaxed, lively atmosphere and the shops attract milling crowds all day long.

Head toward City Hall Way north along Taifa Road past the Law Courts and turn left. You will reach **City Hall,** A3, headquarters of the municipal council. Opposite is the garden side of the Law Courts. You can have a lovely view of the gardens from the terrace of the cafeteria, where the food is simple and unpretentious.

From the cathedral to the mosque

Farther west on City Hall Way, you will come upon the **Holy Family Cathedral,** A3, and the Inter-Continental Hotel, west of Parliament Road at Uhuru Highway.

Backtrack to City Hall and take Wabera Street north, all the way to the end, to the **McMillan Memorial Library,** A2 — its structure is reminiscent of a Roman temple. Go around it to reach **Jamia Mosque****, A2, easily recognized by its lovely dome and white minarets. Don't forget to take off your shoes before entering the mosque.

City market A2

Cross Muindi Mbingu Street to the City Market, an orderly, quiet place with flower, fruit, vegetable and souvenir stands. Souvenir prices tend to be high and it is difficult to bargain here.

The entire district around City Market, bounded by University Way, Uhuru Highway, City Hall Way and Moi Avenue, is filled with good handcraft and curio shops. You'll also find most of the travel agencies, major hotels and restaurants — and the aquarium — in the area.

Marine Aquarium* A2

KCS House, Mama Ngina St. *Open Mon-Sat 10am-5pm*. The aquarium is worth a visit, even if you're going to the coast — or have already been there. A score of 20 large tanks showcase a variety of sea animals, including a shark, scorpion fish and surgeonfish.

National museum*** A1

Museum Rd., ☎ 74 2131. *Open daily 9:30am-6pm. Free guided tours Mon-Thurs 9:30am-noon, 2-4:30pm.*

The museum is situated on Museum Hill Avenue at the northern tip of Uhuru Highway. Several buses heading to Westlands stop opposite the Casino at the bottom of Chiromo Road.

The National Museum, which also houses the African Studies Institute, is designed to provide a popular, instructive look at the civilizations of Kenya.

The Winston Churchill Gallery opposite the entrance offers a diorama presenting animals in their natural surroundings. Mammals are the main focus of the exhibit; of particular interest are the various nocturnal animals, such as the aardvark (ant bear), which you normally can't see in wild because they sleep during the day and come out only at night. The primates, carnivores, rodents and other animals are classified by family.

Take the stairway at the end of the gallery up to the ethnological exhibit on the mezzanine. You'll find a fine display of tribal jewelry, weapons, clothing, musical instruments and other everyday objects. On one side of the mezzanine are hundreds of watercolours painted by Joy Adamson between 1946 and 1960. This remarkable collection offers one of the most comprehensive representations of the people of Kenya.

To the left, the entomological gallery exhibits more than a hundred varieties of insect. The butterfly collection is particularly impressive. Information is given on the tsetse fly, which transmits sleeping sickness, the role of termites and the migration of locusts.

The Aga Khan Hall houses a collection of East African birds, mounted and grouped by family, like the bird of paradise originally from New Guinea.

Go down the spiral staircase for a look at the magnificent, life-size reproductions of the Tanzanian rock paintings of Olduvai Gorge. The palaeontology and prehistory room brings together the archaeological finds of the Leakey family. Don't miss the reconstruction of the elephant fossil carefully uncovered by Mary Leakey.

The next room is reserved for temporary ethnography or geography exhibits. In the following two rooms, you can admire a collection of mounted fish, crustaceans and reptiles, including the rare Siebenrock flat turtle, a 12-in/30-cm long turtle and the Nile perch. The last room of this wing displays botanical watercolors by Joy Adamson.

To reach the other side of the museum, cross the entrance hall, past the museum shop, to the courtyard, where a replica of the elephant Ahmed stands. This old male, renowned for his size, lived in the Marsabit National Park and was given the status of a national monument by President Kenyatta.

A corridor leads to the other exhibits. The upper floor of this wing is devoted to the history of Kenya, presented through documents and photos.

The building is the headquarters of the National Museums of Kenya which manages all the country's regional museums and national monuments (Gedi, Fort Jesus, Olorgesailie, Hyrax Hill, etc.). By becoming a member of the Kenya Museum Society, you can participate in fascinating safari expeditions.

Snake Park* A 1-2

Opposite the National Museum. *Open daily 9:30am-5:30pm.*

This small park opposite the museum contains snakes, lizards, chameleons, tortoises, turtles and crocodiles.

Land-dwelling tortoises like the leopard variety, with its mottled shell, are in the patio. Boomslang snakes slither on the grass, while the poisonous species can be watched in glass cages. The only exceptions are the rock pythons (python sebae) and the Aesculapian snake (the latter is not an indigenous species). More than half of the 50 varieties on display are American, notably the rattlesnake and copperhead. The 24-in/60-cm gila monster, a poisonous lizard from the south-west United States and north-west Mexico is one of the most fascinating species in the Snake Park. The cobra (including the red cobra of Mozambique), the mamba and the puff adder originate in Africa.

In the garden reservoir are American and Nile crocodiles and several species of African turtles. On request, the guard will take the turtles out of the water to be photographed.

African District** B2

The district between Moi Avenue and Tom Mboya Street, half African and half Indian, is a transitional zone between the easy-going animation of the centre and the colourful disorder that reigns in the north-eastern part of the city. To find the heart of this latter neighbourhood, take **Ronald Ngala Street,** B3, off Moi Avenue. The clamour of honking horns, screeching brakes and buses that clank like rolling junkyards, will make your head spin. Bit by bit, though, the cry of hawkers selling maize (corn), fried bananas and other fritters will begin to dominate. Don't wander haphazardly: you can easily lose your way and become confused by the three bus stations in close proximity to each other. What's more, the tumultuous activity make you prey for purse-, camera- and jewel-snatchers.

Turn right on River Road and continue straight along **Landhies Road,** B3, past the first bus station on your left to Kikomba Market at the end of the street. In this clothing market, vendors hawk fabrics and clothing (in particular the colourfully dyed *kombas* that ressemble the loin cloths of West Africa) from stalls lining the alleys shaded by the cloth goods fluttering in the breeze.

At the end of the market a sign indicates Digo Road on the left. When you reach the Agip bus station, turn left to get to Pumwani Road (off map) and continue until the white mosque. There, at the corner of Ronald Ngala Street, Race Course and River Roads, B2, is another bus station. Stroll north with the milling crowds along River Road, which is bordered by covered arcades and fancifully painted houses. At its northern tip, River Road intersects Tom Mboya Street near the **Isma'ilia Mosque,** A2.

Back near the bus station, in an area particularly animated toward the end of the day, you will find two Hindu temples, B3. From Ronald Ngala Street take Uyoma Street south toward Race Course Road: on your left will be Siri Singh Shaba Temple, on your right Swaminarayan Temple, dedicated to Shiva, whose crest — a trident — floats over the façade.

The arboretum** off map A1

West of the city centre lies one of the loveliest residential neighbourhoods of the capital. Take Nyerere and State House Roads, just west of Central Park, A2, toward the north until you reach a dead end street bordered by schools. Botany enthusiasts will be thrilled by this walk through a profusion of jacaranda, frangipani, bougainvillea, hibiscus and a variety of European plants.

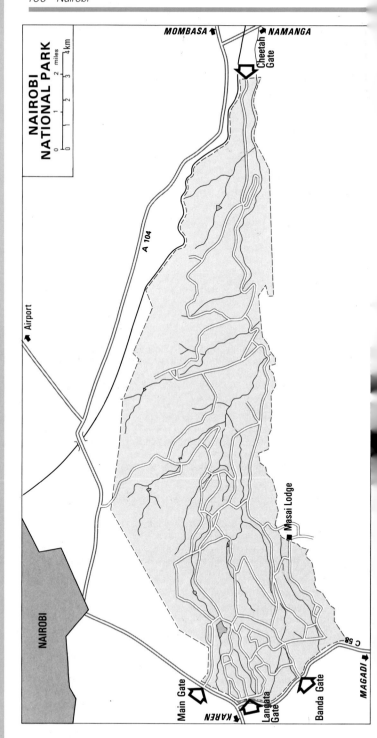

NAIROBI
NATIONAL PARK

MOMBASA
NAMANGA
Cheetah Gate

A 104

Airport

NAIROBI

Masai Lodge

Main Gate
KAREN
Langata Gate
Banda Gate
MAGADI
C 58

0   1   2   3   4 km
0   1   2 miles

Go back the same way to reach the intersection of State House and Nyerere Roads, Uhuru Highway and University Way, A2. This is Nairobi's religious crossroads, with the Presbyterian St Andrew's Church, the Lutheran Church (a small, grey stone chapel), the Catholic St Paul's Cathedral (the resolutely modern polygonal structure consecrated in 1971) and a synagogue.

The railway museum* A3

Station Rd. *Open Mon-Fri 8:30am-4pm, Sat 8:30am-noon, Sun 10am-12:30pm.*

The shortest access is via a path through the empty lot off Haile Selassie Avenue. Otherwise go around Kenya Polytechnic, turn right onto Workshop Road, then right again onto Station Road.

The museum houses a display of locomotives that have operated since the creation of the line and memorabilia from the construction of the railway. For further information, read *The Lunatic Express,* by Charles Miller, and *The Man-eaters of Tsavo,* by P.H. Patterson.

▬▬ *ENVIRONS OF NAIROBI*

Several half-day or day trips in the immediate vicinity of the capital provide a certain insight into the diversity of Kenya.

City park

2 mi/3 km north of Nairobi.

This park is a well preserved remnant, minus the animals, of the woodlands that covered the area before the construction of the railway.

Today, there are lawns, walkways bordered by rare plants, playgrounds and sports fields. Stay in this area of the park, avoiding the southern sector by the river, where you risk being attacked by animals.

Nairobi National Park**

5 mi/8 km south of Nairobi; bus nᵒ 125 or nᵒ 24 from the main bus station. Admission: Ksh 80. No camping allowed. A gas station is at the main entrance. *Open daily dawn-7pm.*

The Nairobi National Park, spreads over 45 sq mi/117 sq km and offers visitors a marvelous chance to see the wildlife wonders of Kenya. The park's main entrance (not very well marked) is on Langata Road just after Wilson Airport. Many companies offer half-day tours to the park (see p. 97).

You will undoubtedly encounter many of the numerous species of herbivores that live in the park: impala, Grant's gazelle, Thomson's gazelle, different types of hartebeest, eland, kudu, zebra, wildebeest and giraffe. If you are keen on seeing some of the predator species (among which, at least one pride of lions), don't hesitate to ask a ranger for advice.

Coming from the main entrance, you will pass the Narogomo Pond, where you can observe, among others, ibis, herons, ducks and secretary birds. Continue through the plain toward Athi Basin at the other end of the park. Drive slowly; the animals are used to being watched and will usually remain motionless as you approach.

You will walk along a path beside the river at Hippo Pool, where crocodiles and hippopotami live. Two armed rangers are on duty in case of difficulty. Impala Hill provides a good viewing point for the whole park.

Picnicking in the park is possible, but you'll have to watch out for black-faced vervet monkeys; they might decide to join you, and are known to sometimes bite.

Don't miss a visit to the Animal Orphanage** (at the main gate to the National Park on the Langata Road), where baby animals that need special protection are raised. Many refuse to leave once they have grown up or have been nursed back to health. The orphanage houses 100 to 150 animals of more than 40 species. Also worth a visit is the aviary which shelters many kinds of birds.

The bomas of Kenya

3 mi/2 km past the main gate of the National Park. You can come here as part of a tour or on your own by car or you can take bus 24 at the Mfangano Street terminus to Forest Edge, near the National Park.

Traditional dances are presented every afternoon in the modern amphitheatre. Nearby is a re-creation of the dwelling of 11 tribes. Vendors sell crafts and souvenirs.

Karen house*

5 mi/8 km south-east of Nairobi; bus n° 24 from Nairobi. *Open daily 9:30am-6pm.*

Baroness Karen Blixen-Finecke (1885-1962) moved from Denmark to Kenya in 1918. In *Out of Africa,* published in 1937, she (using the pseudonym Isak Dinesen) related her experiences on a farm in Kenya.

The village where she once lived was named Karen after her, and her home has been transformed into a museum. It is a romantic place, full of melancholy charm, where it is easy to call to mind the author of *Seven Gothic Tales* and *Winter Tales.*

Ngong Hills**

10 mi/16 km south-west of Nairobi; bus n° 24 from Nairobi; by car, stop at the parking area near the television antenna.

This is a full day's excursion. It is best to go on a Saturday or Sunday when the police patrols and numerous groups of hikers tend to discourage muggers.

Beyond the village of Karen, you'll first pass through a beautiful forest before coming out onto farms and pasture land. From Ngong Town, at the foot of the hills, climb to the summit (7874 ft/2400 m) for an incredible view of the Rift Valley's volcanic craters just beyond the precipitous drop of the Ngong Hills.

On the way up you'll pass sheep and goats, while from the top you can sometimes catch sight of gazelle, giraffe, buffalo or zebra in the valley below. On a clear day, the view extends as far as Mount Kenya on one side and Mount Kilimanjaro on the other.

Olorgesailie*

68 km south-west of Nairobi; by car only — organized tours are unavailable even though the road is well paved all the way to Magadi.

As the road descends in the Rift Valley after Oltepesi, the temperature rises. Many thousands of years ago, before the course of the Ol Keju Nyiro River was changed by an earthquake, the flowing waters formed a lake at Olorgesailie. Animals and the people who hunted them gathered at the lakeshore. Vestiges of the humans and their stone tools, some 200,000 years old, were dug up here and are exhibited in the museum. The stark, barren surroundings become particularly striking when the setting sun patterns the ground with an extraordinary play of colours.

Lake Magadi***

105 km south-west of Nairobi.

The road follows a valley furrowed with ravines. Animals search the muddy ground for some humidity. After a stone bridge you reach Lake Magadi. The water has completely evaporated, leaving in its place large deposits of soda (sodium carbonate). The soda, reflecting the rays of the sun, can turn from crystal to pink. Flocks of flamingoes land here.

The entire zone belongs to the company that mines the soda and the area beyond the village is generally off limits to outsiders. Exceptions are made for individual visitors on Sundays, when they are permitted to go to the hot springs, approximately 19 mi/30 km away.

Kamba country

You'll need a car to follow this itinerary. Take the Mombasa Road (A109) from Nairobi and then turn left on road C97 towards Machakos (39 mi/63 km). There are no specific attactions here except on Mondays, when the market draws the entire neighbouring population, mainly people from the Kamba tribe, renowned as skilled craftsmen.

Continue north-east along the same route to Wamunyu (25 mi/41 km) where a cooperative employs 600 people to make souvenirs, among which are lovely, wood-carved statuettes. One of the vendors, a certain Joseph K. Nzioka, described a group of five men carved in ebony as follows: 'That sad-looking fellow isn't drinking because he hasn't got any money and all he can do is watch the others. The one beside him, happy because he is going to drink, is about to raise his glass in a toast to the third figure, who has already drunk quite a bit. Now he in turn, is thirsty, still thirsty, always thirsty — and he's challenging the others to drink as much as he does. The fourth one can't drink another drop and doesn't even have the strenght to go back home. The old one there is laughing at the others. He's finished with drink entirely, knowing only too well how crazy alcohol can make you.'

From this large village, a magnificent track leads into the hills towards Kangundo where once again the road is paved. At Tala (3 mi/5 km) you'll find a lively marketplace, covered with jacarandas, fig trees and bougainvilleas and surrounded by shops that sell weapons, arrows and a renowned powdered tobacco wrapped in banana leaves.

To get back to Nairobi (34 mi/55 km), take the C98 directly across the dry plain, passing herds of giraffe on the way.

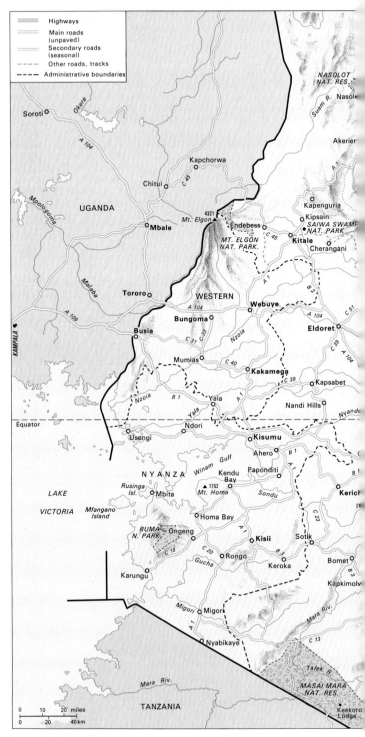

WESTERN KENYA

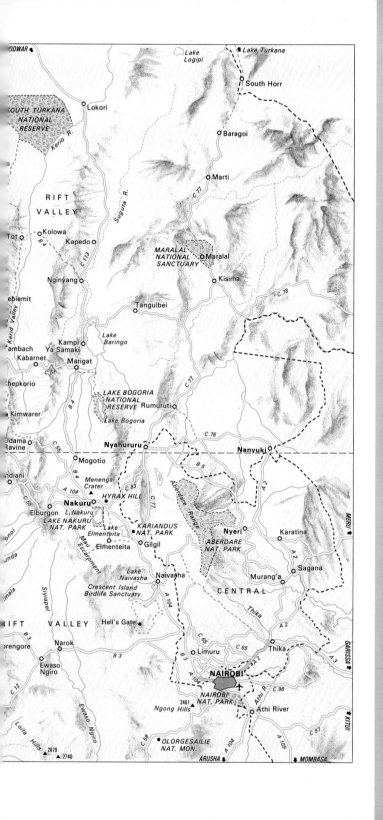

WESTERN KENYA

Organizing your time

- **Four days:** Nairobi - Masai Mara - Naivasha - Nakuru - Nairobi. You'll need a car for this circuit.
- **One week:** Nairobi - Nakuru - Kericho - Kisumu - Homa Bay - Rusinga Island - Ruma National Park (Lambwe Valley) - Eldoret - Kitale - Mount Elgon - Nairobi. A marvelous route in terms of the diversity of both the landscape and the people. It is seldom used by tourists, and no travel agency offers an organized tour package to the area. Except for Mount Elgon National Park and Ruma National Park (Lambwe Valley), you can get to all these places through a combination of bus, taxi and boat. The roads are paved between Nairobi and Kisumu, and the others present no particular problems.
- **One week:** Nairobi - Kitale - Lodwar - Saiwa Swamp - Cherangani Hills - Lake Turkana - Central Island - Cherangani Hills - Kerio Valley - Iten - Lake Baringo - Lake Bogoria - Nakuru - Nairobi. The roads are mostly paved; the only difficult stretch extends from Lodwar to the lodge on the west bank of Turkana Lake. Some travel agencies organize two- to three-day air safaris to Lake Turkana; others feature Baringo and Bogoria lakes (see p. 97). You'll need a car to do the whole circuit, and if you intend to make the excursion through the Elgeyo Marakwet range, a four-wheel-drive vehicule is indispensable.

NAIROBI TO MASAI MARA

About 162 mi/260 km.
Leave Nairobi on Chiromo Road and follow the signs out of town onto the Limuru road. This fertile region is the southern part of Kikuyu country, where the small hills, separated by deep gulleys, are covered with a patchwork of maize (corn) and vegetables, and plantations of coffee shrubs with their fragrant white flowers.

Limuru (18 mi/30 km north west of Nairobi)
Along the roadside, the village women sell basketware and necklaces of small beads while the men are busy selling the sheepskins you see hanging to dry throughout the town.

> ### Food
>
> **Kentmere Club,** POB 39508 in Nairobi, ☎ 42101. Good food, English farmhouse atmosphere, log fire in the dining room.
> **Mrs. Mitchell's Kiambethu Farm.** You lunch in the family farmhouse set in a tea plantation and then may be taken on a walk through the forest, where you are likely to see dramatic black-and-white colobus monkeys.

Blood from the cow's jugular vein mixed with milk is the Masai's main sustenance.

Beyond Limuru, turn right off the new road that heads to Nakuru on a faster, more direct route, and take the old A104. You'll soon forget the discomfort of the rough road when you see the magnificent panorama from 3280 ft/1000 m above the Rift Valley. The road twists through the forested slopes of the escarpment, punctuated here and there by the pink flowers of a cape chestnut in bloom. On one of the steep bends you'll see a charming Italian-built church nestled against the hillside. The constantly changing play of light, colour and perspective is breathtaking.

Masai country

The B3 road descends west along the rocky wall into the Rift Valley. Shortly before Kijabe, about 16 mi/25 km from Limuru, it turns toward Narok (56 mi/90 km) in the Loita Plains. The floor of the valley is studded with volcanic craters, Suswa rising abruptly on the left, and Longonot hiding Lake Naivasha to the north. Over this infinite plain, its gentle undulations emphasized here and there by almost colourless bramble bushes, the play of light creates a marvelous spectacle in constant change. When the sky is lightly studded with rain clouds, patches of shadowed earth washed in a slight drizzle alternate with wisps of scrub brush turned golden by the rays of the sun.

From time to time, you can see in the distance the familiar silhouette of a shepherd tending his flock. Herds of gazelle and giraffe move about randomly.

The road climbs up the other side of the Rift Valley, passing through hills of olive groves and umbrella-shaped acacias. As you approach Narok, the Masai herds become increasingly abundant, and you see *enkang*, the traditional circular villages of huts covered with a mud made of earth and cow urine. At night, the livestock are sheltered in the central enclosure. Stop and you'll find yourself surrounded by groups of children begging for candies and adults selling hand-made necklaces, ear rings and belts. Expect to pay a small fee to take pictures; negotiate the price in advance with the chief. Don't insist if anyone refuses to be photographed.

Narok (100 mi/160 km west of Nairobi)

Narok's main attraction lies in its filling station and supply stores. About 11 mi/18 km beyond the village, you'll find two roads leading to Masai Mara. The road to the left is firm but slightly battered and bumpy even during the dry season. To the right an even rougher road runs along the northern border of the reserve to Oloololo. You can enter the reserve from one side and leave it from the other; in any case you will return to route B 3.

MASAI MARA NATIONAL PARK***

Approximately 162 mi/260 km west of Nairobi. No entry allowed into the park after 6:30pm. Entrance fee: Ksh 200 per person, per day.

One of East Africa's oldest, largest and most beautiful game reserves, Masai Mara is considered to be the northern extension of Tanzania's Serengeti National Park. The reserve has rightly become one of the most popular in the country. It stretches over 646 sq mi/ 1672 sq km. Set aside three days to visit it, changing lodges or camps daily to familiarize yourself with different areas.

At first sight the terrain seems to consist of vast stretches of uninterrupted plains. As you get farther from the easternmost entry at Olaimutiek Gate, however, the savannah spotted with acacia woodlands, gives way to a more varied landscape. Hills and mountains rise higher and higher as you approach the steep Oloololo escarpment on the west, which, by the way, provides a useful landmark if you venture off the roads or trails.

Between the cliff and the southward-flowing Mara River lies the Mara Triangle teeming with animal life. The banks of its tributary, the Talek, flowing in from the west, are overgrown with a lush forest of doum palms, eucalyptus and fig trees.

The mostly permanent water network provides the animals with a year-round supply of water, and the forest offers protective cover for a variety of species. The herbivores can often be seen during the dry season. They are most abundant in July when many of them migrate into Kenya from Tanzania.

Researchers say these seasonal migrations are partly caused by the search for food, but the full reasons for these massive movements remain unknown. Climatic variations can modify the dates from year to year. Zebra usually stay in Masai Mara until mid-November. Wildebeest generally leave the region about two weeks earlier; their departure creates a most fascinating spectacle, as thousands of these strange-looking mammals proceed together across the countryside in almost perfect order.

The reserve is rich with herbivores even outside the migratory period. Besides the wildebeest and Burchell's zebra, the park abounds in topi, hartebeest, and various antelope and gazelle. Finally, Masai Mara boasts the largest on population of Kenya. You can happen upon entire families of lion or elephant in the park Leopards, on the other hand, are extremely rare. Giraffes, hippopotami, crocodiles and herds of buffalo live by the rivers.

In addition to the main track from Olaimutiek and Olemelepo past Keekorok Lodge to Oloololo Gate on the west, there are many secondary tracks. During rainy season tracks running alongside the rivers can become difficult to follow.

Throughout the dry season, of course, the roads are easier to negotiate, but you'll need a good sense of direction; it is always more prudent to hire a professional guide.

It is now possible to fly directly from some of the lodges to Rusinga Island in Lake Victoria, to fish for perch. Reservations are available through the **Lonhro Hotels** in Nairobi, POB 58581, ☎ 27027.

Access

From Nairobi, take the A104, the B3 and the C13, if you are traveling by car. **Sunbird Company** (see p. 30) offers daily flights to the lodges and to Mara Serena, Governor's and Kichwa Temblo camps.

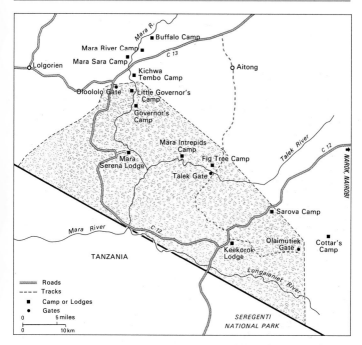

MASAI MARA NATIONAL RESERVE

Accommodation

You should reserve your overnight accommodation through a travel agent in Nairobi, especially if you visit between July and December (see p. 97).

Outside the reserve

▲▲ **Kichwa Tembo,** reservations: Windsor Hotels International Ltd., POB 74957, Nairobi, ☎ 72 6707. 20 tents. ① Swimming pool. Near Olooloo Gate, not far from Mara River.

▲ **Cottar's Mara Camp,** POB 44191, ☎ 88 2408. 30 tents and *bandas,* complete with shower and toilet. ① Situated in a beautiful garden, shaded by bougainvilleas, it is the first camp on the way from Nairobi.

▲ **Mara River Camp,** reservations: POB 45456, Nairobi, ☎ 21 992. 40 beds in bungalows.

▲ **Mara Sara Camp,** reservations: Big Five Tours, POB 10367, Nairobi, ☎ 29 803. 16 bungalows with showers.

Buffalo Camp, POB 20640, ☎ 33 7679. 40 tents along the Mara River.

In the reserve

▲▲▲▲ **Governor's Camp,** reservations: Musaria Ltd., POB 48217, Nairobi, ☎ 33 1871. 27 tents with showers. ① Bar. A mostly American clientele in this camp that offers full comfort and extensive services, including laundering and organized safaris, free of charge. Balloon safaris available.

▲▲▲▲ **Keekorok Lodge,** reservations: Block Hotels, POB 47557, Nairobi, ☎ 33 5807. 60 bungalows. ① ④ Filling station. This is one of the oldest lodges in the park and the first on the road from the

An ornithological paradise: Naivasha Lake.

east. From the bungalows you can see zebras, giraffes, monkeys and other animals drinking from the water hole. Balloon safaris available.

▲▲▲▲ **Mara Intrepid Camp,** reservations: POB 14040, Nairobi, ☎ 33 1688. 21 tents. ① Extremely well-located on the Talek River where the animals come to drink. High-quality comfort. Mostly American guests.

▲▲▲▲ **Mara Safari Club,** reservations: Lonhro Hotels, POB 58581, Nairobi, ☎ 27 027. 40 tents. This is a new luxury lodge that provides graciously appointed tents with four-poster beds. Ballooning is possible and there are 18 new landcruisers for game viewing. All-weather airstrip links the club to Nairobi.

▲▲▲▲ **Mara Serena Lodge,** reservations: POB 48690, Nairobi, ☎ 33 8656. 50 bungalows with bathrooms. ① ④ Filling station. Car rental, new airstrip. Full board only. The lodge's architecture, modeled on the Masai *manyattas,* is one of the most outstanding of the Serena chain. Situated on a crater above the Mara Triangle and River, the bungalows are surrounded by garden terraces where you can watch the animals in the plains. The balloon excursions that leave from Governor's Camp arrive here.

▲▲▲ **Little Governor's Camp,** same management as Governor's Camp, 17 double tents with washrooms. ① Like Governor's Camp, though slightly less expensive, this camp overlooks the Mara River where the animals abound.

▲▲ **Fig Tree Camp,** reservations: POB 40683, Nairobi, ☎ 20952. 40 tents with washrooms. ① The camp is situated in the shelter of fig trees along the Talek River, north-west of Keekorok Lodge. The dining tent is built on a platform above the river where the flow cascades into several small waterfalls. In the evenings a bonfire is lit near the dining tent. Balloon safaris available.

▲▲ **Mara Sarova Camp,** reservations: Sarova Hotels, POB 30680, Nairobi, ☎ 333233. 35 tents with washrooms. ① A fine decor and a wonderful location between two waterways, not far from Keekorok Lodge.

Useful address

Chief Warden, Masai Mara National Reserve, POB 40 Narok, ☎ 4 in Narok.

▬ HELL'S GATE*

Turn off the A104 to the left between the turning to Narok and the town of Naivasha. Hell's Gate can also be reached from the road around Lake Naivasha.

Hell's Gate National Park was created in 1984. Previously the road leading up to these stupendous gorges ran though the private property of the Sulmac company. A strange assembly of pipes marks the entrance. After you register, take the track across the plain between the cliffs and the towers of lava. Antelope, gazelle and zebra graze on the plain. Above them, in the cliffs that give Hell's Gate its name, nest birds of prey like Verreaux's eagles and lammergeyers (bearded vultures).

The track ends 3.5 mi/6 km farther on. The gorges nearby are good places to hike. The steam that once shot out of the rock walls, contributing to the sensational effect of the descent, is diminished now, having been tapped by a geothermal power plant. You might encounter some buffalo or even Masai tribes traveling through.

Take care: the river can swell dangerously when it rains. Be cautious and don't venture out alone. Don't hesitate to ask a guard to accompany you. A project is underway to link this area to Longonot Park (before Hell's Gate on the road coming from Nairobi), which at the moment can be reached only by route B3.

Mount Longonot itself, a volcanic cone, is worth a climb not only for the view into its crater but also for a wonderful panorama of the surrounding Rift Valley.

FROM NAIROBI TO KISUMU (LAKE VICTORIA)

▬ NAIVASHA TOWN AND LAKE

55 mi/88 km north-west of Nairobi.

The town of Naivasha has a filling station and shops where you can pick up supplies. It is renowned for the quality of its wines and of its cheeses which somewhat resemble the French blue cheese. Like most of the towns along this route, the streets intersect each other at right angles; they are bordered by whitewashed houses of various tints, the pavements shaded from the sun by colonnaded verandahs. Many Kenyans of British origins or ancestry still inhabit the region, running large farms and ranches.

Crescent Island Birdlife Sanctuary**

You'll need a full day to visit the island; take a picnic lunch along — you can order it from your hotel the night before.

Crescent Island is an ornithological paradise. Officially private property, the island is open to all and benefits from the natural protection of being accessible only by boat. All the lake hotels provide boats to make the crossing. Note that the water level here, as in all the lakes of the Rift Valley, has been inexplicably and dramatically dropping

Exactly 346 different species of birds have been counted at Naivasha. The ecosystem provides them with a perfect natural habitat. Aquatic species find shelter in the papyrus plants along the shores. The island is overgrown with trees and thickets that open onto lovely glades.

There are no dangerous animals, no carnivores and just a few small predators like mongooses. Few reptiles live on the island nor any crocodiles in the lake. You can explore the island in almost perfect solitude: encounters with other people are rare, and only the monkeys disturb the calm.

The bulrushes make it difficult to move about along the banks of the lake. You may notice fat brown, rat-like creatures swimming in the reeds. These are the harmless coypus (nutrias) that were originally introduced from South America. They bred rapidly and are now also common in Lake Ol Bolossat, north-east of Naivasha. From the summit of the island you can get a clear idea of the region. To the east and north-east are the Rift escarpment and the Kinangop mountains and plateau. Farther back lies the Aberdare (Nyandarua) Range. On the other side of the Rift, to the west, is the Mau escarpment. Mount Longonot, an extinct volcano, and Hell's Gate gorge (not visible from here) are to the south. To the north flow the Morendat and Gilgil rivers; hidden from view by the tall, dense papyrus, they supply the lake with enough fresh water to make it possible to swim without fear of catching bilharzia.

To best observe the birds, some of which are endangered species, be sure to walk quietly. Keep an eye out for the various wading birds (egrets and herons, in particular), kingfishers, Hemprich's hornbills, vultures of a dozen varieties, sunbirds, saddle-billed storks and many more.

Elsamere Conservation Centre

Open daily; tea served from 3 to 5pm.

Part museum and part residential research centre, this former home of Joy Adamson, has been turned into a nature preservation facility, in accordance with her last wishes. Part of the house, in particular her bedroom, has been conserved as a memorial to her work; here Joy Adamson's photos, watercolours and manuscripts are exhibited. The rest of the building has been enlarged to house 13 people involved in nature research.

Resident researchers must belong to any recognized scientific institute or to an association such as the East African Natural History Society, the East African Wildlife Society or the Museum Society. It is, a wonderful place to stay: there are tame animals in the garden, in particular an affectionate zebra. Residents can rent boats to study the fauna and flora of the lake. The centre also organizes expeditions to Hell's Gate, Lake Nakuru and Masai Mara. It is neither difficult nor expensive to join one of the nature societies. For information, contact the Elsamere Conservation Centre, POB 4, Naivasha, ☎ 2Y8 (through an operator).

Access

To reach the lake from Nairobi, turn left about 3.5 mi/6 km before the town of Naivasha. A rough road runs some distance from the shores, which are all private property. Daily buses and *matatus* travel between Nairobi and Maiella, 0.6 mi/1 km from the lodges and camping areas.

Accommodation

In town

▲ **Bell Inn**, POB 532, ☎ 20110. 9 rooms with showers ① A charming and perfectly clean hotel in a lovely little house along the main road. Its souvenir shop sells high-quality merchandise and its restaurant serves delicious pastries.

On the lake

▲▲▲ **Lake Naivasha Hotel,** South Lake Rd., POB 15, Naivasha, reservations: Block Hotels POB 47557, Nairobi, ☎ 335807. 48 rooms and 10 bungalows. ① ④ ⑤ In a superb park that attracts a large number of birds, this hotel is tastefully furnished, though the upkeep of the sanitary facilities leaves something to be desired. Excursions available on the lake, to Crescent Island, and also to Hell's Gate and elsewhere in the vicinity.

▲▲▲ **Safariland Lodge,** reservations: POB 72, Naivasha, ☎ 20441. 56 rooms. ① ③ ④ ⑤ 6 mi/10 km from the intersection with route A106. Recently renovated thatched-roof, chalet-style cottages. Rental facilities: horses, sailboats and motorboats.

▲ **Fisherman's Camp,** reservations: POB 14982, Naivasha; POB 720382, Nairobi. 38 beds in 12 bandas. 5 tents. ⑥ In a magnificent park sheltered by immense acacias. Food shop on premises. Possibility of camping with your own tent and free use of the camp's boats.

▬ *FROM NAIVASHA TO NAKURU*

42 mi/67 km.

Beyond Naivasha, runs a tarmac (paved) road that overlooks Lake Elmenteita. As you drive along, look up at the rocky outcrops beside the road; they sometimes come alive with klipspringers and hyraxes. Like Lake Nakuru, Elmenteita is saline. Its shores are private property and are accessible only if you have an authorization from one of the farm or ranch owners.

3 mi/5 km after Gilgil, take the murram road on the left through the village of Elmenteita. Continue toward Lanet to reach Lake Nakuru.

The new road, on the right upon leaving Naivasha, leads to two historic sites.

Kariandusi

On the right side of road A104, 5 mi/8 km north of Gilgil, is the archaeological site where Leakey uncovered tools and domestic implements made of obsidian, as well as a tooth from an *Elephas antiquus,* an extinct prehistoric species.

Hyrax Hill

This is another prehistoric site (3.5 mi/6 km east of Nakuru) discovered by Leakey. A museum houses a collection of tools and pottery. In the Neolithic cemetery you can see the remains, the women surrounded by their domestic implements, but the men buried with no possessions. This has led to suppositions that the women — like the Kikuyu women of today — were the more active members of society.

▬ *NAKURU*

96 mi/155 km north west of Nairobi.

A lovely avenue shaded by jacarandas and bougainvilleas leads to the city centre. On the left you will see the market, a large rectangular enclosure with covered arcades where Kikuyu and other products are sold. Nakuru is an important agricultural and business centre for the rich surrounding farmland. The annual Agricultural Show is usually held in June.

Accommodation

▲▲ **Waterbuck Hotel,** POB 3327, ☎ 49081. 150 Rooms. ① A new hotel, on the corner of Kenyatta Ave. and West Rd. Conference hall. Organized excursions available to Nakuru National Park (with zoologist), the tea plantations of Kericho, to Naivasha, Baringo and other destinations.

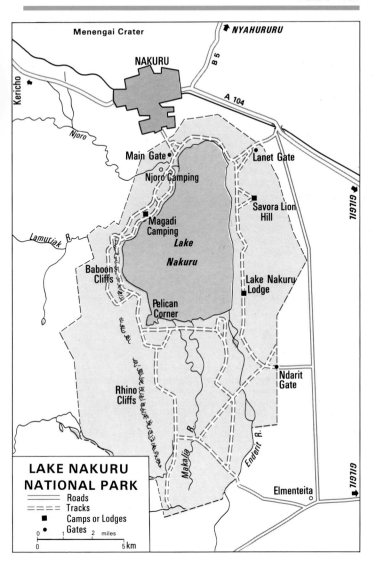

▲ **Midland Hotel,** POB 908, ☎ 41227, 48 rooms. ① Located in the block of houses between Moi Rd., Kenyatta Ave., and Geoffrey Kamau Rd. Car rental and discotheque.

Food

Oyster Shell, on the corner of Kenyatta Ave. and Club Rd., POB 1721, ☎ 40946. Good curries in a restaurant upstairs.

Rift Valley Sports Club, Club Rd., POB 1, ☎ 43821. Peaceful spot for tea with cakes and sandwiches overlooking lovely grounds. Jacaranda trees, tennis and squash courts, swimming-pool.

Useful addresses

There are several garages on George Morara Ave., the continuation of Kenyatta Ave. on the road to Eldoret.

Lake Nakuru National Park

See map p. 121.

Lake Nakuru National Park, famous the world over for the gathering here of millions of pink flamingos, was created mainly to protect these birds. A few years ago pollution of the lake, caused by chemical wastes from a nearby factory, provoked the flight of the flamingos to Lake Bogoria. The water has been cleaned since and many flamingo have returned, but only to the eastern and southern reaches of the lake. Nakuru is unfortunately in the process of drying up, and large sand banks are appearing on its banks. The diminishing area of the lake is blamed on both drought and a growing population that diverts the tributaries, particularly the Njoro River, for its own uses.

While there are fewer flamingo today, there's an abundance of other bird-life: heron, weaver, marabou stork, owl, ibis. The westernmost area of the park is a refuge for primates — baboons, black-faced vervets and colobus monkeys, and others. Among the herbivores, you'll find Defassa and common waterbuck, eland, giraffe, klipspringer, and various gazelle.

In 1979, two leopards were introduced to maintain the park's ecological equilibrium; otherwise, carnivores are rare. Buffalo are difficult to spot. Watch out, however, for the snakes, even pythons, that abound in the forest.

Recently 15 black rhinoceros that had been endangered in Tsavo and Amboseli parks, were brought to Nakuru. It is hoped that the transfer will be facilitated by the park's limited area and the fact that it is entirely enclosed. Observation of the rhinoceros is impossible until they have overcome the trauma of their transfer. A baby rhino was born on Christmas Day, 1988.

Access

Coming from Nairobi, once inside Nakuru, turn left in front of the Midland Hotel; follow Moi Road and then Stadium Avenue to reach the main entrance of the park (2 mi/3 km from Nakuru). Fill your vehicle with gasoline before entering the park since there are no stations inside. You can also enter at Elmenteita, but there is no filling station. Another entrance is at Lanet Gate (turn left before the railway bridge on the way toward Nakuru).

Accommodation

▲▲▲ **Lake Nakuru Lodge,** POB 73667, ☎ 20225 in Nairobi. 12 rooms. ① ④ Half board. Situated on the lakeshore.

▲▲▲ **Sarova Lion Hill,** reservations: Sarova Hotels, POB 30680, Nairobi, ☎ 333233. 66 rooms. ① ④ Superb view of the southern shore of the lake. Car rental.

Camping

At **Njoro, Magadi, Makalia** and inside the park.

Useful address

Chief Warden, Lake Nakuru National Park, POB 539, Nakuru, ☎ 2470.

Menengai Crater**

Leaving Nakuru from Showground Road, take route B5, toward Solai. Follow the signposts to the crater, 5 mi/8 km away.

This 8169 ft-/2490 m-high crater is a fine example of the Rift Valley's extinct volcanos. The view from the summit is spectacular. Because the rim is 7 mi/11 km across, you can't really see the other side except on perfectly clear days. The bottom of the crater (approximately 19 sq mi/50 sq km) is rich in animals. Unfortunately, access is extremely difficult.

Menengai means 'the place of corpses' or 'dead spirits' in Masai. Believing that the dead stay in proximity to the volcano, the Masai come here to pray for the spirits of their families. It is also the site of a mythic battle in which many Masai met their death at the bottom of the crater. It is said that the desperate voices of the dead and the bells of their cattle can still be heard at night.

▬ *FROM NAKURU TO KERICHO*

If you continue to Kericho on the A104 (68 mi/110 km west of Nakuru), you will pass near Molo, a farming centre that, due to the altitude, is chilly in the early morning and often shrouded in mist. These once thick forests were home to the Ndorobo and Okiek hunter-gatherers, descendants of Kenya's earliest inhabitants. Today, because the forests and hunting grounds have been largely cut down or turned into farms, these people have mixed with other groups and some have themselves turned to agriculture.

Kalenjin country

The highway cuts through a prosperous agricultural region, where you can take part in any number of sporting activities (horseback riding, fishing, hiking). This is Kalenjin country. Once herdsmen, the Kalenjin have turned to agriculture.

Subsistence crops such as maize, bananas, and sugar cane, grow amid enclosures of prickly shrubs. Coffee, tea and sisal are cultivated on the plantations. You'll also notice plants with white flowers; these are pyrethrum, a variety of daisy that is an important source of a natural insecticide, pyrethrin, capable of replacing synthetic products. Kenya is the principal producer of pyrethrin.

Subsistence crops gradually give way to tea plantations, which cover the hills around Kericho on the spectacular western side of the Rift Valley.

▬ *KERICHO★*

160 mi/256 km north-west of Nairobi.

Kericho is a lovely, tranquil, town renowned for the surrounding tea plantations. Covered with neatly planted rows of tea bushes, the whole area seems from a distance to be cloaked in green corduroy. Worthwhile visits include a plantation tour, the arboretum that shelters numerous bird species, and the immense forests of eucalyptus and of conifer along the Itare, Kipsoni and Kiptiget rivers. Spending a night in a trout fishing camp on the Kiptiget River is a perfect way to observe the local bird life; information is available at the Tea Hotel.

These superb woodlands are typical of the highlands above Kisumu. They surprised the early British settlers, who little expected to find such forests in Africa, and who dubbed the region 'white man's country'.

Access

You can take a train, bus, taxi or *matutu* from Nakuru to Kericho. If you're driving, take the A104 and then turn left on the B1 signposted to Kericho.

An alternate route to Kericho from Nairobi passes through Narok. Take the A104 to the Narok turning, then take the B3 through Narok to Sotik and finally the C23 to Kericho. There is no filling station from Mara Serena Lodge or Governor's Camp at Masai Mara until Sotik, and the road can often be difficult to negotiate.

Accommodation

▲▲▲▲ **Tea Hotel**, reservations: African Tours & Hotels, POB 30471, Nairobi, ☎ 336858; or POB 75, Kericho, ☎ 20280. 43 rooms. ① ③ ④ ⑤ In colonial times, this fine hotel was highly appreciated by British visitors. The clientele has changed, but the hotel still attracts many guests, especially among residents of Kisumu drawn to the region's marvelous climate. Tea plantation tours and fishing expeditions available.

In Kenya, 10% of the land is set aside to protect its precious wildlife.

▲▲ **Midwest Hotel B & B,** POB 1175, ☎ 20611. 41 Rooms. ① ⑤
Tastefully decorated, this hotel is situated on the road leaving town
toward Kisumu.

Useful address

Garage Kericho Farm & Machinery, Kenyatta Rd., POB 78, ☎ 20521.

▬ *FROM KERICHO TO HOMA BAY*

98 mi/157 km via Sotik and Kisii.

If you'd like to make a journey off the beaten track, drive or take the bus
to Sotik and then to Kisii. The Bantu-speaking Kisii are the subject of a
book, *The Kenya Magic*, by John Schmid, who lived in this region among
the farmers. He notes among the customs of the Kisii, the requirement
that 12-year-old boys reside alone in a hut separated from the others for
three weeks before being circumcised.

From Kisii, you can continue to Homa Bay by car or bus (see p. 127). As
you drive through the area, notice the picturesque ridged thatching on
, the huts, unlike any other in Kenya.

▬ *FROM KERICHO TO KISUMU*

52 mi/83 km.

Proceed along the B1 to reach Kisumu. The road descends from the high
plateau into the plains that surround the Kavirondo gulf on Lake Victoria.
This is Luo country, the dominant tribe of the region.

Bird lovers can take advantage of two side trips along the way. Some
19 mi/30 km after Kericho, immediately after the C37, turn right at Awasi
onto a track that crosses an open prairie, where only isolated trees
interrupt the emptiness. Park and continue on foot. On your right,
219 yd/200 m on, you can observe the birds that live in the reeds.

Return to the B1. Turn left 438 yd/400 m past the signpost indicating

'Kisumu 8 km'. Continue about a kilometre until you reach the Orongo school, where you'll leave your car. A 1.5 mi/2.5 km walk (keep left at the fork) brings you to a marshy area where there is a heronry, which was made into a National Reserve in 1980.

The climate of the plain that lies before Kisumu seems hot after the highlands, though the plain is, in fact, 3609 ft/1100 m above sea level. Here and there, you'll see groups of thatched-roof houses surrounded by hedges of dried branches, standing out against the emptiness of the flat expanse, like islands in a sea.

═══ KISUMU

213 mi/343 km north-west of Nairobi.

Kenya's third largest city, with an estimated population of 150,000, Kisumu was once a major transport and communications centre, but its harbour suffered greatly from the dissolution of the East African Community. Today, Kisumu is isolated at the western end of the country, and the rich agricultural produce of its hinterland is often shipped through Nakuru and Nairobi. The government has to a certain extent maintained the city's role as a regional economic centre. Hotels have been improved and communications with the rest of the country is good. Nevertheless, Kisumu remains outside most tourist itineraries.

The city has a surprisingly Asian air to it, with a large community of followers of the Moslem sect Ismailiyah. You'll see many people dressed in saris and notice Indian and Pakistani names on shop signs.

The markets

The modern downtown district, which you'll recognize by the plaza surrounded by banks, includes two market places. At one, you can pick up some beautiful pottery; the other, at the end of Anaawa Avenue, (leading to the station), is a Sunday flea market. More interesting than the actual merchandise is the local atmosphere of the marketplace, with its performers, preachers and medicine men.

The port

The rhythm is slower in the old part of town. Here the sloping streets are lined with single-storey houses, fronted with covered porches: the shop signs carry Pakistani names.

Go down any one of these streets to Obote Road, which parallels the shore where the workshops factories are located. Turn left to the train station and follow the rails until you reach the port. Once a bustle of activity with the continual shipping of products to Uganda, the port today links only the small towns and islands of the Kenyan shore of Lake Victoria. From here, you'll have a very good view of the lake.

Jamhuri gardens

These gardens on the outskirts of the city are a lovely place for a walk.

Hippo Point

To reach Hippo Point in the residential sector in the south of the city, turn right on the street after the one that leads to the Yacht Club. This is a superb site. Nearby the fishermen sit on the rocks while the children play in the water. Don't go swimming, though. Crocodile and hippopotamus inhabit the area, and there's a risk of catching bilharzia.

Access

There are bus services to Kisumu from Nairobi, Kitale and Kisii. Most of the bus companies are at the corner of Konzi Lane and Odinga Idinga Road, or on New Station Road.

The train station is at the end of New Station Road. There is a daily train to Nairobi.

Kenya Railways operate ferry services to Kendu Bay and Homa Bay. Daily departures for Kendu Bay at 9am; service to Homa Bay three times a week. Reserve at least an hour before departure. Don't bother to look for boats to cross the lake; since the breakup of the East African Community, Kenyan boats are confined to Kenyan territorial waters.

Accommodation

▲▲ **Imperial,** Jomo Kenyatta Highway, POB 1866, ☎ 41485. 86 rooms. ① ④ A very comfortable, air-conditioned hotel in the city centre. The Imperial bar on the side of the hotel is under separate management.

▲▲ **Sunset Hotel,** reservation: POB 215, Kisumu; or Nairobi, ☎ 41100. 50 rooms. ① ④ Located on Jomo Kenyatta Highway towards Hippo Point, the Sunset Hotel provides a remarkably beautiful view of the lake.

▲ **Lake View Hotel,** B & B, Alego St., reservations: POB 1216, Kisumu, ☎ 3141. 25 rooms. Situated on Alego Street near the lake, this is a clean, modest hotel run by Ismailiyah adherents.

▲ **New Victoria Hotel B & B,** Gor Mahia Rd., reservations: POB 276, Kisumu, ☎ 2909. 28 rooms. Located on Konzi Lane. Modest.

Get-in Hotel, Johana Ouko Rd., POB 807, ☎ 42682; and **Casanova,** Kibbos Rd., POB 920, ☎ 43159, are two modest hotels where you can find decent and inexpensive accommodation. Good value for the price.

Camping

1.2 mi/2 km to the south near the Dunga restaurant.

Food

Alfirose, Oginga Odinga Rd. POB 158, ☎ 41677. Indian cuisine.

Bodega, Tom M'Boya Rd., ☎ 42045. This Indian restaurant is managed by Nizar Vitrani who organizes boat trips (see Yacht Club below). *Closed Sundays.* Fish specialities.

Dunga, near Hippo Point. There's a great view of the lake from this Indian restaurant.

Expresso Coffee House, Otuoma St. , POB 74, ☎ 43067. Indian management.

Yacht Club, POB 226, ☎ 42076. You must take out a tempory membership to enter. On Sundays you can meet Nizar Vitrani who organizes boat excursions — single day or week trips (private ☎ 41675). Other members of the club might offer to take visitors on their sailboats.

Useful addresses

Garages
Cooper Motor (Rover, Leyland, Volkswagen), POB 508, ☎ 40136, Obote Rd.
Rainbow (Peugeot), Obote Rd.
Kenya Motor Corporation (Renault, Toyota), Oginga Odinga Rd. POB 1950, ☎ 44128.

SOUTH OF KISUMU: HOMA BAY

It is preferable to go to Homa Bay by bus in the morning — when the visibility is better — and to make the return trip by boat, although you can, of course, drive there and back. Buses travel as far as Mbita, opposite Rusinga Island.

After Kendu Bay, the route goes by the 2133 ft-/650 m-high Mount Homa, not far from Homa Bay. A hike to the peak makes for a nice side trip on your way south. From the village of Mbita, a ferry crosses to Rusinga Island in several minutes. There is also a causeway linking the island to the mainland. Prehistoric fossils were discovered on the island. On Mfangano Island, to the south, are ancient rock paintings, testifying to early settlements here.

If you have a car, you might want to visit the Runa National Park (Lambwe Valley National Park), 10 mi/16 km south-west of Homa Bay. Follow the signposts on the road from Homa Bay. You should devote an entire morning to exploring this valley, locked between the Gwasi hills and the Kaniamwia escarpment. This setting, completely untamed and rarely visited, shelters roan antelope and a large variety of other herbivores, who are not too skittish because few people come to bother them. It is well worth the detour.

From Homa Bay, you can take a ferry to the south of Nyanza province, a territory that stretches from north-west of Kisumu to the Tanzanian border.

Accommodation
▲ **Msafiri Inn**, POB 42013, Homa Bay, ☎ 330820 in Nairobi. 21 rooms. At the foot of Mount Homa.

FROM KISUMU TO MOUNT ELGON NATIONAL PARK

NORTH OF KISUMU: KAKAMEGA

32 mi/52 km north of Kisumu.
Take the A1 from Kisumu. Kakamega Forest is 11 mi/17 km from the town of Kakamega on the road to Kapsabet. You can park by the Forest Rest House. From Kapsabet, the C39 goes to Eldoret.
Bird watchers will want to make a special trip to this part of the country to visit Kakamega Forest. The surrounding landscape continually changes as

the road from Kisumu rises into the hills and valleys to the north. Grassland and farmland give way to forests of conifer or thickets of eucalyptus and acacia.

Kakamega is in the centre of a prime agricultural region where cereals and pyrethrum are cultivated; the forest is now protected from further incursions by adjacent farms. The forest extends all the way to Kapsabet and Kwari Hills at the foot of the Nandi escarpment. It is home to a rich concentration of birds, including many that migrate from Europe in the winter. Whatever the season, the forest is a wonderland. Bring a pair of binoculars.

Continue north to the town of Webuye, where the paper industry is the major economic activity. Turn right onto the route leading to the B2 that links Eldoret with Kitale.

Accommodation

▲ **Forest Rest House,** 11 mi/17 km from town, reservations: Kakamega Forest Department, POB 88. Only a few rooms. No food or drinks.

▲ **Golf Hotel,** Khasakhala Rd., POB 118, ☎ 20460. 62 rooms. ① ④ Inexpensive, good-quality hotel.

▬ ELDORET

193 mi/310 km north-west of Nairobi.

This little town seems rather commonplace at first glance, despite a certain air of pleasant prosperity. To appreciate it better, you should read an account of its origins in Elspeth Huxley's *The Flame Trees of Thika*. Eldoret of 1908 to 1914, as depicted in the book, seems quaint when compared to the town today, but just think of the terrestrial paradise it had been even earlier, when hundreds of thousands of animals lived in the area without fear of being hunted. Now it is a booming agricultural town with textile factories and a university nearby.

A handful of Africaners trekked to Eldoret in ox-drawn wagons to start a new life after losing the Boer War to the British in 1902. There was hardly an inhabitant in the area. Since then, much of the game has disappeared as the land was cleared for farming. The magnificent conifer forest (cedar, pine, fir) remains impressive, though, despite the losses it has suffered. There are also acres of dull wattle plantations exploited for the extraction of tannin.

Eldoret is growing rapidly because it has the good fortune of being close to the Kerio Valley, Kakamega Forest, Lake Victoria and Mount Elgon National Park. It is less than a day's journey from the western side of Lake Turkana.

Accommodation

▲▲ **Highlands Inn,** POB 2189, ☎ 22092. A good alternative when the Sirikwa Hotel is full.

▲▲ **Sirikwa Hotel,** Oloo St., POB 3361, ☎ 31655. Due to frequent conferences held here, reservations are necessary all year round: ATH, POB 30471, Nairobi, ☎ 336858. 100 rooms. ① ④ Conference hall. A lively modern hotel catering mostly to business travelers.

▬ KITALE AND MOUNT ELGON NATIONAL PARK★

236 mi/380 km north-west of Nairobi. The entrance to the park is 12 mi/20 km west of Kitale.

The prosperous province of Trans-Nzoia benefits from a perfect climate. It's an area well worth exploring. If you have a car and are not pressed for time, visit some of the surrounding villages on market days. At the very least don't miss a tour of Mount Elgon National Park.

Lake Turkana: the Sea of Jade.

To visit the park, you'll need a car, assistance from the rangers and an authorization from the management of the lodge (at the entrance to the park).

The best way to get around is to rent the lodge's Land Rover and be accompanied by an armed ranger. Don't try walking in the lower altitude area around the lodge. The elephants, buffalos, and leopards that inhabit the woods will attack if confronted, especially if they are protecting their offspring. On the other hand, you will be perfectly safe in a car. The animals are hard to spot in this dense forest of bamboo, moss-covered podo trees, acacia and other species, but you will doubtless catch sight of gazelles, impalas and monkeys.

At this altitude, the only place where you can feel free to get out of the car is at the entrance to the caves, some of which are several kilometres long. Note, however, that in 1988 they were closed to the public due to an unidentified disease caught by visitors to the caves. Scientists have been looking for an explanation.

Above approximately 10,000 ft/3000 m is moorland where the heather, groundsel and lobelia rise above the generally low foliage.

At about 12,500 ft/3800 m and above you can walk without fear of animals; they cannot survive at this altitude. On the other hand, Mount Elgon (14,173 ft/4320 m) sits on the frontier between Uganda and Kenya and there have been reports of attacks by Ugandan soldiers or bandits in this area. Do not venture beyond the rim of Mount Koitoboss, the limit recommended by the rangers, which is located entirely in the Kenyan zone. It is unfortunate that visitors cannot safely explore the crater and breathe in the steams of vapour that continue to rise from the volcano. Nonetheless, the surroundings are superb and dotted with astonishing miniature plants.

Accommodation

▲ **Kitale Club,** POB 30, ☎ 20030. ① At the southern entrance to the town.

▲ **Mount Elgon Lodge,** reservations: Mount Elgon Lodge Endebess Reservations, POB 30471, Nairobi, ☎ 29751. 15 rooms. ① ⑤ At the entrance to the park, this one-time farm has been transformed into a lovely hotel. Guest rooms in the main building are paneled in teak and cedar. An annex overlooks a superb 150 ac/60 ha park.

FROM KITALE TO LAKE TURKANA

▬▬ *NORTH OF KITALE AND MOUNT ELGON*

Don't count on hailing a bus or *matatu* out here! To make the most of the this trip, especially the last leg, you'll need a four-wheel-drive vehicle, preferably a solid Land Rover.

The route is tarmac until Lodwar, 178 mi/287 km north of Kitale, leaving only 37 mi/60 km of track to reach the lake. It would be a shame to miss that final stretch, so rich in beauty and animal life.

Saiwa Swamp National Park**

Take the B4 towards Lodwar. About 19 mi/30 km from Kitale, just before Kapenguria, you should see a signpost for the park on the right. The entrance is located a couple of kilometres ahead on an easy track road. Leave your car at the guard station and continue along the path to the observation platforms.

To get from here to Cherangani Hills, continue about 37 mi/60 km on the rough road to Lodwar.

Saiwa Swamp National Park, situated near Kipsoen, also known as Kipsain, was created specifically to protect an extremely rare antelope, the sitatunga.

The swamps are at the bottom of a valley about a hundred metres wide and some 3 mi/5 km long. In the woodland above, three platforms have been constructed to make it easier to see the antelope.

The sitatunga is an aquatic antelope resembling a kudu. It has splayed hoofs that support it on marshy, or swampy ground. The sitatunga swims well and spends hours immersed in water with only its nostrils exposed. You'll need a good deal of patience to observe and photograph the animal since it is extremely timid. Colobus and full-bearded Brazza monkeys live in the forests around the platforms.

The Cherangani Hills are part of the national park but you'll need to go back to your car to reach this impressive and deserted range, which you can then explore on foot.

Accommodation

You can stay in either Kitale or Eldoret or at a campsite in the Cherangani Hills.

Cherangani Hills

This is a lovely place to spend a few days, but because the roads are difficult, to make the most of this immense natural setting, you should certainly make several stops. There are mountain streams everywhere, so you won't need to carry stocks of water.

The road runs through the plains until Kapenguria and then winds tortuously up the western side of the Elgeyo Marakwet escarpment and the Cherangani Hills, where it overlooks the Trans-Nzoia province. Soon the road meets the Marun River and runs next to it until the end of the range, 60 mi/96 km from Kitale, after 5 mi/8 km of deeply sunken gorges.

You'll need a full day to climb to the top of **Mount Mtelo** (11,811 ft/3600 m). Park your car at the village of Akeriemet, and camp at the foot of the mountain near the Marun River. You'll have to start out at dawn. Take a guide.

The road that takes you down to the floor of the Rift Valley proceeds at Marich to Lake Turkana. If you don't plan to go on to Lake Turkana from here, you might choose to go up the other side of the escarpment. It is one of the most beautiful trips that you could possibly undertake in Kenya. You must have a four-wheel-drive vehicle.

A tarmac road runs through the valley until Tot (28 mi/43 km); thereafter it becomes a track that rises abruptly up the western escarpment of the Rift; the steeply climbing track overlooking the unforgettable **Kerio Valley** continues for some 30 mi/50 km or so. The road then turns inland until Iten where once again you'll find a tarmac road leading south-west until to Eldoret and south-east to Tambach and beyond.

If you choose not to make this magnificent but difficult journey via Tot and are not going on to Lake Turkana, return to Kitale and continue to Eldoret and Tambach. At Tambach, the road to Kabarnet descends into the Kerio Valley and climbs up the other side.

TOWARD THE WESTERN SHORE OF LAKE TURKANA

If you have the time, head on to Lodwar and then to Kalakol, along a magnificent desert route that you'll take again on your way back. From Marich to Lodwar the rather monotonous road marks the dividing line between Pokot country on the right and Turkana territory on the left.

At the Weiwei River crossing you might see a score or more natives busy in the water: they are panning for gold. This activity, which yields only meagre results, is destined to disappear with the construction of the Turkwel Gorge dam, which will transform the whole area into a lake.

The heat rises sharply as you leave the escarpment and arrive at **Lodwar***. Here the Kikuyu passing through stop to pay tribute to Jomo Kenyatta in front of the house where he was imprisoned by the British.

Only part of the town is shaded by the doum palms of a small oasis. A picturesque market place is enlivened by nomads with their camels and local artisans selling handsome basketware at bargain prices. Be sure to stop at the filling station in Lodwar for jerry cans of petrol and water: this is the first filling station after Kitale and the last toward the north. The station is closed during the siesta between noon and 3pm.

After Lodwar, a rough track heads north; it will take you about two hours to cover 37 mi/60 km. You can visit **Elye Springs*** by turning right onto a track 15 mi/24 km past Lodwar. You can camp next to the lodge (now closed) by the hot springs. The area is full of many different kinds of birds, especially birds of prey.

Lake Turkana**
See also p. 142.

Known as the Sea of Jade, Lake Turkana is almost 186 mi/300 km long, with a surface of more than 3000 sq mi/8000 sq km. It is a veritable inland sea, where the winds reign. Although Ferguson's Gulf is fairly well sheltered, the lake itself is exposed to winds that from gentle breezes can in no time gust to violent, dangerous storms.

Count Teleki, an Austrian explorer of Hungarian origin, named the lake after the crown prince Rudolf, son of emperor Francis Joseph. In 1975

Lake Rudolf became Lake Turkana in honour of the tribe that has lived on its shores for the last three centuries.

Traditionally nomadic herders, the Turkana (see p. 77) have spread over a vast territory, all the way north to the Sudan, south to Pokot and Samburu country and east to the lands of the Rendille, Gabbra, Boran and Somali. They drive their herds of cattle and camels before then, using donkeys to help carry the heavier loads. The Turkana are reputed to be fierce and intelligent; raiding neighbouring groups is common and considered almost as a sport. The tribe also adapts easily to changing circumstances: fishing, farming or fighting when necessary. They also pan for gold along the banks of the Weiwei River.

Near Kainuk many Turkana have permanently settled down to agricultural activities, growing cabbage, millet, sugar cane and maize in the land irrigated by the river.

You'll find Turkana children selling aprons made from goat skins and decorated with fish vertebrae; the women wear these around bare waists for traditional dances.

Accommodation

▲ **Lake Turkana Fishing Lodge,** reservations: POB 44082, Nairobi, ☎ 26623. 16 bungalows. ① ④ Situated on a strip of land in Ferguson's Gulf. You will need a boat to get to the lodge. Use the optic signals on the shore, and someone will come to fetch you. From the dining room overlooking the lake, you can watch the birds. Excursions available for boat fishing or to visit Central Island National Park (one hour's crossing).

Central Island National Park

You can reach the island by boat from the Lake Turkana Fishing Lodge or by negotiating a ride with a local fisherman.

Even though Central Island is a protected area, the Turkana still come here to fish and build fires that destroy the plant life. The island is the nesting ground of many large colonies of birds. It is also a stop in October and in March for European migratory birds. In December, one of the island's crater lakes, known as Flamingo Lake, is swelled by rainwater and becomes the meeting ground for hundreds of flamingos.

The lodge boat leaves visitors at the foot of a steep cliff on the northern shore. Climb to the top, 164 ft/50 m above Lake Turkana. From here you will have an exceptional view of all of Lake Turkana and of the crater lake, surrounded by rocks whose colours seem to change with the weather.

Undoubtedly, the single most exciting site on Central Island is the crater lake filled with crocodiles. These several metre-long reptiles are hard to observe since they hide under the water as soon as they catch sight of anyone. Nevertheless, if you follow the path near the lake, you can make out the shape of the reptiles on the surface of the water and watch them motionless on the other side of the lake.

While the crocodiles might be uncooperative, many visitors manage to come home with photographs of themselves standing beside a tilapia or Nile perch — sometimes as big as the fishermen themselves. These fish, which also inhabit the Nile, are found in Lake Turkana because it was once a tributary of the Nile network. For geological reasons not yet fully clear, Lake Turkana became a separate body.

In September 1984, in this very region, Professor Richard Leakey uncovered the remains of a 1.6 million-year-old child belonging to the family *Homo erectus.*

A fisherman on Lake Turkana.

FROM KITALE TO BARINGO AND BOGORIA LAKES

If you aren't using a four-wheel-drive, you'll have to return on the tarmac road from Lodwar to Kitale (196 mi/315 km) and then to Eldoret (43 mi/70 km). The shortest way to Nairobi is via Nakuru. The landscape changes radically as you climb from the Rift Valley to its western escarpment and cross the highlands from north to south, with Eldoret at the centre.

If you have the time, stop overnight in Eldoret and then take a magnificent drive on the newly surfaced road to Lake Baringo via Tambach and Kabarnet. You can do this trip in a single day. The road is easy and the views are superb.

In a four-wheel-drive, on the other hand, you have several options to get to Lake Baringo. One is to take the tarmac road from Lodwar to Lokichar and then to turn east on the road leading to Lake Baringo that passes through Lokori, Kapedo, Loruk and Kampı Ya Samaki. But be warned, there are absolutely no filling stations or water sources en route, nor will you encounter anybody to help give you directions if you get lost. Yet this itinerary is easy compared to the trip some adventurous visitors undertake: traveling overland from Lodwar to the eastern shore of the lake by way of the Loriu Plateau and Suguta Valley (reputed to be one of the hottest places on earth). If you decide to venture overland, be sure to stock up on supplies, petrol and water; and take along a guide who speaks Turkana and Pokot.

Lovers of wide open, deserted spaces can opt for an easier journey that consists of a five-hour or more trip through the Kerio Valley (94 mi/152 km). At Marich, follow the rough track east toward Sigor, through Tot, Kapsowar, Chebiemit and Iten. The road is paved between Iten and Tambach. You won't find any places to stay between Lake Turkana and Kabarnet, so make sure you bring along camping gear; a good place to stay is in the vicinity of Tot.

If you like, you can head back to spend the night at Eldoret; the next day you can try a trip beginning with the tarmac C54. The excursion is

65 mi/105 km long, of which 39 mi/62 km are track road; along 25 mi/40 km there are some extremely rough sections; count on half-a-day. From Eldoret, head toward Chepkorio; near Kachebelel (27 mi/43 km), a track on the left descends to the Fluorspar fluorite mines at the bottom of the Kerio Valley. The mines are private property, although visitors are allowed to pass through. After the mines, turn left toward the north, taking the valley road along the mountain side.

About 25 mi/40 km on, turn right; another half mile and you'll come to a bridge that crosses the Kerio gorges. The track then goes through the village of Kibohino, winds up the eastern slope of the valley and then crosses a second bridge before reaching Kabarnet. From there the route is surfaced to Marigat.

Final option: coming from Sigor, take the road at Tot along the Kilo Pass to arrive at Loruk on the northern edge of Lake Baringo. Relatively easier but less impressive than the other routes, this trip, too, requires a four-wheel-drive.

By *matatu*, you'll go from Eldoret to Marigat via Kabarnet; from Marigat, the *matatu* arrives in Nakuru at the end of the day.

KABARNET

34 mi/55 km west of Baringo; 180 mi/290 km north-west of Nairobi.

This small mountain village overlooking the Kerio Valley to the west and the Rift escarpment to the east is well worth a visit. The climb from the west of the Kerio Valley is splendid; the terrain changes in a matter of miles from dry, thorn tree country to high, cool, cedar and podo forests. The villagers are very warm to the rare tourist passing through. The local school is proud to have had as one of its teachers the current president of Kenya, Daniel arap Moi.

Accommodation

▲▲ **Kabarnet Hotel**, POB 42013, Nairobi, ☎ 2035. 29 rooms. ① ④ ⑤ This hotel has a nice layout and decor, a lovely large verandah and a shop.

LAKE BARINGO

165 mi/265 km north-west of Nairobi.

The best vantage point for a view of the whole lake is from Loruk. Baringo is a freshwater lake with no visible outlet; according to one theory, it has an underground tributary that resurfaces at Kapedo. This is the last large Rift lake before Lake Turkana, and it attracts many birds: cormorants, pelicans, herons, eagles, plovers, winchats, starlings and more. To make the most of the trip, take along a bird guide book. You can also go on an early morning birdwalk (7am) with an ornithologist from Lake Baringo Lodge (inquire there). Be sure to take binoculars. The walk usually covers an area near some impressive cliffs set back about a mile from the lake. The cliffs themselves, as well as the surrounding bush, abound in fascinating bird life.

Accommodation

▲▲▲ **Island Camp,** on Ol Kokwe island in the middle of Lake Baringo. Managed by Block Hotels, POB 1141, radiocall: 2261. A boat from the lodge takes you across the water to the island. 25 luxurious double tents on the steep slopes of the hill afford a superb panoramic view of the lake. Boat rental and water sports.

▲▲ **Lake Baringo Lodge,** reservations: Block Hotels, POB 47557, Nairobi, ☎ 335807; or Nakuru, POB 1375, ☎ 335807. 50 rooms. ① ④ ⑤ Friendly, hospitable lodge that unfortunately lost some of the charm of its Spanish-style architecture during a recent expansion. Lake excursions available and also visits to Njemps villages. Filling station. Airstrip nearby.

▲ **Mrs. Roberts' Campsite,** near the lodge (about Ksh 50 per person), with the possibility of using the lodge restaurant. The campsite is beautifully located among trees on the lake shore. You may well see hippos and crocodiles (the former can sometimes be heard grazing on the shore at night). Attractive beachwear and kimonos made of brightly dyed fabric can be bought from a small store just beside the campsite.

LAKE BOGORIA NATIONAL RESERVE

27 mi/44 km south of Lake Baringo.

Over the last few years the roads leading to the reserve have been improved, making Lake Bogoria an increasingly popular site. The flamingos migrated here when the waters of Lake Nakuru became polluted and many have stayed, even though Nakuru is now in better condition. Other bird species also thrive near the lake's steaming waters and heated atmosphere. Scalding geysers gush from the sand.

Upon entering the reserve, you will first encounter the Emsos River, one of the two rivers in the southern area. You can drink the water of the second river after boiling and purifying it.

With a four-wheel-drive vehicle, circle the lake to see the greater kudus on the eastern shore. On your way back to Nakuru on the B4, stop at any of the villages in the area of Mogotio for a look at some interesting handcrafts made from sisal.

Access

Take the B4 south of Lake Baringo and then the track road 2.5 mi/4 km south of Marigat. If you hope to continue your visit in the Aberdare (Nyandarua) and Mount Kenya region (see pp. 152-157), an attractive road leads through the Subukia Valley north-east of Nakuru via Subukia to Nyahururu. The valley floor has lovely trees, and the climb up to Nyahururu offers striking views.

Accommodation

A lodge is under construction near the entrance. In the meantime you can stay overnight in Nakuru or camp out by the lake.

CENTRAL AND NORTHERN KENYA

The central region of Kenya, with its invigorating climate, was seen as a sort of paradise to many of the early European settlers. It consists of the central highlands dominated by the Aberdare Mountains, now known as Nyandarua, and the 17,060 ft-/5200 m-high Mount Kenya. It includes the rich agricultural terrains of the Kikuyu and Meru countries, extensive grasslands to the north and east of Nyahururu and forests covering the mountain flanks between 2000 and 3000 m (6500 and 10,000 ft).

Organizing your time

● **One month:** Nyahururu — Maralal — Loyangalani — Sibiloi — Marsabit — Kitich — Samburu — Buffalo Springs — Shaba — Isiolo — Meru — Embu — Nanyuki — Mount Kenya and Nyandarua (Aberdare) national parks — Thika — Nairobi.

The complete circuit requires a full month. If you skip Meru and Embu, you can cover the region in two or, better still, three weeks.

● **Ten days:** the following itinerary is more suitable for a shorter trip. Nyahururu — Maralal — Losiolo escarpment, Wamba — Kitich — the Samburu National Reserve — Buffalo Springs — Mount Kenya National Park and Aberdare (Nyandarua) National Park.

● **Ten days:** A different itinerary would be to go directly from Nairobi to Naro Moru, then visit Mount Kenya National Park (including a two-day trek) and Meru National Park and return to Nairobi by way of Embu.

At the very least, you will need a week to visit a region filled with violent, magnificent contrasts. You'll pass from mountains to plains, from alpine flowers to tropical trees, from cold weather and snow to dusty heat, from excellent tarmac roads to precipitous tracks. Above all don't miss Mount Kenya and Aberdare (Nyandarua) parks, nor the Samburu National Reserve.

While there are both trains and buses in the central region, the national parks are accessible only by car. Tour operators offer separate tours to the important sites but not to the area as a whole. Renting a car is therefore the best solution.

To visit Northern Kenya, you can either go through a travel agency or rent a four-wheel-drive vehicle — but only if — the driver knows how to operate it on the often difficult roads.

A typical camping tour of the north will take you in a large truck to Loyangalani (via Nyahururu and Maralal) and return along the western side of the Marsabit reserve by way of Samburu, Isiolo and Naro Moru. Upon special request, some tour operators will arrange a visit to Sibiloi and Koobi Fora, by plane and in a four-wheel-drive vehicle.

One of the many natural wonders of the Nyandarua Range.

You can follow the same itinerary in your own rented vehicle. The trip takes about a week and an extra two days if you decide to visit Marsabit. From Marsabit you may be obliged to join the official convoy (including police cars) that goes daily from Marsabit to Isiolo and back. This region is considered dangerous because of attacks by armed bands, 'Shifta', from Ethiopia or Somalia. A bus with an armed escort runs from Isiolo to Marsabit and on to Moyale at the Ethiopian border several times a week.

No public transport is available from Marsabit to Lake Turkana, and you can visit the Marsabit Massif only by car. Note that cars cannot be rented in Marsabit.

FROM NYAHURURU TO SIBILOI NATIONAL PARK

▬▬ *NYAHURURU*

123 mi/198 km north of Nairobi, 51 mi/82 km north of Gilgil.

A few miles before Nyahururu, the C77 from Gilgil crosses the equator. Tourists traditionally stop here to be photographed under the sign. If you do so too, you'll doubtless be approached by the numerous souvenir vendors.

The route then traverses the grazing pastures of the Land Settlement Project (which distributed to the Kenyans land bought from European settlers) and arrives at the agricultural village of Nyahururu.

Nyahururu was formerly known as Thomson's Falls after the English explorer Joseph Thomson, the first European to cross Masai country. He came to the falls in 1883.

At an altitude of 8530 ft/2600 m, amid the pastures that border the Marmanet forest at the foot of the Aberdare (Nyandarua) mountains, Nyahururu has an exceptional climate.

Just to the east of the village, are the 249 ft-/76 m-high **waterfalls*** of the Ewaso Narok River. You can see them from the terrace of Thomson's Falls Lodge. The river meanders peacefully atop the plateau before cascading down through a fault in the rock.

You can hike down the steep and slippery path on the left side of the terrace, but go only with a group because people have been attacked here. The best time to take pictures is in the early afternoon when the sun is directly opposite the falls; by 4pm there is not enough light at the bottom of the falls for a good picture.

You can observe many different kinds of birds, particularly kingfishers. A large colony of rock hyraxes nest in the upper part of the cliff.

It will take you only ten minutes to reach the bottom but at least a half hour to climb back. You could also cross the bridge and walk along the other bank of the river for an equally lovely view.

Access

From Gilgil: take the C77 (a good tarmac road).

From Nakuru: take the C69 and then the C77, or alternatively, the road via Subukia for the best views.

From Nairobi: a bus runs to the entrance of the Thomson's Falls site (transfer at Gilgil).

Nyahururu can also be reached by private planes to a nearby airstrip.

Accommodation

▲▲ **Thomson's Falls Lodge,** POB 38, Nyahururu, ☎ 22006; reservations: Central Booking Office, POB 21855, Nairobi. 35 rooms. Half-board only. To the east of the village, this is one of

Kenya's oldest lodges. It is charmingly old fashioned and surrounded by beautiful gardens. Horse rental available.

Camping

You can camp by the lodge and use its showers and sanitary facilities.

FROM NYAHURURU TO MARALAL

22 mi/35 km.

From Nyahururu to Rumuruti, the C77 is tarmac. Beyond, the road makes for some difficult driving. The woods of the Rumuruti forest are swarming with black-and-white colobus monkeys noted for their spectacular leaps of some 20 yards or so.

Samburu country

For some time, the road runs along the Ewaso Narok River, which flows sinuously through the swamps; little by little the savannah of the Laikipia Plateau appears, its pastures nestled beneath the foothills. If you are lucky, you may see some long-haired, bright orange Patas monkeys sitting on top of fence posts beside the road. The plateau was once the domain of the Masai, who were driven out by the British in 1911. Today, there are large cattle ranches, and the area is partially inhabited by the Samburu, who are of the same family as the Masai. Both tribes tend livestock, they dress in a similar fashion and they live in huts made of interwoven branches and covered with cattle dung.

Despite the legends about the warrior-like Masai, they, like the Samburu, are peaceable. Most of the Samburu are still nomadic shepherds, though many have opted for sedentary activities. Many have taken part in recent collective actions to plant trees in the very forests which they or their parents once burned in order to nourish their herds on the tender grass that grew in the ashes. Others have joined the army. You can meet up with the Samburus as far as Lake Turkana in the north and Marsabit and the Shaba Reserve in the east. They generally greet strangers with large smiles and a big welcome.

The women exhibit an elegant bearing, their closely cropped or shaven heads ornamented by a large band of multi-coloured beads from which hangs a metal pendant with a point that rests on the forehead or even between the eyebrowns. Their necks are adorned with dozens of coils of the same beads.

After Laikipia, the route traverses the striking **Lerochi Plateau**** (also known as Lerogi Plateau), which is crossed by rivers and bristling with high hills.

After passing through Kisima, the road begins to climb up the Maralal massif and the temperature drops sharply.

If you don't have enough time to go all the way to Lake Turkana, you can take the C78 that branches off to the right at Kisima. This fairly good road links up with the A2 north of Samburu. From the Kisima junction to Wamba, south of the hills of Mathews Range Forest, the scenery is superb, especially when the road rises above the Ewaso Ngiro.

Just before Wamba, an extremely difficult track leads to the Kitich camp (see p. 145). You can easily spend a day here, because of the excursions in the area. Then continue to Wamba and take the A2.

Useful address

Ewaso River Camel Hikes, POB 243 Gilgil, radiocall: 3933. These hikes are run by Simon Evans, POB 9 Rumuruti, and usually last between eight and ten days. Clients can either ride camels or walk, if they prefer. The terrain is fascinating, wild Samburu country, where no vehicle can pass.

MARALAL NATIONAL SANCTUARY

205 mi/330 km north of Nairobi.

As the road rises the plant life changes: the acacias or thorn trees give way to eucalyptus and to conifers covered with moss and lianas.

The village of Maralal has a population of about 5000, half Samburu and half Turkana. It is the last stop on this northern leg for *matatus*. It is also where the electricity and telephone wires end. The region beyond Maralal, with its extremely perilous roads, is for the truly adventurous.

The Maralal National Sanctuary, which includes the village, was set up to protect Grevy zebra, oryx and gerenuk. The leopards in the sanctuary can be seen only from the lodge.

Accommodation

▲▲▲ **Maralal Safari Lodge,** reservations: POB 42475, Nairobi, ☎ 25641; or POB 70, Maralal, ☎ 2060. 24 cottages. The cottages are very comfortable. From the lodge's terrace, in the evening, you can safely watch the leopards, baited by meat hung from the trees. Don't venture out to the paths around your cottage, where wild animals often prowl.

▲▲ **Maralal Safari Camp,** 10 km south of the village. 14 luxury tents set up in a former hunting ground.

Camping

There is a non-equipped site north of the village on a tree-encircled plateau.

FROM MARALAL TO LOYANGALANI (LAKE TURKANA)

133 mi/214 km.

After the plateau, the road winds through a mossy forest and then comes out onto open pastures where zebra mingle with hump-backed cattle. Both species eat the same vegetation and in case of attack the zebra find they can escape more quickly than the cattle, leaving behind a young calf as easy game for predators.

Losiolo Escarpment**

Take the track that branches off from the main road on the left. It leads across fields of Samburu crops to the western side of the Losiolo Escarpment. This is a detour not to be missed. On either side of the Rift Valley, the cliffs' multiple ridges plunge almost 6600 ft/2000 m into the depression below. The effect is as spectacular as the Ngong Hills near Nairobi or the old road from Limuru to Naivasha.

Continue on the main road that slowly descends into the valley and curves toward the north-east. The view changes continually as the track winds back and forth down the slope.

The mountains give way to a golden savannah, bristling with prickly shrub, among which are the 'wait a bit' bushes, so called because its thorns catch onto your clothes and hold you back as you walk by.

Ngoroko country

These wide expanses continue to be the site of fighting between Turkana and Samburu herdsmen. The Ngoroko (part of the Turkana tribe) are reputed to raid the cattle and camels of everyone, even their tribal brothers. The Turkana, with their beautiful headresses and sophisticated jewelry, vie for elegance with the Samburu at Baragoi (a small village situated in the plain 60 mi/97 km from Maralal).

They are a graceful race: tall, with an elegant build and delicate facial features. Seeing them leaning on their long spears and gazing dreamily at outsiders or watching them leading their herds rapidly into the distance, you find it hard to picture any of them as fierce bandits.

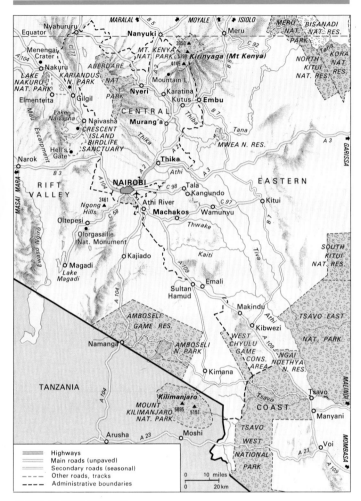

CENTRAL AND SOUTH-EAST KENYA

South Horr Valley★★

After Baragoi — surprise! The jagged, difficult track suddenly leaves the arid plain and drops into an incredibly lush, narrow valley, with South Horr on the far end. The road then runs along the verdant banks of the Ol Doinyo Ngiro River. Paradoxically, the Suguta Valley, one of the hottest parts of Kenya, lies behind the mountains to the west of the river.

The road leaving the valley becomes even more treacherous. Not only will you need a sturdy vehicle but also an excellent driver. At the end of the trying climb, you will finally arrive above Lake Turkana, with the **Teleki Volcano★★** rising on the south-west behind it.

Accommodation

▲▲ **Kurungu Lodge,** South Horr, run by Safari Camp Services, Loyangalani (just north of the camping area); or Koinange St., POB 44801, Nairobi, ☎ 28936 or 330130.

Camping

Also run by the Safari Camp Service.

▬ *LOYANGALANI*★

304 mi/490 km north of Nairobi.

In a small Somali café on the village's main road, on the right side as you head toward the lodge, you'll find a good spot to meet the locals over tea and tasty snacks. The village itself is a good place to pick up inexpensive semi-precious stones (quartz, agate, garnet).

Note that there is no filling station in Loyangalani. The last stations on the way north are in Baringo, Nyahururu, Nakuru, Isiolo, Nanyuku, Meru and very irregularly, at Marsabit. Be sure to bring along a stock of petrol in jerry cans.

South of Loyangalani you will notice a small, steep hill called Por. It is an interesting climb, with a good view of the lake from the top.

Mount Kulal is slightly farther afield, east of Loyangalani. If you can negotiate the track, you'll be rewarded with beautiful, cool forests, contrasting with the heat of the plain below, and, more dramatically, hosts of glorious butterflies.

Accommodation

▲▲ **Oasis Safari Camp,** reservations through any travel agency, no telephone, 27 bungalows. ① ④ Good restaurant. Possibility of using one of the lodge's Land Rovers to visit Koobi Fora, Sibiloi National Park and the El Molo villages. Several fishing boats are available and the lodge operates dhows on the lake. The lodge's German-born owner is a radio enthusiast and possesses equipment capable of capturing radio signals world over.

Camping

Near the lodge.

Safari Camp Services are located just north of the camping area.

▬ *LAKE TURKANA FROM THE NORTH*

Whether you arrive here by road or by air, the first sight of Lake Turkana is overwhelming. It is so immense — 186 mi/300 km long with a surface area of more than 3000 sq mi/8000 sq km — that its northern shore is lost in the distance. The sunlight plays with the colours of the water that continually change, reflecting the ochre, red, violet, mauve and black rocks of the surrounding volcanos. As you stand overlooking the perpetually changing surface of the lake, sculpted by violently gusting winds, you are overwhelmed by an impression of freedom and of infinite timelessness.

The waters seem inviting but don't forget that many crocodiles and hippopotami live here. It is far better to simply admire the birds (flamingo, avocet, pelican, cormorant) attracted to the lake's abundant fish and to the shelter of the vegetation along the shore. There are also, wild herbivores, such as waterbuck, oryx, and hartebeest, although they are rarer in the southern part of the lake. Near Loyangalani you'll be surprised by the sight of cattle immersed in the lake up to their necks, feeding on the water plants that float on its surface.

A delicate coexistence

To whom do these cattle belong? Many of the tribes around Loyangalani seem to have achieved a delicate balance between a nomadic and a settled sedentary way of life. What's more, Samburu, Turkana and Rendille have, at least partially, overcome age-old ethnic rivalries; each tribe lives in peace in its own area of town. Relations with the Luo are less harmonious. The Luo are leaders in the fishing industry, and the economic rivalry between them and the Turkana can be particularly sharp.

The Turkana have been extremely adaptable: they have become skillful fishermen and farmers while continuing their traditional raising of cattle and camels. In fact, their rapidly expanding millet farming is not necessarily incompatible with nomadism: the seeds are sown before the rainy season and the millet is harvested before the Turkana move the cattle to a different grazing area.

The Turkana are also artists, fashioning tasteful objects from metal and leather and creating imaginative jewelry of seeds, bones, ligaments, feathers, fish vertebrae and, of course, the familiar, tiny, coloured beads used by many tribes.

Somewhat different are the Cushitic speaking Rendille, who came from Ethiopia. They can be found all over north-eastern Kenya, from Loyangalani to the borders of Ethiopia and Somalia.

While they do raise goat and sheep, the camel is the basis of their traditional economy and way of life. To the Rendille, the camel is not only a beast of burden, but also a source of food (mainly milk) and a symbol of social values. Unlike the related Somali, Gabbra and other Orma groups, the Rendille are a generally peaceable tribe. They are not known to fight or carry out raids, and while they move frequently to assure the survival of their herds, they have never tried to expand their territory. Their commercial needs are minimal: apart from tea, sugar and some clothing, their major purchase these days is a plastic jerry can. They use it to carry water, which is synonymous with survival when they leave the lake area.

The El-Molo

The El-Molo live in two villages a little to the north of Loyangalani. Their huts are made of interwoven branches, fixed to the ground to withstand rough weather. The El-Molo have been the subject of much controversy. Some claim that they have all disappeared and that the people known as El-Molo are, in fact, Turkana. Ethnologists, though, dispute this theory. To be sure, the El-Molo number fewer than 1000 and have borrowed much linguistically and culturally from neighbouring tribes — in particular, from the Samburu — but they still constitute a distinct group although its ethnic origin remains unknown.

The inhabitants of the two villages give visitors a friendly welcome. You will be asked to pay for the right to take pictures; this fee, the El-Molo explain, enables them to purchase food and thus vary their diet. Despite the hostile environment, they have no desire to leave the lake that supplies them with hippopotamus meat and fish.

SIBILOI NATIONAL PARK*

90 mi/145 km north of Loyangalani.

After a four-hour drive up to Kokoi, north of Alia Bay, report first to the park headquarters. Signposting is non-existent, and rough roads make for extremely difficult driving. You'll need a four-wheel-drive vehicle and a good stock of water and petrol; the only spring, near the entrance to the park, is hard to find, and there is no petrol anywhere. You'll use up a lot more fuel, too, if your vehicle gets trapped in one of the numerous stretches of sand.

Sibiloi National Park (formerly East Rudolf National Park) holds an interest for animal-lovers and paleontologists. On the north edge of the lake, it lies in a region not far from the Ethiopian mountains that receives a good amount of rainfall. You can run across many kinds of animals, such as oryx, zebra and topi. Some people claim they have seen lions swimming in the lake. Visitors are enthusiastic about the park, which offers a rich variety of possiblities: observation of animals and of fossils, visiting pre-historic sites, swimming, fishing and more in an isolated area where the visitors can feel alone.

Koobi Fora

This is one of the richest archaeological sites in East Africa, covering an area of 463 sq mi/1200 sq km inside the park, midway between Alia Bay and Iletret. Excavations conducted here by a team working with Richard Leakey have revolutionized theories about the earliest ages of human development. An almost-complete skeleton of a hominid who lived more than 2.5 million years ago was uncovered and reconstituted. Coded 1470 and classified as *Homo habilis*, the skeleton is characterized by a femur adapted to walking upright and a cranial capacity of 49 cu in/800 cu cm. This discovery pushed back by a million years the date when scientists believe members of our own genus began to walk.

In the same geological layer, the scientists found fossils of a genus called *Australopithecus*, which Leakey believes is not the ancestor of man but represents a divergent evolutionary branch. These excavations were conducted in the Omo River Valley. The river is the main tributary of Lake Turkana and forms a delta of 31 mi/50 km across to the north at the Ethiopian border. Older fossils uncovered here have permitted investigators to set back even earlier the date when the upright position appeared.

All these discoveries have convinced many paleontologists that the fossils can no longer be examined as links in the same evolutionary chain, but rather as evidence of the evolution of parallel but different forms. Koobi Fora continues to be a rich source of discoveries, and to protect the relatively fragile ground, the whole research zone is off limits to the public.

For a permit to visit the site of the excavations, contact in advance: **National Museums of Kenya,** Direction of Paleontology, POB 40658, Nairobi, ☎ 74 2131, ext. 17.

Accommodation

The closest lodges are in Loyangalani and Marsabit (see pp. 142, 145-146).

Camping is possible but you'll need permission. Contact **Sibiloi National Park,** c/o Marsabit Warden, POB 42, Marsabit.

The **Museum Society of Nairobi** (see p. 104), has some *bandas* that are available when they are not occupied by scientists or students. Contact the museum in advance for information and permission.

▬ *FROM LOYANGALANI TO MARSABIT*

The drive from Loyangalani to Marsabit via North Horr passes through the **Chalbi Desert★★★** inhabited by Rendille, Somali and Galla tribes all of Cushitic origin. Throughout the journey, where you are unlikely to meet a single person, you will be constantly accompanied by winds that raise maelstroms of golden dust. More dangerous than the ecological conditions, however, is the presence of *Shifta* (Somali bandits).

To avoid taking any unnecessary risks you can reach Marsabit another way by first heading south from Loyangalani to Maralal and Kisima, and then taking the C78 east toward Wamba.

In a four-wheel-drive vehicle, you can make a worthwhile detour off the C78 to Kitich (28 mi/45 km from Wamba and 239 mi/385 km from Nairobi). About 43 mi/69 km after Kisima, turn left 9 mi/15 km to Ngalai and then 7 mi/12 km toward Kitich. Yellow stones vaguely indicate the track.

Kitich is in a valley at the edge of the rain forest that covers the slopes of the Mathews Range. The forest shelters giraffe, gerenuk, Grevy zebra, buffalo and elephant. During the day you can go for walks beside the river. The vegetation, bird and animal life are extremely rich and varied.

Return to the C78 and follow it to the A2 which it intersects 14 mi/22 km north of Archer's Post. Check with the police station at Wamba or Isiolo (19 mi/31 km south of Archer's Post) to find out if you will be required to join up with a convoy. In any case, you need a sturdy vehicle to drive north on the rough, corrugated road and should keep at a steady 43 mi/70 km per hour. Don't forget that the last filling station is at Isiolo and that the availability of petrol in Marsabit is irregular.

The buses leaving Isiolo for Marsabit are usually filled to capacity with inhabitants from Marsabit returning home after shopping in Isiolo.

Rocky hills break the monotony of the landscape, their colours turning from pink to grey to violet depending on the time of day. After the village of Marile, where you can sometimes find excellent *chapatis* (unleavened Indian bread), the road passes through the unmarked boundaries of the Losai National Reserve. A mission in the village of Laisamis, on the northern edge of the reserve, can be of help in case your vehicle breaks down. Many Samburu, whose herds have been decimated by drought, live here; the women sell straw brooms and bracelets of tiny beads on the roadside. Some Samburu have gone north to Marsabit in search of new grazing land.

The Marsabit massif can be seen on the horizon from a long way off. You'll be entering it a good 19 mi/30 km before reaching the town of Marsabit. The climate here is strikingly mild after the heat of the Kaisut Desert; you might unexpectedly find yourself wrapped in a heavy mist or caught in a downpour.

Accommodation

▲▲▲ **Kitich Camp**, reservations: Let's Go Travel Ltd., POB 60342, Nairobi, ☎ 29539. 10 tents. ① Situated on the Njeng River, with natural pools where swimming is possible, this luxurious, tented camp provides a remarkably hospitable welcome and good food. In the evenings, you can observe elephant, buffalo and sometimes leopard at the river. Guided walks and camel safaris are organized. Possibility of air travel to Wamba and car transport to camp. Ksh 3700 for a double room with full board.

Camping
Possible near **Kitich Camp**.

▬▬ *MARSABIT NATIONAL RESERVE***

171 mi/275 km north of Isiolo, 336 mi/540 km north-east of Nairobi.

Created in 1960 as the Northern Reserve, Marsabit is one of Kenya's greatest reserves. It is renowned as the natural habitat of big-tusk elephants and, in particular, of the now deceased Ahmed, whose replica can be seen in the Nairobi Museum. Jomo Kenyatta declared Ahmed to be a national monument. After Ahmed's death in 1974, Abdul became the king of elephants of Marsabit, only to die four years later. The current king, Abdou 83 (1983 being the first year of his 'reign') is continually tracked by the rangers, who can tell you where he can be found in the park.

Marsabit's reputation is also due to its exceptional location. A million years ago a volcano rose in the middle of the Chalbi Desert, forming a range 5600 ft/1707 m high, with craters that have evolved into *gofs* (lakes) of salty water. The hot air of the surrounding desert picks up moisture over Lake Turkana, which condenses into clouds of mist and rain over Marsabit, the only well-watered region of the north.

The reserve covers the south-eastern side of the mountains. The relatively dry terrain in the foothills of Mount Marsabit soon gives way to a forest of giant trees. Broken by sheer cliffs, the forest surrounds two of the largest *gofs*.

The Marsabit area has a number of factors in its favour: luxuriant plant life, proximity to a town with a mostly semi-nomadic population, the fertile agricultural terrain and roads that are negotiable except during the rainy season.

Besides elephants, the reserve shelters the greater kudu, a stunning antelope with a bounding gait, spiral horns and white stripes on its back. The nocturnal kudu tends to hide in the thickets during the day, but since the sparse forest vegetation here is interspersed with pools you are almost sure to catch sight of one or two.

Marsabit is a zoological paradise. Besides an impressive population of elephant and greater kudu, the forest shetters aardwolves (hyena-like insectivores), caracals, African wild cats (difficult to observe) and various viverrids like civets, large grey mongooses, and different genets. During the dry season, lions draw near the edge of the lodge to drink from the permanent *gof,* Sokorte Diko. During the rainy season (March-April and October-November), which is generally less favourable for watching animals, whole herds of buffalo and troops of baboon approach the lake and, one or two may sometimes venture onto the lodge's verandah. Marsabit Lodge is an excellent base for visiting the reserve.

The setting becomes even more romantic during the rainy season. Suddenly the heavy clouds of mist disperse and you can spot animals dashing off into the forest cover. Violent gusts of wind are followed by tense, sudden silences.

Everything changes during the dry season; leaves and moss turn yellow and then wither to dust. Yet, to the north-west of the mountain range, in contrast to the desert that covers most of north-east Kenya, fields are still being cultivated by the Samburu and Borana. The Rendille and Gabbra continue their traditional pastoral lifestyles. In Marsabit, the shops are run by the Turkana and Somalis.

Visiting the reserve

The main itinerary (25 mi/40 km) leaving from the lodge gives the visitor a good grasp of the park's two natural settings: bush and forest. Set out early in the morning for the market town and then west At the first crossroads, 1640 yd/1500 m on, continue straight ahead for 11 mi/17 km, then turn left at the second crossroads and left again 2 mi/3 km later.

This part of the park is essentially the site of herbivores: zebra, elephant, gazelle, impala and waterbuck. Return to the main track and take it to the right until crossroads 14 which marks the beginning of the forest.

Outside the reserve, you can hike the 5 mi/8 km from the lodge to observe the animals that come in the afternoons during the dry season to drink from Lake Paradise or Sokorte Guda. Don't miss a visit to Gof Bongole.

The Singing Wells

Difficult to reach, these deep wells are never waterless. During the dry season, when sources of water fail elsewhere, men come to these wells and, forming a chain at different levels within, pass filled buckets to the top.

> Accommodation
>
> ▲▲ **Marsabit Lodge,** reservations: POB 30471, Nairobi, ☎ 33 6858; or POB 45, Marsabit, ☎ 2044. 24 rooms. ① Sitting room and bar with beautiful fireplace. Two Land Rovers available for excursions. The lodge needs to be renovated and its cuisine improved.
>
> *Camping*
> Two sites in the park; the one near Lake Paradise is unequipped.

▬ BORANA VILLAGES★★

During the dry season don't miss a visit in the morning to the marketplace, where you'll see Borana tribespeople in *kangas,* their heads covered with veils. The women also wear silver chains draped from their foreheads and held in place by a headband.

The road over the plateau from Marsabit to Moyale (on the Ethiopian border) leads through Borana villages; on either side are fields of maize and other vegetables. The villages are surrounded by papaya, eucalyptus and banana trees.

The Borana, like the Galla, speak Orano, a language of the Cushitic family. They migrated from Ethiopia in the mid-16th century. Their tribe suffered greatly during the troubles with Ethiopia in the 1960s, their economy ruined first by the loss of part of their cattle herds to Ethiopian Somali raiders and then by drought. Today, they have again begun to cultivate the land and to raise new herds.

The Borana are extremely hospitable and willingly invite strangers into their homes. Each hut is a circular structure with smaller rooms inside formed by dried-grass dividers. Each group of huts houses an extended family of a father, two wives and all their children (approximately six each), the grandparents, uncles and so forth.

The Borana create imaginative art work, including metal jewelry and gourds decorated with finely woven grass and cowrie shells that can take the women up to a year to make.

▰ *FROM MARSABIT TO CHALBI DESERT*

Continue north through the Chalbi Desert along the road to Moyale: you'll come to Gof Jobae. Its impressive crater, usually dry, is 0.6 mi/1 km across.

To return to Loyangalani, head back to Marsabit and take the C77 on the left just after leaving the village. This is the route to Lake Turkana via North Horr. Stock up on water, food and petrol because you won't find any on the way. You won't have any problem finding your way up to North Horr, even over the sandy stretches of the road, but beyond, you'll need a guide to cross the Bura hills and you should travel in a convoy with other vehicles.

FROM SAMBURU TO MERU NATIONAL PARK

▰ *SAMBURU NATIONAL RESERVE**

152 mi/244 km south of Marsabit, 22 mi/35 km north of Isiolo.

This reserve actually consists of two adjoining reserves: the Samburu and the Buffalo Springs reserves (officially called Isiolo), separated by the Ewaso Ngiro River.

Samburu Reserve

Right in the midst of semi-arid savannah, the reserve's river and fresh-water springs attract a profusion of animals, especially near the end of the dry season. Another striking feature is the rich, reddish-brown colour of the soil.

The major attractions here are the reticulated giraffe, also called Samburu Giraffe, which live in herds of about a dozen. Other mammals abound, including Grevy zebra, Beisa oryx (a large grey antelope with black markings on the face), elephant and lion. Undoubtedly the most visible animals in the reserve are the striped ground squirrel.

The juncture of arid and humid environments has attracted thousands of birds. There are several species of guinea fowl and pigeon and almost as many birds of prey as in Marsabit. Ornithologists have spotted some less common species such as the spurwinged plover.

Buffalo Springs (Isiolo) Reserve

Lush vegetation and superb palm groves cover the banks of the river which can be crossed by a bridge (sometimes flooded during the rainy season). South side of the river, the many springs and pools make the area swampy and greener than to the north: the countryside is a humid savannah bordering the **Champagne Hills** to the east. The road along the hills provides a good view before it reaches the valley. Koitogor Hill to the north marks the frontier of the arid savannah, a striking contrast to the greenery of the reserve.

The road network is generally good, and the only place where you're likely to get bogged down is the track that parallels the river. In the dry savannah, you'll need a four-wheel-drive vehicle everywhere except on the Koitogor circuit, which is negotiable, if sometimes with difficulty, in an ordinary car.

The charm of these reserves lies in the abrupt contrast between north and south, in the play of light on the Champagne Hills and in the mountains looming on the horizon north and west of Koitogor. The abundance of animal life justifies a two-to three-day stay at one of the magnificent lodges.

The Springs

Buffalo Springs lies in a rocky hollow east of the reserve that carries its name. It forms a pool where you can swim, though you should watch out for crocodiles, which are seen here from time to time. A little farther on, the same springs creates another fresh-water pool where animals come to drink.

Accommodation

▲▲▲▲ **Samburu Lodge,** reservations: Block Hotels, POB 47557, Nairobi, ☎ 33 5807. 65 rooms. ① ④ Filling station and resident mechanic. The lovely thatched-roof bungalows built of stone and cedar from Mount Kenya line the Ewaso Ngiro River bank. From the lodge, you can observe the crocodiles, hippopotamuses, birds and, in the evenings, leopards.

▲▲▲▲ **Samburu Serena Lodge,** reservations: Serena Lodges & Hotels, POB 48690, Nairobi, ☎ 33 8656. 50 rooms. ① ④ Also along the river, these luxurious, straw-covered bungalows are situated opposite Koitogor hill, near the Buffalo Springs Reserve. The terrace permits observation of hippopotamuses, crocodiles and, in the evenings, leopards.

▲▲▲ **Buffalo Springs Lodge,** reservations: ATH, Utalii House, Uhuru Highway, POB 30471, Nairobi, ☎ 33 6858. 38 luxury tents. ① Bar. On the southern bank of the river, these former *bandas* have been recently renovated.

▲▲ **Larsen's Camp,** reservations essential: Block Hotels, POB 47557, Nairobi, ☎ 33 5807. 15 tents. ① Bar. This more modest camp, 1.2 mi/2 km from Samburu Lodge on the southern side of the river, is somewhat difficult to find. Good food.

▬▬ SHABA NATIONAL RESERVE★★

19 mi/31 km north of Isiolo.

Its name comes from the cone of a volcano; spectacular traces of the volcano's lava flow mark the entire landscape. The banks of the Ewaso Ngiro River, which borders the reserve on the north, are covered with trees that stand in stunning contrast to the surrounding savannah. At the spectacular Chanler's Fall's at some distance to the east, the river drops abruptly to a basalt slab below.

The setting, with its numerous small hills, is magnificent. Watered by four springs, Shaba is more humid than the two neighbouring reserves to the west and attracts even more wildlife. You'll need a four-wheel-drive vehicle, and since the tracks are badly signposted, you should get a detailed map of the area from the Public Map Office on Harambee Avenue in Nairobi.

Shaba was where Joy Adamson was living and reintroducing leopards to the wild when she was murdered.

Accommodation

Camping is possible on several roughly equipped or non-equipped sites, in particular in the **Champagne Hills**. Make reservations through the reserve's rangers.

Useful address

Chief Warden, POB 28, Isiolo, ☎ 21Y2 (through an operator).

ISIOLO ★★

169 mi/272 km north-east of Nairobi, 51 mi/82 km north-east of Nanyuki.

The village, consisting of one main street, with attractive trees and colourful tribespeople, is the gateway to the north. There is a filling station and a police barrier. In the past, one needed special permission to make the journey north. While this is no longer the case, you may be asked by the police where you are heading and be told whether or not you should travel with a police convoy. If you don't stay with the convoy you've joined, you risk being stopped at the next police station, obliged to get into one of the convoy's trucks and abandon your car to the Sololavi police, one hour's ride away from Archer's Post.

The quickest route to Meru National Park is to head east 19 mi/30 km to the village of Muriri on the C91. A tarmac road on the left leads to Maua (14 mi/22 km) where you will turn left onto the track that goes to the park entrance (22 mi/35 km).

Lewa Downs

South of Isiolo, take the track marked 'Trails Camp'. There's an airstrip between Ngara Rhino Sanctuary and Lewa Downs.

The managers of Lewa Downs, a privately owned ranch, will put up small groups who are then taken on excursions to explore the region south-west of Isiolo. You'll see lion, elephant, antelope and even leopard and cheetah.

A few kilometres away, David and Delia Craig have set up a rhinoceros sanctuary. The animals are sheltered in a giant enclosure, several dozen square kilometres in area. The entrance fee is Ksh 100.

Accommodation

▲▲ **Lewa Downs Farm,** reservations: Wilderness Trails, POB 42562, Nairobi, ☎ 27048. 7 rooms. ① Good cooking. Horse rental; excursions on foot and by vehicle.

MERU

18 mi/29 km north-east of Nairobi, 31 mi/50 km south of Isiolo.

Meru is a hillside agricultural centre with a population of 5000. In this region, north-east of Mount Kenya, subsistence farming dominates, in particular the cultivation of maize. Meru overlooks the plains to the east like a terrace shaded by a wide variety of fragrant trees.

Along the main streets, you'll find filling stations, a post office, several banks, two hotels, bookstores and shoes and clothing shops. The best way to discover this lively town is simply to wander about on foot.

Meru, particularly known for the national park nearby, is also the capital of one of the largest ethnic groups in Kenya: the Meru (about 500,000). Essentially farmers, the Meru raise livestock, as well as crops like maize, potatos, tea and coffee.

The town has a museum that you'll find marked on the road to Nanyuki and Isiolo. Inside, Meru tools and clothing are displayed in a traditional homestead, and the characteristic plants of the region grow in the museum garden. You may be told about the Miraa tree here, which is widely grown in the area and is appreciated for its leaves that are used as a stimulant. You might hear talk of the *molon*, which is, in fact, the local name for the cola tree.

Accommodation

▲▲▲ **Meru County Hotel,** Kenyatta Highway, POB 1386, ☎ 20427. 47 rooms. ① Lovely rooftop terrace. Car rental.

▲▲ **Pig & Whistle Lodge,** POB 268, Meru, ☎ 20574. 24 rooms. An agreeable hotel with an old-time atmosphere. Organized activities include fishing, golf and butterfly catching.

▬▬ *MERU NATIONAL PARK*★★★

199 mi/320 km north-east of Nairobi, about 62 mi/100 km east of Meru.

On your way from Meru, make a stop after Kangeta to admire the superb scenery. As you approach the park, the wattle trees give way to savannah and then to bushland.

Meru National Park stretches from the eastern face of the Nyambeni range, at an altitude of 2821 ft/860 m, to the Tana River; the river's source is in Mount Kenya. The park area includes 15 permanent rivers, small springs and swamps, yet much of the terrain, especially in the north, is typical savannah.

The Rojewero River divides the park into two very different ecological areas. To the north lies a plain studded with solidified lava and shaded here and there by thorny acacias and bushes. To the south, the red, sandy earth supports a much denser vegetation of brushwood, baobab and other tall trees.

The park owes its fame to Joy Adamson; it was here she undertook her first experiments, reacclimatizing first the lioness Elsa and then the cheetah Pippa into their natural habitat. Joy's husband, the park warden, was forced to kill Elsa's mother when Elsa was just a cub. After a few years of care, the Adamson's decided to release Elsa to the wild. Joy Adamson wrote several books describing the experience from which she and her husband had learned so much about the social life of the animals. She used the proceeds to set up the Elsa Fund, a private foundation for the study of animal life and the protection of endangered species.

Several sites at the park are named after the Adamsons, though nothing remains of the camps they set up. Before she was murdered in 1980, Joy had moved near Shaba, while her husband continued his work in the Kora National Reserve until he, too, was murdered in 1989.

Meru National Park is a great place to observe lion and cheetah attracted by the many grazers, notably the hartebeest, Burchell's and Grevy's zebra, and Grant's gazelle. At midday you'll find them escaping the heat under the shelter of doum palms along the river banks. The rare Rothschild giraffe, with its three or five horns and a coat resembling that of the reticulated giraffe, can be seen here. Herds consisting of hundreds of elephants and hundreds of buffalo gather by the water courses. Monitor lizards and tortoises abound, but it is hard to catch a glimpse of these reptiles.

One of the park's main attractions is the white rhinoceros of South Africa, which has been introduced successfully. The small size of the park has facilitated surveillance of the rhinoceros. The 'white', or square-lipped, rhinoceros is actually dark grey; it owes its name to the Afrikaner word *wijd*, meaning 'wide'. It is larger than the black rhinoceros, has a wide, square muzzle and a longer, more tapered horn. The white rhinoceros is reputed to be fairly docile and can be approached without difficulty.

The bird life of the park is also very rich and includes birds of prey, notably vultures, and wading birds along the river banks.

Despite its beauty, Meru National Park is rarely visited, and thus much of its vegetation and animal life has remained intact. Poachers, however, continue to plague the park, as Joy Adamson described in her books. The rangers are more available to accompany visitors than at busier parks; they will show you where you can best observe the animals, as well as the spot where Pippa and Elsa are buried (the latter is midway between Adamson's Falls and Ura Gate). There are plans to construct a small museum here.

To get the most from a visit to this paradise, a two- or three-day stay is recommended. Avoid coming during the rainy season, when the grass

Meru National Park: the setting of the fabulous story of the lioness Elsa, recounted by J. Adamson in Born Free.

A Lion's Tale

'Only one thing is certain,' mused Joy Adamson in an autobiography published in the spring of 1979, 'people get out of life exactly what they put into it.' Both she and her husband, George Adamson, nurtured a great passion for the life they had adopted in Kenya and especially for the great cats whose welfare they cared more about than their own.

Austrian-born Joy Gessner moved to Kenya in 1937 after she 'fell in love with this wonderful country' during a safari. In 1944 she met George Adamson, a game warden, and they were married the same year. Together this legendary couple fought a daily battle against Kenya poachers and successfully experimented in re-acclimatizing lions to the wild. Their real fame came as a result of Joy's novel (and subsequent motion picture), *Born Free*. It immortalized the lioness Elsa they reared after George was forced to shoot the cub's mother in self-defense.

Born Free and Joy's other well known books, *Living Free* and *Forever Free,* have reached across the globe to acquaint less adventurous animal lovers with the wonders of Kenya's wildlife. With her book and movie income, Joy launched an international conservation project called the Elsa Wild Animal Appeal. Her work did not benefit lions alone; other personal endeavours included working with cheetahs and leopards.

In January 1980 Joy Adamson was murdered at the Shaba Game Reserve in Central Kenya. An original report blamed 'the great claws' of a lion. Later, it was found that the killer was a former servant Joy had accused of theft.

Although the Adamsons had been amicably separated since the mid-1960s, George was determined to continue the fight on behalf of the lions — despite a growing feeling of resentment that had been developing among poachers, who felt threatened by his work. With his own life in danger, he slept with a revolver by his bedside and continued to struggle for his cause with meager funds.

But in Kenya's Kora National Reserve, George also met with sudden, violent death. Coming to the rescue of friends attacked by poachers, the 83-year-old Adamson was killed, leaving the future of his cause still unfulfilled. About the tardy identification of Joy's killer ten years earlier, George had written, 'far better had it been a lion.' What he realized was that the most dangerous creature in the wilderness of Kenya was not the one endowed with great claws and teeth, but rather the one armed with guns and knives.

and water are abundant and the animals are more dispersed, and don't miss a visit to Adamson's Falls, 37 mi/60 km south of Meru Mulika Lodge, on the Tana River.

Accommodation

▲▲▲ **Meru Mulika Lodge,** reservations: Safari Inns, POB 46582, Nairobi, ☎ 338471. 66 rooms. ① ④ Full board only. Filling station. The bungalows of this superb lodge are built on a natural terrace; an ideal vantage point for watching the animals. Airstrip about 100 yd/m from lodge.

▲ **Leopard Rock Safari Lodge,** reservation: AA Travel, POB 14982, Nairobi, ☎ 337900. 10 bungalows. No restaurant but cooking equipment is available.

Camping

Nine partially equipped or non-equipped sites.

Useful address

Chief Warden, Meru National Park, POB 162, Nanyuki; radiocall Nairobi 3700.

Returning to Nairobi

83 mi/134 km.

You can head straight back to Nairobi, taking the B6, which is tarmac to Embu. The road runs on the eastern side of the Mount Kenya range, through brightly coloured scenery: the blood-red laterite clay is overgrown with foliage of different shades of green, and farmlands stretch up to the abruptly rising, tree-covered slopes. The new road provides picturesque views of the valleys to the east, carved by turbulent streams.

Accommodation

▲▲ **Izaak Walton Inn,** POB 1, Embu, ☎ 20128. 27 rooms. ① Situated in a garden 1.2 mi/2 km north of Embu, this is a good base for trout fishing.

ABERDARE (NYANDARUA) RANGE AND MOUNT KENYA

▬ *NANYUKI*

118 mi/190 km north of Nairobi, 51 mi/82 km south-west of Isiolo.

Situated at an altitude of 6381 ft/1945 m, with Mount Kenya towering impressively above, Nanyuki is an important communications crossroads and regional centre with a population of 13,000. It is also a business centre for the large cattle ranches to the north-west of town on the Laikipia plains. You will find banks, shops, bars, the post office and filling stations along the main street. Just off it are colourful markets and an interesting craft centre (as you leave town to the north on the Nyahururu road), the **Nanyuki Spinners and Weavers,** where you can visit workshops and be tempted by the fine produce for sale (rugs and mats, among other things). Nanyuki is a good base for excursions to the Mount Kenya massif and the Aberdare (Nyandarua) Range.

In July and August the summits of the mountains are usually wrapped in heavy cloud and mist known as *gathano* to the Kikuyu. The temperatures are cool in October through December, ranging from 46 to 77° F/ 8 to 25° C.

Access

You can reach Nanyuki from Nairobi by air, bus and *matatu.* Buses and *matatus* link the town to Meru, Isiolo, Nyeri and Nyahururu.

Accommodation

In Nanyuki

▲▲▲▲ **Mount Kenya Safari Club,** reservations: Lonhro Hotels, POB 58581, Nairobi, ☎ 27027; or Intercontinental, POB 43564, Nairobi, ☎ 330621. Cottages and garden suites, altogether 133 bedrooms. ① ③ ④ Sauna, golf, horses, footpaths on the mountainside, trout fishing, safaris. A former hotel converted into an exclusive club frequented by American movie stars (foremost among them William Holden) and reopened to the public in 1962. A Ksh 200 entrance fee is required, even for a simple visit. Adjoining the extensive grounds are the William Holden Wildlife Education Centre and the Mount Kenya Game Ranch which shelters young abandoned animals.

▲▲ **Sportsman's Arms Hotel,** POB 3, Nanyuki, ☎ 23200. 25 rooms. A clean, old-world hotel run by Indians. Lovely view of Mount Kenya.

Outside Nanyuki

There are two possibilities of luxury accommodation on Ol Pejeta ranch west of Nanyuki (reservations: Lonhro Hotels, POB 58581, Nairobi, ☎ 27027):

▲▲▲ **Mount Kenya Safari Lodge,** 11 bedrooms. Cottages in a beautiful garden setting. Swimming pool, tennis courts. Splendid view of Mount Kenya.

▲▲▲ **Sweetwaters Tented Camp,** 25 tents overlooking a floodlit water hole. Swimming pool, game lookout bar, land cruisers for game drives, camel rides. Animals on the ranch include elephant, zebra, giraffe, hartebeest, Thomson's and Grant's gazelle.

Camping

In a less luxurious but delightful setting beside the Ewaso Ngiro river is the campsite on **El Karama** ranch, about 27 mi/43 km north-west of Nanyuki. You can rent horses if you want to explore the ranch and see the game.

NANYUKI TO ABERDARE (NYANDARUA) NATIONAL PARK

South of Nanyuki, the new A2 is still under construction; you have to drive along a series of deviations through the wide agricultural valley between Mount Kenya on the left and the Aberdare (Nyandarua) Range on the right. Almost immediately on leaving town you pass the Equator, where to mark the point there is a colourful signboard and a row of souvenir stalls.

Nyeri

Coming from Nanyuki you first pass Naro Moru on the A2 and continue south to a junction, where you take the B5 (tarmac) to the right.

Nyeri, the kingtown of jacarandas, is an important agricultural centre with a lively market. On the outskirts of town, toward Mweiga, lies the grave of Robert Baden-Powell (1857-1941), founder of the Boy Scouts. He retired to Nyeri in 1938.

Accommodation

▲▲▲ **Naro Moru River Lodge,** south of Nanyuki, POB 18, Naro Moru, ☎ 22018. 31 cottages and 7 bandas. ① ③ ④ ⑤ Sauna, conference room. Not far from the entrance to the Mount Kenya National Park. Perfect base for excursions up the mountain. Hiking and climbing equipment for hire. Trout fishing possible in the Naro Moru river.

▲▲ **Bantu Lodge,** south of Nanyuki, POB 333, Bantu Rd., Nanyuki, ☎ 1 in Burguret. 14 rooms. ① Nightclub on Wednesday, Saturday and Sunday. The cottages are in a large garden beside a river.

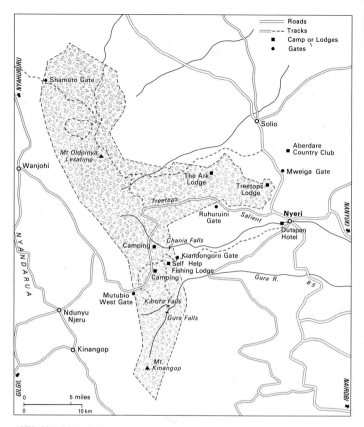

ABERDARE NATIONAL PARK

━━ *ABERDARE NATIONAL PARK*** (Nyandarua National Park)*

In January 1979, the name of the park and the mountain range was changed from Aberdare to Nyandarua after its second highest mountain (12,815 ft/3906 m). The name Aberdare was given to the range a hundred years ago by Joseph Thomson in honour of the president of the Royal Geographical Society who had encouraged Thomson's expeditions. It continues to be used today, even in official documents.

The whole mountain range, favoured with abundant precipitation stretches from north to south over some 43 mi/70 km but only the heights generally over 9842 ft/3000 m are within the park limits. One exception is the Treetops Salient, which slopes down to an altitude of 6998 ft/2133 m toward Nyeri. Two lodges, have been built in this area, which was once a migration zone for elephants on their way to the Mount Kenya massif. Today, fenced-off fields and the road prevent the elephants from following this route. Animal life in the park remains abundant, however, and includes buffalo, elephant, giant forest hog, bush pig, genet cat and civet.

Both the animals and the vegetation change with the altitude. Covering the slopes between about 6500 ft/2000 and 10,000 ft/3000 m is thick rainforest; evergreens, including the superb podo, give way to bamboo, ferns and camphor trees. This is where most of the animals live: elephant, rhinoceros, buffalo, warthog and other wild hogs, and a

A view of Mount Kenya from Aberdare National Park; it is the sacred mountain of the Kikuyu, the home on earth of their god, Ngai.

profusion of various antelope. It is even possible to admire the rare bongo (an antelope with white stripes on its flanks and face), leopard (including the black panther), numerous primates (among which, the black and white colobus monkey) and a wide range of bird life, particularly the superb crowned eagle. A very aggressive species of lion characterized by a thicker coat than that of the savannah lion lives in the southern part of the park.

Above the forest lie open fields bristling with alpine growths of scrub brush and heather as tall as trees and groundsel that, with its yellow flowers, resembles the artichoke or lobelia plant. These highest reaches are the habitat of the rare black serval cat and the gregarious rock hyrax; the latter will not hesitate to come and poke its nose in your belongings.

The moorland that covers the rounded summits of the Aberdare Range is one of the most stunningly beautiful parts of the park. Rarely visited, this wild region shelters few animals. Numerous streams cross the entire range. Waterfalls are everywhere. Don't miss the spectacular Chania, Karuru and Gura falls in the southern area (entry via Mutubio West Gate). Trout fishing is extremely popular, but don't forget to ask the rangers for a permit.

Access

The three entrances on the eastern side, from south to north, are Kiandongoro Gate, Ruhuruini Gate and Mweiga Gate. The latter leads to the two lodges in the Treetops Salient — Treetops and The Ark. To visit the northern area near Nyahururu, enter by the Shamato Gate. Coming from Naivasha and Gilgil, beyond Kinangop, you'll use the Mutubio West Gate. The track linking Mutubio Gate and Ruhuruini Gate is rarely open anytime but January and February.

There is no track between the north and south of the park; after a visit to the falls in the south, you'll have to leave the park by the Ruhuruini Gate, pass through Nyeri, go around the park to Nanyuki and take the road toward Nyahururu to enter again via the Shamato Gate. Mountain climbers use this entrance to reach the foot of Mount Ol Doinyo Lesatima (13,120 ft/3999 m).

Accommodation

▲▲▲▲ **Treetops,** POB 23, Nyeri; reservations: through Block Hotels, POB 47557, Nairobi, ☎ 335807. 45 rooms. ① Few amenities.

Suites are the only rooms with private bathrooms. Full board only. After lunch at the Outspan Hotel in Nyeri, minibuses will drive you here for tea and dinner. The lodge, built on stilts, towers above a pond and makes for a great observation platform, especially at night. On February 5, 1952, the then princess Elizabeth was visiting here with her husband, Philip, en route to Australia and New Zealand when her father, King George VI, died and she became queen.

▲▲▲ **Aberdare Country Club,** reservations: Lonhro Hotels Bruce House, Standard St., POB 58581, Nairobi, ☎ 27027. Coming from Nanyuki along the A2, turn right just before Kiganjo toward Nyeri. 15 rooms. ① ③ ④ ⑤ Lovely building with a tile roof overlooking the valley (stupendous view) and the Nyandarua Range on the horizon. Good food. Excursions on foot and on horseback and trout fishing are organized. Game sanctuary. Aviary. Guests en route to the Ark first lunch here.

▲▲▲ **The Ark,** reservations: POB 59749, Nairobi, ☎ 335900. 45 rooms. ① After lunch at the Aberdare Country Club, you are driven to the lodge for tea and dinner. A narrow footbridge leads to the Ark, which is an ideal spot to watch animals at night. A signal buzzes in your room when especially interesting animals are visible. Among the house rules: visitors are not allowed to venture out alone, luggage is limited to one small travel bag per person, and the lodge is not open to children under eight.

▲▲▲ **Outspan Hotel,** reservations: Block Hotels, POB 47557, Nairobi, ☎ 335807. On the road from Nyeri to Mweiga. 35 rooms. ① ③ ④ ⑤ Excellent cooking. Lovely decor in a magnificent park. Organizes visits to the private ranch, Solio Game Reserve. Guests en route to Treetops first lunch here.

▲ **Self-Help Fishing Lodge,** between Chania and Karuru falls. An excellent choice for trout-fishing enthusiasts. Check with the rangers for information.

Camping

Seven unequipped sites in the park: **Magura, Gachage, Mwathe, Kiguru, Chania, Honi, Wandari.** Chopped wood available. Be especially careful in the southern areas of the park, where you could be attacked by lions.

Useful address

Chief Warden, Nyandarua National Park, POB 22, Nyeri, ☎ 24 in Mweiga.

▬ *MOUNT KENYA NATIONAL PARK*★★

Naro Moru Gate is 12 mi/20 km from route A2.

Mount Kenya is an extinct and eroded volcano; jutting from the massif are three peaks, **Batian** (17,044 ft/5195 m), **Nelion** (16,998 ft/5181 m) and **Lenana** (16,299 ft/4968 m). They form a crown at the summit of the range and each might seem to tower over the others depending on your vantage point. The formation is almost circular and its diameter is 37 mi/60 km. Its slopes rise about 10,000 ft/3000 m over the valleys that surround it. Mount Kenya holds a central role in the beliefs of all the peoples in the region: the Embu, Meru, Kamba and Kikuyu. The god of the Kikuyu is believed to reside in the mountain.

A belt of dense evergreen forest covers the slopes. There are cedar and, on the western flank, podo, mixed in with olive trees at the base. Higher up, bamboo predominates alongside palm trees on the eastern flank up to about 10,000 ft/3000 m. Beneath the trees, the ground is overgrown with flowers, ferns, liana and moss. These woodlands provide excellent living conditions for the proliferation of many animal species — practically the same as those in the Nyandarua Range.

Mount Kenya National Park encompasses the area above the forest, starting at about 10,500 ft/3200 m, although most of the entrances are lower down. This is moorland, broken by numerous streams that have formed 32 lakes and tarns within many valleys. The vegetation is the same as that in the Nyandarua Range at the same altitude: alpine foliage, giant heather, groundsel, lobelia and rosewood (hagenia). The playful rock hyraxes abound here while the primates, especially colobus monkey, are found higher up. Within the dense forest live elephant, buffalo, all kinds of antelope (including the extremely shy bongo), leopard (equally difficult to observe) and rhinoceros.

Most of the animals can not easily be watched since they take cover in the forest thicket. Staying at a lodge is the best way of seeing them, particularly the bongo; their appearance near the lodge is always signaled and causes much excitement.

Fishing and mountain climbing

Several trout streams flow by the Mountain Lodge area, making it a perfect place to combine mountain hiking, animal-watching and fishing. If looking at the animals is not a priority, you might opt for the **Naro Moru Lodge** for its fishing and hikes. Teleki Valley and the approaches to Mount Lenana are easily accessible. The mountain — its name comes from the Masai prophet Olana — is also called 'Tourist Peak' since it is easy to reach from the Mackinder camp. Hikers should be careful about the effects of the altitude (about 13,000 ft/4000 m).

Accommodation

▲▲▲▲ **Mountain Lodge,** advance reservations necessary in Nairobi, POB 30471, ☎ 336858. 38 rooms. A recently renovated luxury lodge built on stilt foundations. It is situated on the south-western flank of Mount Kenya on a former migration path of elephants moving from Kihari to Nyandarua. It is 14 mi/22 km from Kiganjo (if you come from the north, it is just before Karatina town). Excellent place to observe animals that come to drink from the pool. Be sure to close the windows of your room to keep out the monkeys.

▲▲ **Karatina Rest House,** POB 141, Karatina, ☎ 71404, Nyeri. 25 rooms. ① Grill.

▲ **Mackinder Refuge,** situated at the foot of the glaciers at an altitude of more than 13,000 ft/4000 m. 50 beds in rooms and dormitories.

▲ **Met Station Refuge,** at an altitude of about 10,000 ft/3000 m. Wooden *banda* dormitories, with 30 beds and communal showers. Both refuges are run by **Naro Moru Lodge** (see p. 153).

▬▬ TO NAIROBI

Route A2 to Nairobi passes through a region inhabited by the Kikuyu and covered in fields of coffee plantations. If you want to visit the towns of Muranga (formerly Fort Hall), Sagana, Maragua or Thika, you'll have to get off the main road.

Thika

26 mi/42 km north-east of Nairobi.

Thika was made famous by Elspeth Huxley, a writer who spent some time here and told of it in her book *The Flame Trees of Thika*. The town, which is situated in an area of banana, sisal, pineapple and especially coffee production, has changed greatly since then. Today it is a regional agricultural centre and industrial town with fruit-canning and tannery factories.

Accommodation

▲▲▲ **Blue Post B & B,** POB 42, Thika, ☎ 21303. Coming from Nanyuki, get off the A2 at the Chania Falls signpost before Thika. 15 rooms. ① ③ ④ Discotheque. Situated in a lovely flower-filled garden at the edge of Chania Falls, the hotel makes for a pleasant stopover.

SOUTH-EAST AND EASTERN KENYA

Organizing your time

- **One week:** beach lovers and marine life enthusiasts will opt for the resorts along the coast: Shimoni, Malindi or Watamu Island. History buffs will turn to Bamburi, Jumba la Mtwana and Gedi. Amboseli and Tsavo West are good choices for a safari, and Lamu is ideal for dhow excursions, sightseeing and swimming.

- **Ten days:** you'll have time to tour the whole coast from Shimoni to Lamu. Alternatively, you can go on a safari in Amboseli, Tsavo East and Tsavo West parks and still have time to visit Mombasa and Malindi.

- **Three weeks:** this is sufficient time to follow the itinerary in this chapter.

FROM NAIROBI TO MOMBASA VIA AMBOSELI

Leave Nairobi by the road leading south toward Jomo Kenyatta International Airport and Mombasa. At Athi River, the way to Amboseli and Namanga (on the Tanzanian border) forks to the right. Alternatively, a more pleasant option from Nairobi is to cross Nairobi National Park to Cheetah Gate where you can pick up the A104 near Athi River.

This is Masai country. The *enkangs*, 'villages' in the Masai language, blend perfectly into the surroundings. A circular thornbush fence encloses the dome-shaped Masai huts, which remain constantly dark and cool inside. At night the herds are sheltered in the centre of the *enkang;* they leave behind heaps of dung attracting flies that can be particularly bothersome to the unaccustomed visitor. If you want to take pictures, you will generally have to pay a few shillings.

The tarmac A104 passes through the important regional centre of **Kajiado** (47 mi/75 km south of Nairobi). The Masai come here to study at the agricultural school. On a clear day, you can see Mount Kilimanjaro from this region of verdant, undulating hills.

Namanga

55 mi/88 km south of Kajiado, 102 mi/164 km south of Nairobi.

Namanga is the gateway both to Tanzania and to Amboseli National Park. The border, long closed between the two countries, can now be crossed by visitors holding a Tanzanian visa. Beyond this small town, an extremely difficult track crosses superb hillside country to the park.

The arid plateau of Tsavo East National Park

Accommodation

▲▲ **Namanga River Hotel B & B,** POB 4, Namanga. 45 rooms.
① ④ Fishing.

▬▬ AMBOSELI NATIONAL PARK★★★

150 mi/240 km south of Nairobi via Namanga.

Amboseli is a park of fantasy. The sheer spectacle of night falling on Mount Kilimanjaro — which the Masai call 'Oldinyo Oibor', or 'the White Mountain' — was enough to fascinate and astonish Ernest Hemingway. Its proximity to Nairobi makes it a popular tourist stop.

Around Lake Amboseli, which is dry 11 months a year, the landscape is open, bushy savannah dotted with thickets and some acacias. From a hill in the centre of the park you can watch hundreds of wildebeest and other grazers. And, of course, the volcanic Mount Kilimanjaro towers from across the Tanzanian border over the entire region at 19,340 ft/5 895 m above sea level. In the early morning light of dawn, its crown of snow turns a stunning pink. Its summit then disappears behind clouds during the day only to reappear, ever more majestic, at sundown. Photographers should remember to use a filter to cut through the haze that might be hanging around the mountain.

Amboseli is criss-crossed by an extensive road network that includes several main murram roads and numerous tracks. For the sake of protecting the natural habitat of the wildlife, don't venture off the tracks, even if you are tempted to cut across an open plain to get a closer look at a rare species. The damage left by the wheels of your vehicle will contribute to the loss of the vegetation and thus of the animals that feed on it. Drought has already damaged the land; over the past few years the lack of rain has caused a build-up of salts that will become detrimental to plant life unless the drought stops. Though dry weather predominates, in March and April torrential downpours can make the tracks impassible.

Despite all the weather problems, Amboseli offers a profusion of animals. You can find herds of buffalo in the Ol Okenya Swamp and of elephants along the Sinet River. There are common giraffe, Grant's and Thompson gazelle, impala and mixed herds of wildebeest, hartebeest and zebra.

In the northern part of the park, you can easily observe gerenuk, prides of lion, hyena, hunting dogs, black-backed jackal and sometimes the bat-eared fox, with their large, round ears.

On the other hand, you are unlikely to spot either leopard or cheetah. White rhinoceros have been completely exterminated by poachers, and while you might still encounter a black rhinoceros, that species too is diminishing.

The park boasts a rich bird life. An abundant variety of wading birds nest in the swamps. They include the ibis, egret, avocet, common and saddle-billed stork, secretary bird and heron, accompanied by vultures, ducks, and geese such as the Egyptian goose.

Access

The three main entrances are Namanga Gate on the west, the central Lemeiboti Gate and Kimana Gate on the east.

There is an airstrip in the park near the lodges.

Accommodation

In the park

Advance booking is recommended.

▲▲▲▲ **Amboseli Serena Lodge,** reservations: POB 48690, Nairobi, ☎ 338696. 90 rooms. ① ④ Full board. Filling station. You'll find the solicitous service and friendly welcome of the Serena chain. The architecture uses stylistic elements of Masai dwellings: dome shaped buildings covered in reddish ochre earth open onto patios overrun with luxurious vegetation. Masai dance show nightly.

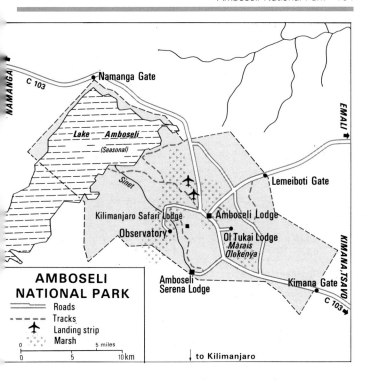

**AMBOSELI
NATIONAL PARK**

══════ Roads
─ ─ ─ ─ Tracks
✈ Landing strip
▷ ▷ ▷ Marsh

0 ─── 5 miles
0 ─── 5 ─── 10 km

↓ to Kilimanjaro

▲▲▲ **Amboseli Lodge,** reservations: POB 30139, Nairobi, ☎ 337510. 106 rooms. ① ④ Full board only. Magnificent view of Mount Kilimanjaro. Car rental.

▲▲▲ **Kilimanjaro Safari Lodge,** reservations: POB 30139, Nairobi, ☎ 337510; in Amboseli, ☎ 12. 70 rooms. ① ④ The thatched-roof cottages open onto a pool. Four-wheel-drive rental.

▲ **Ol Tukai Lodge,** reservations: Travel Bureau Ltd., University Way, POB 43230, Nairobi, ☎ 21716. 11 double bandas with bathroom and kitchen; bedding provided. No restaurant or shop.

Camping

Possible in park. Be careful not to leave food in your tent; it attracts animals and insects.

Outside the park

▲▲▲▲ **Kilimanjaro Buffalo Lodge,** POB 73, Loitokitok, or POB 72630, Nairobi, ☎ 76324. On the Kimana Gate road. 103 rooms. ① Cottages made from blocks of lava rock. Nice view of Mount Kilimanjaro.

▲▲ **Kimana Leopard Camp,** POB 16004, Nairobi, ☎ 62696. 2.5 mi/4 km off the main road from Makutano. 26 tents. ① This quiet lodge on the banks of the Kimana River attracts Nairobi residents. Guided treks organized.

▲▲ **Kimana Safari Lodge,** reservations: POB 30139, Nairobi, ☎ 377510. On the Makutano road, 2 mi/3 km from Kimana. 24 rooms. ① ④ The pavilions are spread over a garden where a salt pool attracts animals. Beautiful view of Mount Kilimanjaro.

▲ **Gona Safari Camp,** POB 41257, Nairobi, ☎ 506006. 4 tents and 4 bandas. Another lovely camp, also along the Kimana River.

Useful addresses

Chief Warden, Amboseli National Park, POB Namanga, ☎ radiocall Nairobi 2240.

Filling station, near the ranger post.

▬▬ *FROM AMBOSELI TO TSAVO WEST*

81 mi/130 km.

Leave Amboseli by the Kimana Gate and go east, through Masai country. Beyond Kimana you'll cross a plateau studded here and there with termite mounds.

As you near the **Chyulu Hills** (7132 ft/2174 m), blocks of lava cover the road making it even more jagged and difficult to drive along. This young volcanic chain becomes the splendid 'devil's flow' at **Shaitani Flow.**

▬▬ *TSAVO WEST NATIONAL PARK**

205 mi/330 km south-east of Nairobi to Voi on the A109.

Stretching over an area of 2700 sq mi/7000 sq km, Tsavo West requires a visit of a least two or three days. The park shelters an enormous variety of game. Its brushy savannah is the favourite habitat of lions.

The park is divided into three parts. North of the Tsavo river lies a landscape of arid hills and valleys. Between the river and the road leading from Voi to Taveta (on the Tanzanian border) rise scarcely noticeable plateaus covered with savannah bush. South of the road extends an area of monotonous plains.

If you are pressed for time, limit your visit to the northern sector, the lodge circuit (9 mi/14 km). This was also the site of several battles between the British and the Germans during World War I.

Numerous species of mammals and reptiles are drawn to the area's watering holes. Islands of bulrushes are ideal nesting places in the autumn for many migratory birds.

Mzima Springs* is the most spectacular site in Tsavo West. Some 10 million litres of water an hour gush out of this natural spring south of Kileguni. Filtered by the lava, the water is crystal clear. Three quarters of it is sent through pipelines to Mombasa. The remainder fills two lakes on different levels linked by a waterfall and surrounded by bulrushes, palms and tamarinds.

To visit Mzima Springs, leave your car in the parking area. Take the path toward Mzima (328 yd/300 m) to the first lake. A wooden footbridge leads to an underwater observatory in the centre of the lake. Through its glass windows you can watch hippopotamus, crocodile and all sorts of fish. This is a delightful, impressive experience.

This is a perfect place to spend the hotter hours of the day before setting out on a trek. The banks of the Tsavo River are also rewarding, especially when the elephant come to drink at the end of the day.

Poacher's Lookout, near Kitani Safari Camp (intersection numbers 30 and 32), provides a fine view of the whole park.

Proceed down the road, a good one, that follows the river and then an extremely well-shaded canal that goes through an area where the Taita live. You will mostly see herbivores here: elephant, gathered in herds of up to a hundred, gregarious buffalo, small antelope, zebra, Beisa oryx and the lesser kudu. Near Lake Jipe you might catch sight of lion, or at least hear them. There are also leopard and cheetah. Il you have the time, visit the well-situated **Ngulia Sarafi Lodge,** nicely situated on a hill, and the beautiful **Kilaguni Lodge.**

To leave Tsavo, take a shortcut from Lake Jipe to the A23, Taveta-Voi, in the direction of Maktau Gate.

The snow-covered summit of Mount Kilimanjaro; from Amboseli National Park.

Access

There are many entrances to the park. Counterclockwise from the north-west, the gates are Mtito Andei, Mbuyuni, Jipe, Kasigau, Maktau, Manyani and Tsavo. The excellent inner road network has numbered crossroads. If you enter the park through Kasigau Gate, you'll need a four-wheel-drive vehicle to reach the northern section.

Accommodation

▲▲▲▲ **Kilaguni Lodge,** reservations: ATH, POB 30471, Nairobi, ☎ 33 6858. 53 rooms. ① Full board only. Filling station. With a superb view of Chyulu Hills, this is one of Kenya's best lodges. Two pools attract the animals and birds.

▲▲▲▲ **Ngulia Safari Lodge,** reservations: ATH, POB 30471, Nairobi, ☎ 33 6858 or POB 90604, Mombasa, ☎ 20627. 50 rooms. ① ④ Full board. Filling station. The lodge's site, less beautiful than that of Kilaguni Lodge, offers an ideal place to look out over the entire Tsavo River valley.

▲▲▲ **Lake Jipe Safari Lodge,** reservations: POB 31097, Nairobi, ☎ 27623; radiocall 2016. 2 mi/3 km from the lake. 36 rooms. ① ④ Excellent kitchen. Built in 1988, the lodge is in a protected area where animals abound. Fishing, treks and bird-watching.

▲▲ **Kitani Lodge,** reservations: Let's Go Travel, POB 60342, Nairobi, ☎ 29539. 6 *bandas* with kitchen and bathroom, shop and bedding rental.

▲ **Ngulia Safari Camp,** reservations: POB 720382, Nairobi, ☎ 72 0382. 6 rustic *bandas* with kitchen and bathroom; bring your own bedding. No restaurant or shops.

Camping

Sites include **Rivergate, Mtito Andei Gate, Chyulu Gate, Ziwani** and **Jipe.**

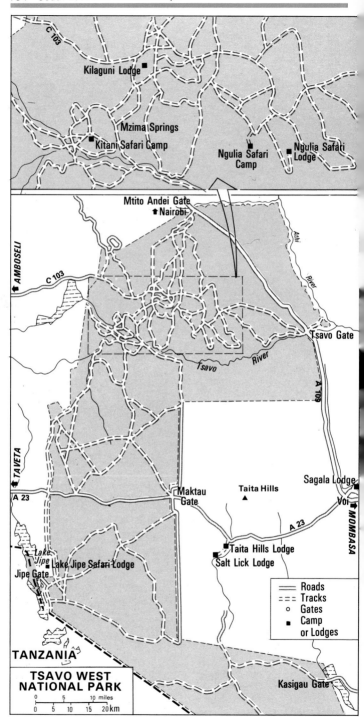

Kilaguni Lodge ■

Mzima Springs
■ Kitani Safari Camp

Ngulia Safari
Camp ■

Ngulia Safari
Lodge ■

Mtito Andei Gate
↑ Nairobi

← AMBOSELI

C 103

Athi River

Tsavo Gate

A 109

Tsavo River

← TAVETA

A 23

Maktau
Gate

Taita Hills
▲

Sagala Lodge ■

Vor

MOMBASA →

A 23

■ Taita Hills Lodge
■ Salt Lick Lodge

Lake
Jipe
■ Lake Jipe Safari Lodge

Jipe Gate

Roads
--- Tracks
○ Gates
■ Camp or Lodges

TANZANIA

**TSAVO WEST
NATIONAL PARK**

0   5   10 miles
0 5 10 15 20km

Kasigau Gate

Information

Chief Warden, Tsavo West, POB 66, Voi. ☎ 28 in Voi.

From Tsavo West to Tsavo East

The A23 crosses the beautiful Taita Hills and links Tsavo West via Maktau Gate to Tsavo East where it intersects the main Nairobi-Mombasa highway. The road more or less parallels the railway, which crosses the Tanzanian border at Taveta.

Turn right off the A23 for a stop at **Salt Lick** and **Taita Hills lodges.** While both are lovely, Salt Lick Lodge is farther from the road and has more wildlife.

Accommodation

▲▲▲▲ **Salt Lick Lodge,** reservations: Hilton International, POB 30624, Nairobi, ☎ 33 4000. 63 rooms. ① Filling station. Present your reservation voucher at Taita Hills Lodge on your way through. The cottages are separate from one another and built on stilts. A network of raised footbridges connect one with the other and to the lobby and restaurant. The pools and salt licks at the foot of the lodge attract many animals.

▲▲▲▲ **Taita Hills Lodge,** reservations: Hilton International, POB 30624, Nairobi, ☎ 33 4000. 58 double rooms with baths. ① ③ ④ Discotheque, tennis court, pool. Full board. Filling station. Less striking architecturally than Salt Lick Lodge.

TSAVO EAST NATIONAL PARK*

A monotonous, arid plateau extends over the entire park, which is divided into two parts by the Galana River. To visit the northern area, you must have permission and be accompanied by a professional guide who organized the expedition. The accessible area, covering about 1500 sq mi/4000 sq km between the Galana River on the north and the Voi River on the south, is one of open plains overgrown with dry scrub. The Voi is dry part of the year, but verdant thickets and palm groves thrive on its banks all year round.

The best period to visit Tsavo East is during the dry season, from December to March, when the springs draw a sizeable group of animals. Observation is easier at this time because of the diminished vegetation. You'll be able to watch some of Kenya's largest herds of elephant. Altogether, some 15,000 to 20,000 elephants roam the park. Their voracious appetites 330 lb/150 kg a day, have resulted in widespread destruction of shrubs and bushes.

Buffalo travel in herds of more than 200, accompanied by white oxpeckers and the occasional hyaena and jackal ready to attack the weak, young or sick. You might have to wait hours in this harsh landscape to catch sight of these giant herds; you'll be treated, though, to an unforgettable spectacle well worth the wait.

Count on two days for Tsavo East, including one day along the Galana River, which is the best watering area during the dry season. In the morning, groups of greater kudu mix with Defassa waterbuck and smaller antelope. Gerenuk too are common. The best area to see the remaining rhinoceros — their numbers continue to diminish — is in the less accessible eastern sector of the park.

The lion, the species that has most contributed to Tsavo's reputation, still inhabits the park, as do the cheetah, caracal, jackal and leopard. They are, however, particularly difficult to see; the visitor is more likely to encounter groups of hyena or wild dog crossing the road.

The Galana River is formed from the combined waters of the Tsavo River, which flows through Tsavo West, and the Athi River, which crosses the plains of Nairobi. At **Lugard's Falls,** the river cascades into a narrow gorge between multi-coloured rocks. Climbing is dangerous here. If you follow the river, you will, eventually reach Crocodile Point, a series of pools, not far from the park exit, where you may see crocodile.

Accommodation

▲▲▲▲ **Voi Safari Lodge,** reservations: POB 30471, Nairobi, ☎ 33 6858. 5 mi/8 km from the main entrance from Voi. 53 rooms. ① ④ Full board. Filling station. Animal observation. Outstanding location on a rocky bluff overlooking the plain.

▲▲▲ **Crocodile Tented Camp,** reservations: POB 500, Malindi, ☎ 20481. On the outskirts of the park, 3 mi/5 km from Sala Gate on the road to Malindi. 24 tents. ① ④ Luxury tents along the Sabaki (the name the Galana River takes as it flows to the coast).

▲▲ **Tsavo Inn,** reservations: Kilimanjaro Safari Club, POB 30139, Nairobi, ☎ 33 7510. On the outskirts of the park at Mtito Andei. 32 rooms. Half board. Frequented by groups.

▲▲ **Tsavo Safari Camp,** advance reservations necessary: Kilimanjaro Safari Club, POB 30139, Nairobi, ☎ 33 7510. ☎ 3899 in Mtito Andei. Coming from Nairobi, 16 mi/25 km from Mtito Andei. 30 tents. ① ④ Half board. Leave your car beside the Athi River and a boat will carry you across to the camp. Organizes expeditions to the northern sector of Tsavo East, accessible by permit only.

▲▲ **Aruba Lodge,** reservations: Let's Go Travel, POB 60342, Nairobi, ☎ 29 539. Inside the park 22 mi/35 km from Voi, the lodge is on the edge of a dam, which forms an artificial lake to which birds are attracted. 6 cottages. Small food shop nearby. Rental of bedding. Also accessible from Manyani, Sala and Buchunia entrances.

▲▲ **Bushwacker's Safari Camp** (also known as Musalani Camp), reservations: AA Travel, POB 14982, Nairobi, ☎ 337900. 16 mi/26 km from Kibwezi. 10 *bandas.* Bring your own bedding. No restaurant or shops.

▲▲ **Tsavo Game Ranch Safari Cottages,** reservations: Let's Go Travel, POB 60342, Nairobi, ☎ 29539; or POB 3, Voi, ☎ 2564. 9 mi/15 km from Voi on the road to Mombasa. 10 cottages. ① ④ A tranquil spot rarely used by tour groups.

Camping

At **Voi Gate** (lavatories and water), **Aruba Lodge** and **Buchuma Gate** (water) and **Bushwacker's Safari Camp** outside park.

Useful address

Chief Warden, Tsavo National Park, POB 66, Voi. ☎ 28 in Voi.

MOMBASA

95 mi/153 km south-east of Voi, 73 mi/118 km south of Malindi, 303 mi/487 km south-east of Nairobi.

Mombasa provides a relaxed and tropical alternative to the (relative) bustle of Nairobi. There are few high-rise buildings, and life moves at the pace of a small town. Although it is a major tourist destination, Mombasa is also Kenya's second largest city; it is a busy port and you will see as many sailors on the streets as tourists. In fact, most travelers to the coast don't stay long in Mombasa; the hotel facilities to the north and south are generally more complete, luxurious and 'international', and of course for sun-seekers the beaches are much more attractive.

Yet the island city of Mombasa, which is linked to the mainland by bridges and a ferry, deserves more than an after-

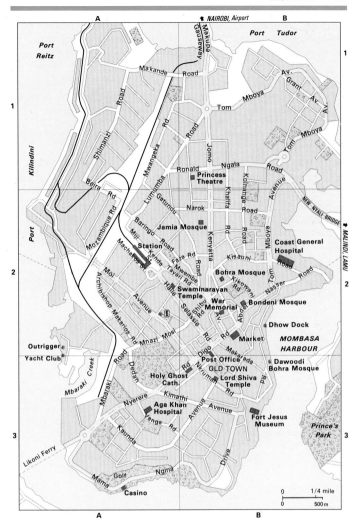

MOMBASA

noon excursion. The ethnic diversity of the town can be seen by the number of mosques (50) and temples (dozens). The Swahili, Asian and Arab communities reflect the long and varied history of what was, successively, a Portuguese stronghold, an Arab outpost and the capital of the British East Africa protectorate.

Mombasa in the past

Mention is made of Mombasa by 12th century chroniclers, as the capital of the King of the Zenj ('coastal people'). Vasco da Gama arrived in 1498, received a cool welcome and moved north up the coast to Malindi, where the inhabitants were markedly more friendly. The next foreign incursion took place in

1505 when the Portuguese, in an effort to limit Arab control over the Indian Ocean (and therefore over the spice trade), attacked the then-important port, staying no more than two days.

In their wake they left little of value, having murdered hundreds, plundered the city and burnt it to the ground.

The Portuguese returned regularly during the 16th century, and in 1593 confirmed their hold over Mombasa by beginning the construction of Fort Jesus. They managed to hold the fort until 1698, when they were beseiged and finally conquered by the Omani Arabs.

Although struggle for control over the small island territory continued, Oman's influence as a naval power in the region overpowered that of the Portuguese, and Mombasa remained an an outpost of the Arab rulers for two centuries.

By the 19th century, the British were well rooted in the area and were making strong efforts to limit the slave trading carried out on Africa's eastern coast. They were finally able to persuade the Omani ruler to cede the Kenyan coastal area to Britain and, in 1888, the British East Africa Protectorate was set up, with Mombasa as its capital. The British remained in Mombasa until independence in 1963.

▬▬ *PRACTICAL INFORMATION*

Map coordinates refer to the map p. 167.

When to go

High season lasts from December to March. April to July are also good months to visit Mombasa, despite the occasionally brief but heavy thunderstorms; prices are appreciably lower then. During the rainy season, though, the grass grows high and the muddy roads become less negotiable, often hindering excursions to nearby Tsavo National Parks and Shimba Hills.

Access

Boat

Boat services to Lamu via Malindi leave from Kilindini Harbour or from the Old Harbour. **Shipping Company of India,** Moi Ave., POB 82364, A2, ☎ 26336 or 26337, operates a monthly Mombasa-Bombay line.

Bus

The bus station is on Kenyatta Avenue near Digo Road, B2. Several bus companies provide services to Malindi, Garissa (with transfer at Garsen for Lamu) and Nairobi. The offices are on Mwembe Tayari Road, B2: **Coast Bus Services,** POB 82414, ☎ 20916; **Goldline,** POB 83542, ☎ 20027; and **Kenya Bus Services,** POB 90380, ☎ 24851.

Plane

Moi International Airport in Port Reitz is 9 mi/15 km north of Mombasa by Makupa Causeway. **Kenya Airways** operates a regular shuttle between the airport and Moi Avenue in the city centre, A2. You can also take a bus from the airport to Digo Road, B2, or a taxi. See 'Useful addresses' pp. 171-172, for a list of airline companies.

Train

The station is at the end of Haile Selassie Road, A2. Daily trains leave for Nairobi at 5 and 7pm, arriving in Nairobi at 8 and 8:30am the next day.

Accommodation

▲▲▲▲ **New Outrigger Hotel,** Ras Liwatoni, POB 8235, A2, ☎ 20822, tlx: 21368. 44 rooms. ① ④ Air conditioning. Boat rental. Deep-sea fishing. In its peaceful location, the New Outrigger is one of the island's best hotels. Excellent cuisine.

▲▲▲ **Manor Hotel B & B,** Nyerere Ave., POB 84851, A3, ☎ 31 4643. 70 rooms. ① Long the meeting place of British colonial officials, the Manor now caters to Kenyan business people.

▲▲▲ **Oceanic Hotel,** Kaunda Ave., POB 90371, A3, ☎ 31191/2. 132 rooms. ① ④ ⑤ Discotheque, golf. Some air-conditioned rooms. Magnificent view of the Kilindini port and the forest of baobab trees on the tip of the island. Free shuttle service to hotel's private beach 6 mi/10 km away. The hotel is well situated.

▲▲ **Castle Hotel,** Moi Ave., POB 84231, A2, ☎ 23403 or 21683, tlx: 22591. ① Bar, conference hall. Centrally located and air conditioned.

▲▲ **Hotel Hermes,** Msanifu Kombo St., POB 98419, B2, ☎ 31 3599. Near the centre. 19 rooms. Indian restaurant.

▲▲ **New Carlton Hotel B & B,** Moi Ave., POB 86779, A2, ☎ 23776. 23 rooms. ① Centrally located (opposite the Castle), with a lively, if unimaginative, restaurant.

▲▲ **New Palm Tree Hotel,** Nkrumah Rd., POB 90013, B3, ☎ 31 1756 or 31 2169. 30 rooms. Midway between the modern centre and the old sector of the city, this hotel offers quality, tranquility and cleanliness, at a reasonable price.

Food

You can enjoy excellent fish dishes and quality Indian cuisine in Mombasa.

Capri, Ambalal House, Nkrumah Rd., POB 90574, B3, ☎ 311156. Meat specialities, in an elegant atmosphere. E.

Fontanella, near Nyerere and Moi Aves., POB 82515, B3, ☎ 23756. Very popular café that serves meals all afternoon. R.

Galaxy, Archbishop Makarios Rd., POB 81692, A2, ☎ 311256. Chinese food. I.

Harlequin, in Nyali near the Tamarind restaurant (off map), POB 85378, ☎ 472373. Excellent French cuisine. E.

Hermes, Msanifu Kombo St., POB 98419, B2, ☎ 313599. In the hotel of the same name, near the centre. R.

Indo Africa Bar, Haile Selassie Rd., POB 82662, B2, ☎ 21430. Asian food. I.

Kutin, Moi Ave., POB 9970, A2, ☎ 314752. Vegetarian Indian food. I.

Libba's, Nyali Ratna Sq., POB 83167, ☎ 471138. Good Italian restaurant. R.

Nawab, Moi Ave., POB 83451, A2, ☎ 311302. Hearty servings; Asian cuisine. R.

New Outrigger, Ras Liwatone, POB 8235, A2, ☎ 20822. Located in the hotel, this French restaurant is undoubtedly one of the city's best. E.

Le Pichet, Marineland, Mtwapa Creek, POB 45, Kikambala (north of Mombasa), ☎ 485923 or 485865 (see p. 182). *Closed Mon.* French restaurant specializing in seafood. Boat rentals for the day, complete with picnic meal furnished by the restaurant. E.

Shahnai, Mungano St., near Moi Ave., A2, northern Indian cuisine; no alcoholic beverages. I.

Singh, Mwembe Tayari Rd., near Haile Selassi Rd., POB 83860, B2, ☎ 493283. Good Indian food, air conditioning. R.

Tamarind, in Nyali, POB 85785 (off map), ☎ 471747. Top-quality service in this seafood restaurant. The house speciality is lobster. Open daily. Reservations necessary. There is a great view of the Old Harbour. E.

Getting around

On foot
The distances are short, but don't underestimate the heat, which can make walking unbearable. Even in the cool season, daytime temperatures vary between 73° F/23° C and 90° F/32° C. Set aside at least a day to visit the downtown area.

By bus
Buses are practical for getting to the airport and traveling along the coast. In the city, you're better off taking a taxi or walking.

By taxi
The Mercedes taxis, as in Nairobi, belong to the Kenatco Transport Company; the yellow-banded independent taxis are easily recognizable. Don't forget to negotiate the price before starting off.

By car
For a complete tour of the island, rent a car, if only for half a day (see p. 172).

Organized Tours

Across Africa Tours, Moi Ave., POB 82139, A2, ☎ 314394 or 315360, telex: 21108.

African Tours & Hotels, New Carlton Hotel, POB 90604, ☎ 311022, regional ☎ 20627, telex: 21018.

Big Five Tours & Safaris, Nkrumah Rd., POB 86922, B3, ☎ 311426 or 20421.

Bunson Travel Service (Mombasa), Southern House, Moi Ave., POB 90291, A2, ☎ 311331.

Coast Car Hire & Tours Ltd., Ambalal House, Nkrumah Rd., POB 90789, B3, ☎ 311752 or 312532.

Flamingo Tours, Ambalal House, Nkrumah Rd., POB 83321, B3, ☎ 311591 or 311978/-9.

Nilestar Safari Centre, Ambalal House, Nkrumah Rd., POB 90090, B3, ☎ 315283 or 313226.

Rhino Safaris, Nkrumah Rd., POB 83050, B3, ☎ 311755 or 20194.

United Touring Co., Moi Ave., POB 84782, A2, ☎ 316333 or 313274. Desk at Moi International Airport, ☎ 433211.

Universal Safari Tours, Ambalal House, Nkrumah Rd., POB 99456, B3, ☎ 316576 or 314174.

Shopping

In Mombasa you can find a wide variety of merchandise in every price range: jewelry, fabrics, clothing, wood carvings, mats, sisal basketware, artefacts made from banana leaves, sandals, bags, belts, boxes, leather cases and more.

Majengo market*, off Kenyatta Avenue, B2, is a major shopping area that remains relatively unknown to tourists. There are food stands (try the freshly grilled cashews) and all sorts of wickerware. Avoid bringing your camera into this busy neighbourhood.

On **Biashara Street,** in the city centre, parallel to Kenyatta Avenue, B2, a series of shops sell Indian fabrics and clothing, including *kikois, kangas* and saris. The second-hand items are often more beautiful and more expensive than the new ones. Unfold the fabric to make sure that it is all in good condition.

The old harbour of Mombasa.

Noopy's Boutique, on Moi Avenue opposite Barclays Bank, A2, sells fabric to make saris and ready-made outfits complete with skirt, bolero and scarf.

Also on Moi Avenue are two antique shops worth stepping into: **Gallerie Ghalia,** next to Barclays Bank, A2, and **Labeka,** A2, for its furniture and attractive woodwork.

Tototo, on Haile Selassie Road, B2, is a good place to pick up inexpensive wickerwork, pottery, fabric (including batiks), soap-stone statuettes, and handcrafts made by the disabled. No bargaining.

Mombasa Housewares, on Digo Road, B2, sells antique copperware. You can pick up everything from a pepper grinder to a coconut grater and the shop offers a basket to all buyers.

Anils Arcade, on Biashara Street near Digo Road, B2, offers a wide variety of goods, including semi-precious stones.

In the old town, browse around the fish market on **Government Square,** B3. Opposite, in a charming old house, is **Lamu Gallery,** where you can buy combs, statues, fabrics and furniture.

Masha'Allah Gallery, on Government Square (to your right upon leaving Lamu Gallery), B3, specializes in carpets imported from the Middle East.

Ali's Curio Market, opposite Fort Jesus, B3, is a Yemenite antique shop in an old building that offers a wide variety of objects. You'll find a restaurant on the upper floor. Reasonable prices.

Prices at **Bahari Boutique** on Ndia Kuu Road, opposite Fort Jesus, B3, are also reasonable.

Stop at **Fontanella Gallery,** B3, in the heart of the modern city centre near the Castle and Manor hotels, for metal artwork and wood sculptures.

Useful addresses

Airlines
Air Kenya Aviation, Moi Ave., POB 84700, A2, ☎ 433320 or 433196. Two flights daily to Lassir.

Cooper Skybird, Moi International Airport, ☎ 433059. Flights to Kiwayu, Malindi, Lamu and Nairobi.

Kenya Airways, Savani House, POB 99302, B2, ☎ 21251; airport, ☎ 433211; flight information, ☎ 433400. An average of five flights daily between Nairobi and Mombasa, and one to Malindi.

Pioneer, ☎ 432355. Malindi, Lamu and Nairobi.

Sunbird Aviation, Moi International Airport, POB 84700, ☎ 433220. Two flights daily to Lamu.

Banks

They are open Monday to Friday 8:30am-12:30pm and the first and last Saturday of each month 8:30-11:30am.

American Express, c/o ETCO, Nkrumah Rd., POB·90631, B3, ☎ 312461.

Bank of Credit and Commerce, Ambalal House, Nkrumah Rd., POB 85349, B3, ☎ 25721 or 215875.

Barclays Bank, Nkrumah Rd., POB 90182, B3 ☎ 311660; Digo Rd., POB 90184, B2, ☎ 316045; and Moi Ave., POB 90183, A2, ☎ 26520 or 21136.

Commercial Bank of Africa, Moi Ave., POB 90681, A2, ☎ 24711 or 314860.

National Bank of Kenya, Nkrumah Rd., POB 90363, B3, ☎ 311736 or 311150; Moi International Airport, POB 90363, ☎ 433211.

Standard Bank, Treasury Sq., POB 90170, B3, ☎ 24611 or 314972.

Boat rental

Bahari Club, POB 90413, ☎ 471316, on the road to Kilifi and Malindi, after the Nyali Bridge on the left. Not only does the Bahari Club build its own boats and sell those of the major international manufacturers, but it also organizes fishing trips and rents boats and scuba equipment. Boats are rented with a crew for half or full days. You have to buy a temporary membership.

'K' Boat Services, Ras Liwatoni, near the Outrigger Hotel, POB 82345, A2, ☎ 20822. Be sure to make reservations 48 hours in advance. Prices are about the same as those of the Bahari Club.

Car rental

The same selection of models at similar prices are available at most agencies. For an extra fee, Avis and Hertz will allow you to drop off the car in Nairobi or Malindi. In Mombasa, unlike Nairobi, you can rent a beach vehicle such as an Austin Minimoke or a motorcycle.

Across Africa Safaris, Moi Ave., POB 82139, A2, ☎ 314395 or 315360.

Avis, Moi Ave., POB 84868, A2, ☎ 23048 or 20465.

Bellerive Tours, Moi Ave., POB 99031, A2, ☎ 20651.

Big Five Tours & Safaris, Nkrumah Rd., POB 86922, B3, ☎ 311426 or 20421.

Central Rent-a-Car, Moi Ave., POB 99753, A2, ☎ 20171 or 312070.

Coast Car Hire & Tours, Ambalal House, Nkrumah Rd., POB 90789, B3, ☎ 311752 or 312532.

Diani Car Hire & Tours, POB 17, Ukunda, Diani Beach, ☎ 2195.

Glory Car Hire, corner of Digo and Buxton Rds., POB 85527, B2, ☎ 21159 or 20265.

Hertz, Moi Ave., A2, ☎ 316333 or 316235; also at Moi International Airport, ☎ 433211.

Leisure Car Hire, Moi Ave., POB 84902, A2, ☎ 24704 or 314846.

Rhino Safaris, Nkrumah Rd., POB 83050, B3, ☎ 311755 or 20194.

United Touring Company, Moi Ave., POB 84782, A2, ☎ 316333 or 313274; also at Moi International Airport, ☎ 433211.

Consulates

Great Britain, Mr. J. Walters, E.A. Comfers Ltd., 7th floor, POB 90180, ☎ 25913.

United States, Palli House, Nyerere Ave., POB 88079, A3, ☎ 315101.

Garages

Cooper Motor Corporation, Archbishop Makarios Rd., POB 99200, A2, ☎ 314088. Leyland, Land Rover and Volkswagen.

Kenya Motor Corporation, Moi Ave., POB 80315, A2, ☎ 23071. Renault and Toyota.

Marshalls, Moi Ave., POB 90404, A2, ☎ 25093 or 25456. Peugeot.

Hospitals

The Mombasa General Hospital, POB 90294, B2, ☎ 312190 or 312099. State-owned hospital.

Aga Khan Hospital, Vanga Rd., POB 83013, A3, ☎ 312953. Private hospital.

Tourist information

Mombasa Information Bureau, Moi Ave., POB 99596, A2, ☎ 25428. *Open Mon-Sat 8am-noon and 2-4:30pm, closed Sun.* Friendly service and extensive information. You can telephone travel agencies free of charge.

GETTING TO KNOW MOMBASA

Map coordinates refer to the map p. 167.

The island is linked to the mainland by two bridges, a causeway and ferry service. Coming from Nairobi, cross the Makupa Causeway and drive straight on Kenyatta Avenue to Digo Road, B2. This is the heart of the city, the meeting place of its modern and old sectors and the focus of shopping activities. If one of your main interests is shopping, you'll be spending a lot of time in this area. From here you can stroll to the Mwembe Tayari market where spicy fragrances fill the air.

Hindu temple and the tusks B2

Head back to Kenyatta Avenue for a stop at the Shree Cutch Satsany Swaminaryan temple opposite Faza Road. The exotic atmosphere is at its height during the Indian New Year, when the temple is decorated with paintings, colourful floral bouquets and cakes in fantastic shapes.

Take Faza Road, which becomes Bajun Street, and then Aga Khan Road to Moi Avenue, A2. Here you'll see the city's landmark — a **sculpture** representing four gigantic elephant tusks forming two arches, one over each side of the avenue. Nearby is the tourist information office; almost all the travel and car rental agencies, banks, hotels, restaurants and shops are also found on Moi Avenue.

The Old Town*** B3

Bounded by Digo Road, the Old Harbour and Nkrumah Road, the area known as the Old Town is, in fact, no more than 100 years old. Nothing remains of the Arab-Swahili town that the Portuguese discovered in the 15th century. You needn't worry about losing your way in the labyrinth of narrow, winding streets; the sector is fairly compact and the sea marks its eastern edge. You can easily use the Old Town's major landmarks to get your bearings: **Jain Temple** near Digo Road; the **Hindu Temple** off Nkrumah Road opposite the Anglican Cathedral and next to the giant dome of the Baluchi Mosque; and the oldest monument in Mombasa, **Fort Jesus,** erected by the Portuguese in 1593. Be sure to keep a good hold on your handbag and camera equipment.

The Old Town has a specifically oriental character, testifying to the age-old links between the Arab and African cultures. Most of the inhabitants are of Indian descent. In the harbour, you'll see the familiar triangular sails and elegant forms of the dhows; even today they journey across the

Indian Ocean from Arabia, carried by the winds of January, and return in April. They transport spices that perfume the Old Town shops. The houses, too, reflect the mixture of cultural influences: here, Moorish-style, carved wooden latticework; there sculpted brightly painted balustrades.

A lively, often contradictory, charm permeates the Old Town. Wandering through its winding streets, you'll see murram alleys flanked by shanty houses; prosperous residences along paved sidewalks; and luxury cars driven by the wealthy. You'll hear hammering resound from the workshops of carpenters, wood-carvers and tinsmiths.

Fort Jesus** B3
Open daily 8:30am-6:30pm.

The stronghold was built in 1593 by the Portuguese João Batista Cairato on the coral bluff commanding the Old Harbour entrance. In 1698, after a siege lasting two-and-a-half years, Fort Jesus fell into Arab hands. During three full months of the siege, a mere 25 men and 50 women held out, awaiting reinforcements. The Portuguese recaptured the fort in 1728 only to lose it forever on Palm Sunday in 1729.

The fort continued to pass from hand to hand: to the various sultans of Oman, to rebellious governors, and then to the Sultan of Zanzibar. The British attacked it at the end of the 19th century. The stronghold remained unoccupied for some time, during the period when Mombasa was the colony's capital (with Treasury Square at the centre and the administrative district stretching to the fort).

It was converted into a prison and then was architecturally restored between 1958 and 1960, becoming the headquarters of the coast's Archaeological Studies Centre. Today it is a national monument and houses the **National Museum of Kenya,** which supervises the excavations along the coast (specifically Gedi and Jumba la Mtwana).

The museum is situated in the fort's east wing, facing the central courtyard. Its collection comprises Chinese, Arab and Persian ceramics from the 9th to the 18th century; 16th-century weapons and tools; ancient maps and a model of the fort.

After a visit to the museum, climb up to the San Mateus bastion for a view of the Old Harbour. From here it is easy to imagine the Portuguese soldiers awaiting the supply ships from India or resisting the Arab attack. Graffiti discovered from this period is displayed in a small hall.

Fort Joseph and the baobab forest   AB3
Leaving Fort Jesus, you can walk from Treasury Square to the residential Mbaraki district. In the midst of the villas surrounded by gardens stands the **Little Theatre,** Mnazi Moja Rd., POB 81143, ☎ 312101 or 25497, popular for evening shows. Continue toward the golf club to Mombasa's other Portuguese stronghold, **Fort Joseph,** now a ruin, situated on the edge of a sheer cliff overlooking the ocean. Then cross the forest of baobab trees extending to the Oceanic Hotel. Finally, you can follow Nyerere Avenue back to the city centre.

SOUTH OF MOMBASA

▬ LIKONI

The coastal resort towns south of Mombasa are more popular with Kenyans than the northern one because they are considered to be more beautiful and cleaner and their waters to contain more fish. Take the Likoni ferry from Mombasa (at the end of Nyerere Avenue in Kilindini Harbour, A3). After the village of Likoni, continue along the road to **Shelly Beach,** so called because its shores were once filled with shells. Keep in mind that collecting shells is prohibited; in any case, there are hardly any left.

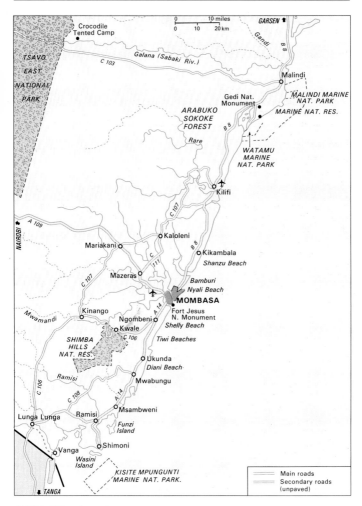

COASTAL AREA AROUND MOMBASA

Accommodation

▲▲▲ **Shelly Beach Hotel,** reservations: POB 96030, Mombasa, ☎ 451001. 101 rooms. ① ③ ④ Bar, discotheque, African show. Full board. In two low, pink-tile-roofed buildings. Daily bus service to Mombasa.

▲ **Savannah Cottages,** reservations: Moi Ave., POB 83644, Mombasa, ☎ 23456. 10 cottages with bathrooms and fully equipped kitchens.

▬▬ *SHIMBA HILLS NATIONAL RESERVE* ★★

24 mi/38 km south-west of Mombasa.

The road through Kwale is tarmac over 21 mi/33 km. Note that petrol is not always available at the filling station in Kwale (5 mi/8 km from the ranger post in the reserve). The entrance is at Kwale Gate. The reserve's road network is extensive, and clear signposts at the crossroads make touring the park very easy.

Shimba Hills was made into a national reserve to protect the superb sable antelope. It is the only place in Kenya where you can be virtually certain to catch sight of them. You will find that these antelope prefer the cover of the woods and can be difficult to photograph.

The sable antelope is large and dark in colour with stunning scimitar-shaped horns. A slightly plunging back, large and muscular chest, and a distinct mane give this species a majestic gait.

Since 1972, Shimba Hills has also been home to the roan antelope which is fawn-coloured and even larger than the sable antelope, though it is characterized by the same horns. The roan antelope, though, lives mostly in the open, and the two species rarely mingle.

Among the other interesting animals inhabiting Shimba Hills are the forest elephants. They differ from the savannah variety in that they are smaller, but tend to be more aggressive, with a rounder head and tusks that curve downward. The elephants often come close to the lodge.

The patches of woodland shelter colobus monkeys, two species of galagos and many duiker antelope. The serval, a large African spotted cat with fine ears, is common in the park. Birds include turaco, woodpeckers and many sunbirds.

Go to **Giriama Point** for a panoramic view of both the interior and the coast. The centre of the reserve, flanked by two escarpments, is covered mostly by woodlands. Open savannah studded with thornbush stretches to the south. You can see coastal beaches as far as Shimoni near the Tanzanian border, the rain forests in the foothills and Digo Plain from the coast to the interior.

Drive from Giriama Point to **Elephant Lookout,** leave your car and climb down the steep trail on your right to the valley. Cross a small river and hike up the other slope to reach **Shedrick Falls**. This is a lovely spot for a picnic.

Since there are no carnivores in Shimba Hills National Reserve (even though the word *shimba* means 'lion'), you can get out of your car and walk around anywhere. Be prudent, however, around the elephants and the antelopes, both of which can sometimes be aggressive.

Accommodation

▲▲▲ **Shimba Hills Lodge,** reservations through travel agencies; POB 83 in Kwale. 31 rooms. Only two with bathroom. Collective showers for the others. Situated in the midst of a forest, the lodge is linked by a trail through the woods to the belvedere above the water hole.

Camping

Possible in the park.

Useful address

Chief Warden, Shimba Hills National Park, POB 30, ☎ 36 in Kwale.

TIWI*

13 mi/21 km south of Mombasa.

Leaving Shimba Hills via Kwale, return to route A14 (10 mi/16 km) and turn right to Tiwi, a small town known for its beach.

Accommodation

There are no hotels in Tiwi, but it is possible to rent a cottage or bungalow on a weekly basis. These are relatively inexpensive but must be booked several weeks in advance.

▲▲ **Twiga Lodge,** ☎ 4061, reservations: POB 80820, Mombasa. ① Fully equipped cottages. Campsite and food shop.

▲ **Capricho Beach Cottages,** ☎ 3068, reservations: POB 96093, Mombasa. ④ 10 fully equipped cottages suitable for six people. Bring your own linen.

▲ **Tiwi Beach Bungalows,** reservations: POB 96008, Mombasa, ☎ 2Y7. 5 bungalows for 4 persons. A staff worker is available.

DIANI BEACH★★

6 mi/10 km south of Tiwi.

Between Tiwi and Diani Beach the road crosses a flat region shaded with palm trees. The houses here are rectangular, with a mangrove framework supporting clay walls that are reinforced with rock and coral. The palm roofs (known as *makuti*) extend over the verandahs as well.

Turn left off route A14 at the village of Ukunda to reach the coast road, which is bordered by hotels. The area is fantastic, overgrown with palm, baobab and eucalyptus trees and bushy, dwarf vegetation like rock blossoms.

The coral reef, furrowed with its small grottoes and organ pipes, stands in vivid contrast to the extraordinary whiteness of the sand. Protected by the reef, you can swim, water-ski or wind surf with no danger. Wear a pair of rubber sandals or tennis shoes to avoid cutting your feet on the sharp coral. At high tide, the undertow throws a layer of white foam to the surface. Low tide is a perfect time to comb the beach for fish and shells trapped in the crags.

Diani is also renowned for the giant baobab tree near the Trade Winds Hotel. Reputed to be more than five centuries old, it was designated a national monument by former president Jomo Kenyatta.

A path to the right of the Jadini Hotel leads into the forest. Today this is the only remaining patch of woodlands from the days when dense vegetation stretched all the way to the beach. Several trails lead through the woods to a pool: a fine spot for a picnic. Colobus monkeys and duiker antelope live here, as do numerous bird species, including the Schalow's turaco, with its lovely emerald-green plumage. Near the Two Fishes Hotel, a path leads to the snake park.

Accommodation

Almost all the hotels have rental facilities (scuba diving equipment, boats, surfboards, wind surfers) and organize ocean-fishing excursions. From north to south along the coastal road, you'll find the following hotels:

▲▲▲▲ **African Sea Lodge,** reservations: Alliance Hotels, POB 49839, Nairobi, ☎ 337501 or 20149. 152 rooms in bungalows. ① ④ ⑥ Discotheque. On the same grounds as the Jadini.

▲▲▲▲ **Diani Reef Hotel,** reservations: Sonotels Kenya Ltd., Wabera St., POB 61753, Nairobi, ☎ 2175 or 2062; POB 35, Ukunda, ☎ 2175 or 2062. 150 rooms. ① ③ ④ Bar, boutique, discotheque, centre for all water sports, beauty parlour. Car rental, safaris. Very luxurious.

▲▲▲▲ **Golden Beach Hotel,** POB 31, Ukunda, ☎ 2172 or 2066 in Diani Beach. 138 rooms. ① ③ ④ ⑥ Bar, discotheque. A big hotel with daily bus service to Mombasa.

▲▲▲▲ **Leisure Lodges,** reservations: POB 84383, Mombasa; ☎ 2011 in Diani. 140 rooms and 7 luxury apartments. ① ③ ④ Discotheque, full board.

▲▲▲▲ **Leisure Lodges,** reservations: POB 84383, Mombasa; ☎ 2011 in Diani. 95 luxury suites. ① ④ Located on the same grounds as the above.

▲▲▲ **Jadini Beach Hotel,** reservations: Alliance Hotels, POB 49839, Nairobi, ☎ 337501 or 20149. 160 rooms. ① ③ ④ Bar, discotheque, full board, parachuting, rental of glass-bottom boats.

▲▲▲ **Leopard Beach Hotel,** reservations: POB 34, Ukunda, ☎ 2111 in Diani. 161 rooms in bungalows with roofs of *makuti,* an indigenous plant used for thatching roofs. ① ③ ④ Discotheque.

▲▲▲ **Neptune Village,** reservations: POB 83125, Mombasa, ☎ 485701, ☎ 2350 in Diana Beach. 86 rooms in bungalows with roofs of *makuti.* ① ③ ④ Bar, boutique, discotheque. Fishing dhows available, car rental. Organizes safaris. Shows.

▲▲▲ **Nomad's Beach Bandas,** reservations: POB 1, Ukunda, ☎ 2155 in Diani. *Bandas* with shower and fan. Camping. ① Known for its seafood restaurant and relaxed welcome.

▲▲▲ **Ocean Village,** reservations: POB 88, Ukunda, ☎ 2188 or 2003. 36 bungalows with fully equipped kitchens and showers in a garden of bougainvilleas and frangipani. ① ③ ④ Food shop. Organizes safaris to Shimba Hills, Marine Park and Wasini Island. Tranquil setting and personalized service.

▲▲▲ **Robinson Baobab,** reservations: POB 84792, Mombasa, ☎ 2026 or 2030 in Diani. 150 rooms. ① ④ Bar, full board. Belongs to a German hotel chain. Recreational activities organized by staff.

▲▲▲ **Safari Beach Hotel,** reservations: Alliance Hotels, POB 49839, Nairobi, ☎ 337501 or 20149; ☎ 2726 or 2088 in Diani. 192 rooms in bungalows with roofs of *makuti* (indigenous plant). ① ④ ⑤ Air conditioned.

▲▲▲ **Trade Winds Hotel,** reservations: ATH, POB 30471, Nairobi, ☎ 336858; or POB 8, Ukunda, ☎ 2016 or 2116 in Diani. 103 rooms. ① ④ Discotheque, bar on terrace shaded by coconut trees, full board. Traditional Swahili architecture. Organizes safaris. Weekly African dancing show.

▲▲▲ **Two Fishes Hotel,** reservations: ATH, POB 30471, Nairobi, ☎ 21855. 117 rooms. ① ④ Full board.

▲▲ **Diani Beachalets,** reservations: POB 26, Ukunda, ☎ 2180 in Diani. 10 cottages without bedding.

Camping

Possible at **Jadini Beach, Leisure Lodge,** and **Trade Winds.**

Food

Ali Barbour's Restaurant, Diani Beach Rd., POB 53, Ukunda, ☎ 2033. Built inside a cave. Extremely expensive prices for average quality meals. European chamber music.

Vulcano, opposite Diani Beachalets. *Closed Sunday.* Very good.

▬ *MSAMBWENI*

32 mi/52 km south of Mombasa.
Take the A14 south to Msambweni. The route crosses a rich agricultural region. Amid the eucalyptus, baobab, palm and fig trees lie plantations where sugar cane, cashew nuts, mangos, bananas and coconuts grow.

Accommodation

▲▲▲ **Black Marlin Hotel,** reservations: POB 80, Msambweni, ☎ 90. 12 three-bedroom villas with kitchen and bathroom. 11 studios. 42 rooms. ① ③ ④ Boutique, beauty parlours, discotheque, conference hall. Fishing boats. Scuba diving school. Organizes excursions.

▬ *SHIMONI**

42 mi/67 km south of Mombasa, road forks to Shimoni (11 mi/17 km). This lovely village lies in the shade of coconut trees, baobabs and

bougainvilleas just opposite the coral reef that encircles Wasini Island. Shimoni is renowned for its caves, which were used as hideouts during attacks by the cannibal Galla tribe in the 16th century. The Arab slave traders used them in the 19th century despite the British interdiction on the trade; they brought their captives here and forced them to climb through the narrow caves to the foot of the cliff where boats to Arabia awaited.

Accommodation

▲▲ **Pemba Channel Fishing Club,** reservations: POB 44, Ukunda, ☎ 5Y2 in Msambweni. At the entrance to Shimoni. *Closed April through July.* This is the best base for ocean-fishing expeditions. Bungalow rental. Full board.

▲▲ **Shimoni Reef Lodge,** POB 82234, ☎ 471771 in Mombasa. 6 bungalows covered with *makuti* roofs, with sink, hot plate and grill. ① Two boats for ocean fishing and two glass-bottom boats. Scuba diving masks.

WASINI ISLAND★★

The Swahili population of the mainland found refuge on this island when they were threatened by Galla marauders and the Masai. During World War I, Shimoni residents brought their goats and cattle here for safekeeping, only to discover that they couldn't get them back after the war. The animals reproduced, and their offspring still run wild on the island although they are rarely visible.

A trail leads to the **Coral Garden** in the interior. This fantastic, open plain of succulent plants and corals resulted from the tides that have periodically flooded the area over the centuries.

KISITE MPUNGUNTI MARINE NATIONAL PARK

Many travel agencies and hotels in Mombasa, Diani and Shimoni organize tours of the marine park. The glass-bottom boat excursion typically includes a stop in Wasini, with a picnic lunch on the island and a visit to the marine park during low tide.

Food

Wasini Island Restaurant, POB 281, Ukunda, ☎ 2331. Excellent. Kisiti Show Tours stops here for lunch.

VANGA★

31 mi/50 km south-west of Shimoni.

You can get to Vanga from Shimoni on a fishing boat or by car. Police control the access and you might have to tip them in order to leave town.

This small old town was first occupied by the Portuguese, then by the Arabs and finally by the Sultan of Zanzibar. Today it is an important fishing centre and probably an even more important focal point for smuggling. The town becomes particularly animated at high tide, with the return of the fishing boats and the sale of the day's catch.

In the port you can watch the fishermen repairing their nets. In the cove, protected from the sea by mangroves and a sand bank, they build boats from mango tree trunks and they dry shellfish to use in the preparation of a condiment that is exported as far away as Japan.

Ocean-fishing excursions are possible from here.

NORTH OF MOMBASA

▬ NYALI**

Head north over the New Nyali Bridge from Mombasa to reach the luxurious and tranquil suburb of Nyali. Splendid residential homes are barely visible in the midst of the enormous gardens that surround them. A fine beach and elegant hotels serve the area, which is conveniently close to the city.

At the northern tip of Nyali, visit the **crocodile farm** of Mamba Village *(open daily 8am-6pm; animal feeding about 4pm)*. You can join one of the three- to seven-day expeditions on the Tana River organized by Mamba Village to capture the crocodiles. Information: **Mamba Village,** POB 85723, ☎ 47 2709.

Accommodation

▲▲▲▲ **Mombasa Beach Hotel,** reservations: ATH, POB 30471, Nairobi, ☎ 33 6858. 151 rooms. ① ④ ⑤ Bar, discotheque. Full board. The hotel is situated in a stunning park. Fishing, scuba diving.

▲▲▲▲ **Reef Hotel,** reservations: POB 82234, Mombasa, ☎ 47 1771. 108 rooms. ① ④ Discotheque, gym, sauna. Full board. Pizzeria. Opposite the beach, the hotel boasts an original architecture of pinnacled roofs.

▲▲▲ **Nyali Beach Hotel,** reservations: Block Hotels, POB 40075, Nairobi, ☎ 33 5807. 235 rooms. ① ④ Shop, discotheque. Full board. Filling station. A large, modern building, surrounded by gardens, near Nyali's 18-hole golf course. There are two cottages for rent in the garden, but they are rarely available.

▲▲▲ **Silver and Bahari Beach Hotel,** reservations: POB 81443, Mombasa, ☎ 48 5521. 105 rooms at Bahari and 99 at Silver. ① ③ ④ Bar, discotheque, air conditionning. Full board only. Car and boat rental. Two hotels side by side with a beautiful decor of *makuti* (indigenous plant) and coral.

▲▲▲ **Silver Star,** reservations: POB 81443, Mombasa, ☎ 48 5521. 123 rooms. ① ④ Bar, night club. Next to the Silver and Bahari hotels and offering the same level of comfort. Lovely *makuti* roofs.

▬ BAMBURI

Jomo Kenyatta Public Beach in Bamburi is signposted 6 mi/9 km north of Mombasa. Named after the former president who used to come here often, it is one of the few beaches along the northern coast that is easily accessible to the public. Elsewhere, private villas, hotels and private parks form a sort of barrier between the road and the ocean.

The beach is consequently crowded and it can be difficult to find parking. Be sure to keep a close eye on your belongings. Hotels line the beach near the **Kipepeo Aquarium**, where a variety of marine life is displayed in a dozen beautiful and well-maintained aquariums. Among the most fascinating is the mudskipper (periophthalmidae), so known because it skips about out of water and lies basking in the sun. These fish are capable of staying out of the sea for several hours.

Accommodation

▲▲▲▲ **Plaza Hotel,** reservations: POB 81269, Mombasa, ☎ 48 5001. 90 rooms. ① Scuba diving school, water skiing, surfing, boat excursions, mini golf course. The sports facilities are run in conjunction with the Severin Sea Lodge. The enormous concrete building with its rounded windows looks somewhat like a beehive.

▲▲▲▲ **Severin Sea Lodge,** reservations: POB 82169, Mombasa, tlx: 21228, ☎ 48 5001. 180 rooms and 15 bungalows. ① ③ ④ Discotheque. Full board. Frequented by group tours. Near the Sunline Tennis Center and a golf course.

▲▲▲▲ **Whitesands Hotel,** reservations: POB 90173, Mombasa, ☎ 48 5926; or POB 30680, Nairobi, ☎ 33 3233. 307 rooms. ① ③ ④ Discotheque. This hotel is constantly expanding its structure and modernizing its facilities.

▲▲▲ **Bamburi Beach Hotel,** reservations: POB 83966, Mombasa, ☎ 48 5611. 122 rooms. ① ④ Bar, discotheque, gym, 200-seat conference hall. Lively atmosphere in the restaurant for the Friday night 'sing along'. Good Chinese restaurant in the garden.

▲▲▲ **Kenya Beach Hotel,** reservations: POB 95748, Mombasa, ☎ 48 5821. 96 rooms. ① ④ Bar, discotheque, air conditioning. Full board. Dinner and dancing nightly. Striking two-floor octagonal buildings.

▲▲▲ **Ocean View Beach Hotel,** reservations: POB 81127, Mombasa, ☎ 48 5601. 103 rooms. ① ④ Discotheque, filling station. The cottages were recently renovated and enlarged.

▲▲▲ **Traveller's Beach Hotel,** reservations: POB 87649, Mombasa, ☎ 48 5121, tlx: 21422. 126 rooms. ① ③ Air conditioning, water sports, excellent Indian restaurant.

▲▲ **Sea Waves Beach Hotel,** reservations: POB 80940, Mombasa, ☎ 485492 or 485421. 25 rooms. ① Discotheque. Nice, friendly, family hotel.

Camping

Behind the **Sea Waves Hotel.**

Cottage rental

Cowrie Shell Apartments, reservations: POB 80674, Mombasa, ☎ 485971; or Jambo Hotels, POB 40224, Nairobi, ☎ 27828. Apartments for four people with a double bedroom, a living room, a kitchen and a bathroom. Entirely equipped, including bedding. Rental arrangements must be made long in advance.

Food

Fontana, POB 83999, ☎ 485934, on Malindi Rd., near Kenya Beach Hotel. Also hotel and night club. E.

Joli Coin, near Severin Sea Lodge. French chef preparing Seychelles cuisine. Friendly atmosphere. I.

SHANZU

Immediately after Bamburi is Shanzu Beach. Here the road begins to run somewhat farther from the ocean. The reef, too, is farther from the beach so that you can swim at low tide.

Accommodation

▲▲▲▲ **Intercontinental,** reservations: POB 83492, Mombasa, ☎ 485811, tlx: 21153. 192 rooms. ① ③ ④ Bars, health club, night club, casino, car rental, conference hall, shops, watersports activities. Luxurious rooms in three plain concrete buildings. Frequented by groups. Restaurant serves hearty meals.

▲▲▲▲ **Serena Beach Hotel,** reservations: POB 48690, Nairobi, ☎ 33 8656; or POB 90352, Mombasa, ☎ 485721, fax: 485453. 120 rooms. ① ④ Bars, beauty parlour, discotheque, scuba diving school, water skiing, African dancing shows. Tasteful Swahili-style architecture and decor. Organizes excursions.

▲▲▲ **Coral Beach Hotel,** reservations: POB 80443, Mombasa, ☎ 485408. 248 rooms. ① ③ ④ Discotheque. Full board. Same management as the Dolphin Hotel; encompasses the former Palm Beach Hotel. Situated atop the cliff in lovely shaded gardens with patios.

▲▲▲ **Dolphin Hotel,** reservations: POB 81443, Mombasa, ☎ 485801. 108 rooms. ① ④ Discotheque. Full board. In two-storey buildings on the slopes of the cliff.

▲▲ **Malaika Hotel,** POB 81443, Mombasa, ☎ 485101. 90 rooms. Full board. The hotel's architecture seems out of place in its surroundings. What's more, the Malaika offers few amenities compared to the other hotels in Shanzu.

▬ FROM SHANZU TO GEDI

North of Shanzu, the road crosses Mtwapa Creek. The calm of the inlet makes Mtwapa a perfect spot for all watersports and a meeting place for fishermen.

On the right immediately after the bridge is **Kenya Marineland and Snake Park.** Here you can observe two sharks, a skate and a dozen or so turtles belonging to three different species *(Chelonia mydas, Carretta carretta* and *Eretmochelys imbricata).* Also on view are snakes and crocodiles.

Unfortunately, they are kept in conditions that leave a lot to be desired; the crocodile pond is filled with muddy water in which there is hardly room to move. On the grounds of the park is a sculpture centre where you can buy Akamba and Makonde pieces at better prices than in Mombasa. Kenya Marineland also offers outings in traditional Arabian boats.

Fishing

MacConnell Company, reservations: POB 82849, Mombasa, ☎ 485230. Organizes ocean-fishing expeditions and scuba diving tours and rents scuba diving equipment.

Food

Le Pichet, POB 45, Kikambala, ☎ 485923 or 485865. *Closed Mon.* Reservations are necessary. The restaurant boasts a view of the creek and an agreeable atmosphere. Transport arrangements can be made through your hotel. E.

Jumba la Mtwana
Open daily 7am-6pm.

This national monument (1.5 mi/2.5 km after the Mtwana bridge on the route to Malindi), under the administrative supervision of the Fort Jesus archaeological department, has been partially explored by James Kirkman. It consists of two mosques, a tomb, and the ruins of a small group of houses. According to Kirkman, in the 13th century the Swahilis constructed the village some distance from the town of Mtwana so they could carry on the slave trade unhindered. It was mysteriously abandoned in the 14th century; the reasons remain unknown, though the Galla may very well have been a factor.

Kikambala

This is a superb 4 mi-/6 km- long sand beach. Unfortunately, the influx of seaweed makes swimming at low tide impossible.

Accommodation

▲▲▲ **Sun 'n Sand Beach Hotel,** reservations: POB 2, Kikambala, ☎ 8 or 55. 152 rooms in bungalows. ① ④ Bar, discotheque, video lounge. Full board. Native-style carved wood decor, with a giant chess board on the terrace floor.

▲▲▲ **Thousand Palms Beach Hotel,** reservations: POB 104, Kikambala, ☎ 110 or 111. 100 rooms in bungalows. ① ③ ④ Bar, ping-pong, horses, ponies and camels. Air conditioned. Swahili-style architecture. Live dance music evenings and private beach.

▲▲▲ **Whispering Palms Hotel,** reservations: ATH, POB 30471, Nairobi, ☎ 336858; or ATH, POB 90604, Mombasa, ☎ 23509. 96 rooms. ① ④ Bar, discotheque, archery. Organizes excursions.

▲ **Kanamai,** POB Kikambala, ☎ 46. Christian hotel providing reasonably priced beds in dormotories for young people.

Cottage rental

Kikambala Beach Cottages, reservations: POB 83344, Mombasa; ☎ 32 in Kikambala. 4 houses with 8, 5, 3 and 2 beds.

Youth hostel

Kanamai Youth Hostel, POB Kikambala, ☎ 46. Dormitory beds; camping on the grounds is also possible.

Kilifi

36 mi/58 km north of Mombasa.

As the road from Mombasa nears Kilifi, it runs through the largest sisal plantation on the coast; Kenya is the world's second sisal producer after Tanzania. You'll also see cashew groves and mango orchards. The road passes by **Takaungu,** a very traditional Moslem town, where fishing, not tourism, is the main industry. Among the other economic activities of the region are cattle raising (the quality of the milk is very high) and chicken ranching. Factories process cashews, sisal and palm oil.

Before taking the ferry across to Kilifi, you can visit a private collection of reptiles at **Reptile House** down to the left. Also on the Mombasa side of the creek lie the ruins of a cemetery and tombs of Mnarani. Ferries cross the Kilifi Creek almost around the clock. Construction of a bridge is now underway.

Accommodation

▲▲▲ **Mnarani Club Hotel,** POB 81443, Mombasa, ☎ 2318 Kilifi; reservations: ATH, POB 90604, Mombasa, ☎ 23509. 90 rooms. ① ④ Discotheque, scuba diving, boat rental, water skiing. Filling station, airstrip. Situated in a superb site at the mouth of the creek, this hotel belongs to a German chain. Reservations must be made in advance.

▬ GEDI NATIONAL PARK

63 mi/102 km north of Mombasa and 10 mi/16 km south-west of Malindi.

By car, the park is just off the main road from Malindi, a few miles from Watamu. You can also reach the park by bus from Malindi and Mombasa (twice daily). Bring a lunch since there is no restaurant. You needn't go on an organized tour: an excellent guidebook is sold at the entrance.

All that remains of the houses, mosques and a palace are their foundations. The site stretches over a large area where dense tropical vegetation flourishes and there is a delightful abundance of butterflies. The ruins are linked by trails. James Kirkman began excavations here in 1948; he believes that Gedi was founded in the 13th century by people from Malindi and was known as Kilimani, a name that appears on 17th-century maps of the area.

The town prospered until it was destroyed in the 17th century by Galla nomads from Somalia. It is thought that the name Gedi was given by the Galla and that it might be the name of the Galla chief responsible for the town's destruction.

Most of the ruins are found in an area of about 200 yd/m on each side. A tomb dating from 1399 is situated at the entrance. To the right are the main buildings — the grand mosque, the palace and homes of the elite. Many questions remain unanswered. Why is the town located so far inland when its prosperity was based on maritime trade? Is it possible that a natural phenomenon, perhaps a gradual silting of the coast, was responsible for the abandonment and ruin of the town? Finally, was Gedi founded at the end of the 14th century, as the date on the tomb suggests, or much earlier with the known advent of East African commerce in the Indian Ocean?

In the surrounding forest are the black-faced vervet monkey, colobus monkey, galagos, various rodents (including the elusive yellow-rumped elephant shrew), numerous bats, and the rare Zanzibar duiker antelopes, with their small horns. Bird enthusiasts will appreciate the population of swallows, martins and turacos.

Accommodation

Camping
Inquire at the park entrance.

WATAMU MARINE NATIONAL PARK

10 mi/16 km south of Malindi.

North of Gedi, the road continues to the ocean and the bay of Mida Creek.

Watamu Marine National Park extends over an area of 4 sq mi/10 sq km, which includes the bay and all the coastal waters between the beach and the coral reef. It is forbidden to fish, hunt, gather or even move any thing in the park (animal, plant or shell). A fee is required for boat excursions.

Beyond the reef is the **Marine National Reserve,** which stretches over 82 sq mi/213 sq km. The same rules apply here, but you can scuba dive free of charge. November to the end of April is the high season for scuba diving: the water is the clearest and the sea life the most abundant.

Accommodation

▲▲▲ **Hemingways,** reservations: POB 182, Watamu, ☎ 32006 or 32052. 59 rooms. ① ④ Glass-bottom boat rental. *Makuti*-roofed bungalows.

▲▲▲ **Ocean Sports,** reservations: Watamu, POB 340, in Malindi, ☎ 32008. 25 cottages. ① ④ Discotheque, car and boat rental. This is the oldest hotel in the region, with extensive sporting facilities. Jokingly referred to as 'open shorts' by local inhabitants because of its friendly, casual atmosphere.

▲▲▲ **Turtle Bay,** reservations: POB 457, Malindi, ☎ 32003 or 32080. 126 rooms. ① ④ Bar, boutique, discotheque, car and boat rental. Classical architecture in lovely gardens.

▲▲▲ **Watamu Beach Hotel,** ☎ 32001 or 32010; reservations: POB 81443, Mombasa, ☎ 471603; or Nairobi, ☎ 25228. 139 rooms in bungalows. ① ③ ④ Discotheque, car, horse and boat rental. Safaris. Mostly German clientele.

▲▲ **Watamu Blue Bay,** POB 163, ☎ 32095. 45 rooms in bungalows. ① ④ Bar. Fans. Mostly Italian clientele.

FROM WATAMU TO MALINDI

Sokoke Forest

Don't leave the fork that goes from route A14 to Gedi and Watamu without passing through Sokoke Forest. Head back slightly in the direction of Kilifi and you'll see a small, somewhat overgrown road leading into a forest. There are three species of birds that you can spot here and nowhere else in the country: the owl, the pipit and a special weaver. In October and in March several small wading bird species migrate here.

Sokoke Forest, along with Mida Creek, is reputed by ornithologists to be one of the best places in Kenya for bird watching.

Accommodation

All along the coast from Turtle Bay to Silversands Beach you'll find new hotels run by Italians. The hotels combine extreme refinement with Swahili-style architecture that blends perfectly into the surroundings.

▲▲▲▲ **African Dream**, reservations: POB 939, Malindi, ☎ 20119. 65 rooms. ① Air conditioned. Luxurious and comfortable hotel. Italian cooking.

▲▲▲ **Coconut Village**, reservations: POB 868, Malindi, ☎ 20923. 35 rooms. ① ⑤ Fans or air conditioning. A large Italian buffet. A nice location, and private club style.

▲▲▲ **The Driftwood Beach Club**, reservations: POB 63, Malindi, ☎ 20155. 27 bungalows and cottages. ① ③ ④ ⑤ Discotheque, Squash court, scuba diving centre. The Driftwood rarely accepts groups and is often fully booked. The management is British.

▲▲▲ **Kivulini Village Beach Hotel,** reservations: POB 142, Malindi, ☎ 20898. 36 rooms. ① ④ Discotheque, library. Excellent Italian cuisine. Situated atop a coral cliff in which small steps have been carved. Excursions.

▲▲▲ **Tropical Village**, reservations: POB 68, Malindi, ☎ 20256 or 20711. 56 rooms. ① ④ Opposite the Malindi Marine Park. Excursions. Extensive sports facilities.

▲▲ **Scorpio Villas**, advance reservations necessary: POB 368, Malindi, ☎ 20194. 16 one-, two- or three-bedroom villas with kitchens and sitting rooms. ④ ⑤

▲▲ **White Elephant Sea Lodge**, reservations: POB 553, Malindi, ☎ 20528. 34 rooms. ① ④ Air conditioned. Breakfast hall 'in the trees'. Calm and relaxed atmosphere.

▬▬ *MALINDI*

74 mi/119 km north of Mombasa, 10 mi/16 km north of the Gedi-Watamu intersection.
Malindi is a pleasant picturesque town. The older part has a distinctly Arabic feel to it, with narrow streets full of children and cats. Among the reminders of the town's ancient history are a house with a wooden balcony dating from the Portuguese era and a memorial to Vasco da Gama's arrival in 1499.

Vasco da Gamma Pillar

Take the road toward Silversands past the fish market and you will see a turn-off left of the monument. The pillar is situated on a cliff at the edge of the cape separating Malindi Bay from Silversands Beach. You'll have good views from the point.

Malindi Marine Park

Continue to Casuarina Point, where you won't want to miss a trip to the marine park. It can be reached by glass-bottom boat (15-minute trip). Snorkeling is a great way to admire the infinite variety of marine life; the colours of the fish and coral stand out brilliantly against the neutral background of the ocean floor.

Snake Park

This is located on Casuarina Point and includes some 50 species of reptile, all captured in the region. The Sieben Rock turtle with its flat, soft shell, is one of the principal attractions, though it is often hidden from view. The privately owned collection is wonderfully displayed and is undoubtedly the most interesting of its kind in Kenya.

Accommodation

In town

▲▲▲ **Eden Roc Hotel,** on the beachfront of Malindi Bay, Lamu Rd., POB 350, Malindi, ☎ 20480. 150 rooms. ① ③ ④ Discotheque, casino, scuba diving, car and boat rental. Full board.

▲▲▲ **Lawford's Hotel,** POB 20, ☎ 20440; or reservations: POB 40224, Nairobi, ☎ 27828. 140 rooms. ① ④ On the beachfront along the bay near the city centre with discotheques, full board, air conditioning. Relaxed atmosphere. Car and boat rental.

▲▲ **Bougain Village,** POB 360, Malindi, ☎ 20317. Situated far from the ocean, near the outskirts of town past the shopping centre and the Again store. 60 rooms. ① ④ ⑤ Bar, boutique. Organizes excursions.

▲▲ **Malindi Chalets,** managed by Jambo Hotels, POB 20, ☎ 20440; or reservations: POB 40224, Nairobi, ☎ 27828. ④ ⑤ Close to the city centre and the ocean. 12 cottages with two double bedrooms, kitchen and bathroom.

▲▲ **New Kenya Hotel,** Jamhuri Street, POB 198, ☎ 20657. Situated in the city centre. Reasonably priced.

Outside town

▲▲ **Club Che-Shale,** POB 492, Malindi, ☎ 20063; or reservations: Nairobi Booking office, New Stanley House, POB 47557, Nairobi, ☎ 331635. 15 mi/25 km north of Malindi on the road to Garsen. 20 *bandas* with two beds and a shower. Accessible only by four-wheel-drive vehicle. Arrangements can be made to be picked up in Malindi.

▲▲ **Palm Tree Club,** POB 180, Malindi, ☎ 20397. Near the golf course. 16 rooms. ① ④ Air conditioned. The swimming pool is in the style of an ancient Roman *impluvium*. Comfortable.

Food

Lamberti's, POB 543, ☎ 20127. African cuisine amid handsome gardens with enormous rubber trees. R.

Lady Cheeta, POB 180, ☎ 20577. High quality Italian cuisine. Near the Palm Tree Club. R.

Stardust, Lamu Rd., POB 350, ☎ 20388. Dinner and dancing until 4am. On the outskirts of Malindi past the shopping centre. E.

Shopping

You won't lack for souvenir shops and clothing boutiques when you stroll along the main streets. You might stop in at Again, POB 449, ☎ 20094, owned by a French decorator, where you can find safari clothes, jewelry, furniture, sculptures and silverwork. Most of the large hotels also have boutiques selling beachwear and curios.

Don't miss the fish market on the southern edge of town.

▬▬ *LAMU*

Despite the obvious decline of this once prosperous little town, Lamu retains a refined atmosphere: beautiful doorways framed in carved wood and the civilized manners of the inhabitants testify to its rich history. It's easy to fall in love with this town after a simple walk through the labyrinth of narrow streets or along the waterfront. In the evening, when the fleet of dhows returns to the port from a day's fishing or trips to other islands, the waterfront becomes a hub of activity.

Lamu seems to be a world apart from the other coastal towns. The fact that no cars are allowed on the island contributes to its special charm. What's more, tourism is not the driving force that is has become elsewhere. There are no discotheques, nightclubs or sports centres. Neither is there a beach; if you'd like a swim, you're in for a good long walk, or you'll need to take a boat — a delightful and rewarding option.

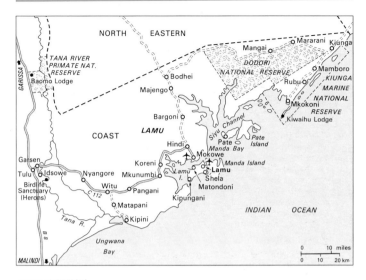

LAMU AND ENVIRONS

The old houses of stucco and carved wood are being renovated. For a look at the architecture, contact Mohamed Lami (see 'Accommodation') or go to the museum, which is housed in a renovated building on the north side of town. Besides period furniture, costumes and jewelry, the museum features an exhibit on the people of the south-east. The museum library contains a copy of J. de V. Allen's *History of Lamu*.

Access

By bus

A bus leaves for Malindi (8-hour trip) and Mombasa early Mondays, Wednesdays and Saturdays. Departures are from the Tawakal office on the waterfront at the dhow port. The bus trip can be particularly tiring and requires a transfer in Garsen (69 mi/111 km north of Malindi).

One of the lovely beaches south-east of Lamu.

By plane

Daily flights link Lamu to Malindi, Mombasa and Nairobi. For information contact: **Sunbird Aviation,** POB 84700, Mombasa, ☎ 433220; **Cooper Skybird,** ☎ 21443, Mombasa, and 3055, Lamu (the office is on the waterfront, next to the museum); **Pioneer Airways,** ☎ 3055, Lamu (the office is on the waterfront, next to the museum); **Equator,** ☎ 3139, Lamu (on the waterfront, next to Petley's Inn). When you arrive by plane, you can easily see the three islands of Lamu, Manda and Pate. You land on Manda Island, and a boat takes you across to Lamu.

By car

A four-wheel-drive vehicle is recommended if you're driving from Malindi. About 2.5 mi/4 km north of Malindi, the main road is no longer tarmac. The ferry service across the Tana River at Garsen (69 mi/111 km north of Malindi) operates from 6am to 6pm. Lock your car doors for the crossing. Driving is prohibited in Lamu, but you can leave your car at the Mokowe parking lot.

Accommodation

▲▲ **Petley's Inn,** POB 4, ☎ 3048; reservations: POB 46582, Nairobi, ☎ 29612. Near the museum, in a 19th-century building on the waterfront. 15 rooms. ① ④ Full board. See 'Food' below for Petley's Inn Garden.

▲ **Full Moon,** above the Papawia restaurant, 1 block north of the Customs offices. 11 rooms. Communal sanitary facilities. Inexpensive.

▲ **New Mahrus Hotel,** Harambee Rd., POB 25, ☎ 3001. 20 rooms. ① The rooms overlook an enormous central stairway. There's a lovely view over the ocean from the restaurant.

For a modest sum you can sleep in a rooftop dormitory at the Castle Lodge, Kiswani Lodge and Dhow Lodging (near the post office).

In Shela

▲▲▲ **Peponi Hotel,** advance reservations necessary: POB 24, ☎ 3029 or 3154. 18 comfortable rooms overlooking the ocean. ① Boutique, patio. A much-sought-after hotel among individual travelers.

Food

Equator, Kenyatta Rd., POB 83, ☎ 3272. Situated in the southern part of town on the waterfront. This British-owned restaurant provides average food in a pretty setting against a background of music from the 1930s. Expect a long wait. E.

New Mahrus, Harambee Rd. Decent cooking, nicely served in a waterfront setting that is particularly attractive at night. R.

New Star, Harambee Rd. A lively restaurant with rock-bottom prices, though its cleanliness is problematic. You can eat curried rice for a few shillings. Especially crowded when the boats come in; singing and guitar playing. I.

Papawia, near Petley's. Unpretentious fare at modest prices with a terrace overlooking the harbour. R.

Petley's Inn Garden, POB 4, ☎ 3107. Bar, tea house and restaurant. High-quality service, excellent food. E.

Yogurt Inn, Harambee Rd., toward the north. Popular café that serves yogurt and *muesli.* I.

Shopping

On **Harambee Road** you'll find many *kikoi* shops open late at night that sell these colourful fabrics that can be used as wrap-around skirts, scarves or wall hangings.

Handcrafted furniture can be found along Harambee Road and at the edge of the waterfront.

ENVIRONS OF LAMU

Take a walk to visit the *shambas* around the country homes of some of Lamu's residents. Here you'll see cattle, goats, sheep and grey donkeys. To avoid the unbearable heat, get an early start.

South-east of Lamu (1.2 mi/2 km) is the village of Shela. You can walk from Lamu town at low tide or reach the village by boat at high tide. A vast beach is bordered by giant dunes; unfortunately there is absolutely no shelter from the burning afternoon sun.

Many of the renovated villas here belong to English people. At Kipungani and Matandoni, the activity at the ship yards has slowed down, but you can still watch the construction or repair of dhows.

Manda Island

After a crossing in a dhow, you arrive on the island at high tide through a narrow channel amid mangroves.

Takwa, the ruins of a 16th-century town is now buried deep in the sand; only a pillared tomb remains visible. The town's inhabitants left it to settle in Shela on Lamu island. Thousands of crabs frequent the shores of this otherwise deserted beach.

Accommodation

▲▲ **Ras Kitau Beach Hotel,** advance reservation necessary: in POB 9, Lamu, ☎ 3206. 18 rooms. ① Fine dining, pleasant, shaded beach, scuba diving. Organizes excursions. Closed April 30-June 15.

▲ **Blue Safari Club,** reservations: POB 41759, Nairobi, ☎ 338838. 10 rooms in huts. Sailboats, motorboats and scuba diving equipment. Italian management.

Dodori National Reserve

Elephants and many kinds of migratory bird can be seen in this park, but because of a lack of facilities and relative inaccessibility, the reserve is rarely visited.

Accommodation

▲ **Kiwayu Safari Village,** reservations: POB 48287, Nairobi, ☎ 331231. 10 cottages accessible by plane or in a four-wheel-drive. Fishing, boat trips, waterskiing, scuba diving, surfing. Full board rates include sports, except for ocean fishing and scuba diving.

BEYOND LAMU

From Lamu, a murram road leads to Garissa (174 mi/280 km north-west of Lamu, 236 mi/380 km east of Nairobi), a town of little interest. To interrupt the monotony of the drive, you can stop at **Witu forest** for some bird watching. Another road heads to Garsen from Lamu. By far the best way to visit the region between Garsen and the sea is to travel up the Tana River on the *African Queen*. This is a four-day safari; you're picked up in Malindi and driven to a small Pokomo village along the river just south of Garsen, from where the boat cruises to the tented camp on the delta. You'll see crocodiles and hippopotamuses along the banks. For information: **Tana River Ltd.**, POB 24988, Nairobi, ☎ 882826.

GARSEN

Garsen is a junction town (68 mi/110 km west of Lamu), with a marketplace and an intermittent supply of petrol.

Along the B8, 31 mi/50 km north of Garsen, you'll find the **Tana River Primate National Reserve**, known locally as 'Mchelelo'. The forest is home to numerous primates, including the red colobus monkey and the

Tana mangabey. Both are rare species indigenous to the Tana River woodlands and endangered by the deforestation of the region. You will also see buffalo, topi, and a large variety of birds. There is no place to stay over in the reserve.

Useful address

Chief Warden, POB 58, Garissa, ☎ 57.

ARAWALE RESERVE

87 mi/140 km north of Lamu, turn right toward the village of Bura on the eastern shore of the Tana.

The reserve was created essentially to protect the Hunter's hartebeest (or hirola). This local species, a relative of the other hartebeests, is becoming increasingly rare. It is thought to number no more than 2000. Among the other interesting species here are the oribi, a small antelope with large, round ears and short, thin horns, and the topi, one of East Africa's most common antelopes. There is no accommodation, although camping is possible.

Useful address

Warden, Arawale Reserve, POB 58, Garissa, ☎ 10.

GARISSA

The marketplace is frequented by Somali nomads and Pokomo farmers who come here to sell the rice and sugar cane that they grow along the banks of the Tana River.

Petrol, water and supplies are available. Two roads run parallel to the Tana. The western one leads north to Kora Wells and the Rahole National Reserve. The eastern road goes to Meru and Kora National Reserve. George Adamson introduced the lions he had nurtured into Kora National Reserve, and Joy Adamson did the same in Meru National Park.

BACK TO NAIROBI

From Garissa to Nairobi, you'll take the murram road through a fairly monotonous region passing through the villages of Kakunika, Mwingi and Thika (see p. 157).

▬ USEFUL VOCABULARY

A note on Swahili

Swahili is basically a Bantu language coloured by borrowings from Arabic and to a lesser extent from Portuguese, Asian tongues and English. It is East Africa's *lingua franca,* believed to be spoken in its purest form by the Zanzibaris. In Kenya it is part of the national school curriculum and is spoken in varying degrees of excellence depending on where in the country it is used. For the coastal Swahili people it is their mother tongue. For other Kenyans living inland it is often a second or third language and is therefore spoken with less attention to grammar then the coastal residents. This Swahili is known as "kitchen" or "upcountry" Swahili.

Swahili has a pleasing emphatic intonation; once you've mastered a few basic rules it is relatively easy to pronounce. With the exception of some Arabic words, stress is invariably on the penultimate syllable. Every syllable is voiced. Here are some guidelines:

Vowels
A like the 'a' in far
AU like the 'ow' in cow
E as in 'end' or the 'ai' in train
I like the 'ee' in feet
O as in on
U like the 'oo' in boot

Consonants
B as in begin, though sometimes pronounced 'p'
CH as in change, sometimes sounds like a 't' (C does not stand alone)
D as in do, sometimes 't' or 'j'
DH like the 'th' in them, or 'dh' in dharma
F as in fill
G as in go
H as in hello
J as in jam
K as in kind
L as in lung, sometimes pronounced 'r'
M as in might. When **M** comes directly before other consonants (**mb**ali, 'far'; **m**chele, 'rice'; **m**vua, 'rain'; **mz**ee, 'an elder') don't precede it by any vowel sound like 'eh' or 'uh' or 'oo', just the 'mmmm' sound on its own is sufficient.
N as in note. **N** is sometimes pronounced like a semi-vowel, 'in', when it precedes monosyllabic nouns like nne, 'four'. On other occasions as in **nd**imu, 'a lime' or **ng**uvu, 'strength', just give an 'nn' sound without preceding it with any vowel. **NY** is pronounced like the 'ni' in companion.
P as in pin
Q is never used
R as in ring, often rolled; sometimes pronounced 'l'
S as in sit
SH as in show
T as in tonic
TH as in think
V as in vision
W as in will
X is never used
Y as in yes
Z as in zebra

Common words and phrases

Hello	*Jambo*
How are you?	*Habari yako?*
Well, fine	*Mzuri*
Very well	*Mzuri sana*
Thank you (very much)	*Asante (sana)*
(The word for please, *tafadhali*, is rarely used, usually only by tourists)	
Good morning	*Habari ya asubuhi*
Good evening	*Habari ya jioni*
Welcome, come in	*Karibu*
Goodbye	*Kwaheri*
See you	*Tutaonana*
Yes	*Ndiyo*
No	*Hapana*
Good	*Mzuri*
Bad	*Mbaya*
I like . . . very much	*Napenda . . . sana*
I'd like	*Nataka*
Sorry	*Samahani/pole*
I don't understand	*Sifahamu/Sielewi*
I don't know	*Sijui*
I don't speak Swahili	*Sesema kiswahili*
Do you speak English?	*Unasema kingereza?*
Where do you come from?	*Unatoka wapi?*
I'm British/American	*Mimi Mwingereza/Mwamerica*
What's your name?	*Jina lako nani?*
My name is	*Jina lango ni*
Friend	*Rafiki*
Mister	*Bwana*
Madam	*Mama*
Mrs	*Bibi*
A person/people	*Mtu/Watu*
Man/Men	*Mwanaume/Wanaume*
Woman/Women	*Mwanamke/Wanawake*
Boy/Boys	*Kijana/Vijana*
Girl/Girls	*Msichana/Wasichana*
Child/Children	*Toto/Watoto*
Me/I	*Mimi/Ni*
You	*Wewe*
He/She	*Yeye*
Us/We	*Sisi/Tu*
You (plural)	*Ninyi*
Them/They	*Wao/Wa*
What?	*Nini?*
When?	*Lini?*
Where?	*Wapi?*
Which?	*Gani?*
Who?	*Nani?*
Why?	*Kwa nini?*
Because	*Sababu*
But	*Lakini*
Fine, Ok	*Sawa*
Here/There	*Hapa/Huko*
And	*Na*
Or	*Au*
Together	*Pamoja*
Perhaps	*Labda*
Just a minute	*Ngoja kidogo*
No problem	*Hakuna matata*
Quick	*Upesi*
Slow	*Pole pole*

Up	*Juu*
Down	*Chini*
Old	*Mzee*
Young	*Kijana*
New	*Mpya*
Where's the lavatory?	*Wapi choo?*
Ladies	*Wanawake*
Gents	*Wanaume*

Numbers

Half	*Nusu*
One	*Moja*
Two	*Mbili*
Three	*Tatu*
Four	*Nne*
Five	*Tano*
Six	*Sita*
Seven	*Saba*
Eight	*Nane*
Nine	*Tisa*
Ten	*Kumi*
Eleven	*Kumi na moja*
Twelve	*Kumi na mbili*
Thirteen	*Kumi na tatu*
Twenty	*Ishirini*
Twenty-one	*Ishirini na moja*
Thirty	*Thelathini*
Forty	*Arobaini*
Fifty	*Hamsini*
Sixty	*Sitini*
Seventy	*Sabini*
Eighty	*Themanini*
Ninety	*Tisini*
One hundred	*Mia (moja)*
One hundred and one	*Mia moja na moja*
Two hundred	*Mia mbili*
Three hundred	*Mia tatu*
One thousand	*Elfu (moja)*

Time

Time in Swahili is told in two 12-hour cycles, sunrise to sunset and sunset to sunrise (6am-6pm and 6pm-6am). This means that when it is 4pm, you interpret the time as 10 hours after sunrise, and so you say 'Saa kumi' (ten o'clock). All you do is look at your watch and read the number opposite your time on the face; in other words, 12 is 6, 1 is 7, 2 is 8, 3 is 9, 4 is 10 and so on. To avoid confusion you can add *ya asubuhi* ('of the morning') or *ya jioni* ('of the evening').

What time is it?	*Saa ngapi?*
One o'clock	*Saa saba*
Two o'clock	*Saa nane*
6 o'clock	*Saa kumi na mbili*
8 o'clock	*Saa mbili*
Noon	*Adhuhuri/Saa sita*
Midnight	*Usiku wa manane/Saa sita*
Quarter past	*Na robo*
Half past	*Na nusu*
Quarter to	*Kasi robo*
Minutes	*Dakika*
Hour	*Saa*
Half an hour	*Nusu saa*
Now	*Sasa*

Immediately	*Sasa hivi*
Early	*Mepema*
Late	*Kuchulewa*
Day	*Siku*
Night	*Usiku*
Morning	*Asubuhi*
Afternoon	*Alasiri*
Evening	*Jioni*
Week	*Wiki*
Month	*Mwezi*
Year	*Mwaka*
Yesterday	*Jana*
Today	*Leo*
Tomorrow	*Kesho*
Sunday	*Jumapili*
Monday	*Jumatatu*
Tuesday	*Jumanne*
Wednesday	*Jumatano*
Thursday	*Alhamisi*
Friday	*Ijumaa*
Saturday	*Jumamosi*

Shopping

To buy	*Kununua*
To sell	*Kuuza*
What time does . . . open/close?	*Saa ngapi inafunguliwa/inafungwa . . .?*
Shop	*Duka*
Bank	*Benki*
Post Office	*Posta*
Letter/Parcel/Stamps	*Barua/Bahasha/Stempu*
Telephone	*Simu*
Money	*Pesa/fedha*
How much?	*Pesa ngapi?*
What is the price?	*Bei gani?*
Cheap	*Rahisi*
Expensive	*Ghali sana*
Can you reduce the price a little?	*Waweza kupunguza kidogo?*
I want	*Nataka*
I will buy it	*Nita nunua*
I don't want	*Sitaki*
Big	*-kubwa*
Small	*-dogo*
There is	*Iko*
There isn't any	*Hakuna*
Blouse	*Blauzi*
Cigarettes	*Sigara*
Magazine/newspaper	*Gazeti*
Matches	*Kibiriti*
Shirt	*Shati*
Skirt	*Skati*
Shoes	*Viatu*
Suit	*Suti*
Trousers	*Suruali*

Health and emergencies

Danger	*Hatari*
Help	*Saidia*
Hurry	*Haraka*
Fire	*Moto*
Thief	*Mwizi*

Stop	*Simama*
Police	*Polisi*
Doctor	*Daktari*
Call the police/doctor	*Ita polisi/daktari*
Hospital	*Hospitali*
Dentist	*Daktari wa meno*
Pharmacy	*Duka la dawa*
I'm ill	*Mimi mgonjwa*
Fever	*Homa*
Malaria fever	*Homa ya malaria*
Head	*Kichwa*
Stomach	*Tumbo*
Tooth	*Meno*
Medicine	*Dawa*
Injection	*Sindano*

Driving

Car	*Gari*
Let's go	*Twende*
Road	*Njia*
Highway	*Barabara*
Right	*Kulia*
Left	*Kushoto*
Go straight	*Enda moja kwa moja*
Near	*Karibu*
Far	*Mbali*
Front	*Mbele*
Back	*Nyuma*
Where are you going?	*Una kwenda wapi?*
I'm going to	*Nakwenda*
I'm lost	*Nimepotea*
Show me the way	*Nionyeshe njia*
Is the road ahead passable?	*Nawesa pita njia mbele?*
Where does this road lead to?	*Njia hii ina-enda wapi?*
Stuck	*Kwama*
Can you help push the car?	*Unaweza saidia kusukuma gari?*
Danger	*Hatari*
No entry	*Hakuna njia*
Watch out	*Angalia*
Fierce dog	*Mbwa kali*
Stop here	*Simama hapa*
Wait here	*Ngoja hapa*
My car has broken down	*Gari yango imevunjika*
Mechanic	*Fundi wa magari*
Petrol (Gas)	*Petroli*
Fill it up	*Jaza tenki*
Check the water/oil/tyres (tires)	*Angalia maji/mafuta/mpíra*

At the station, at the airport

Airport	*Uwanja wa ndege*
Bus	*Basi*
Plane	*Ndege*
Taxi	*Teksi*
Train	*Gari la moshi*
Train station	*Stesheni*
Luggage	*Mzigo*
Suitcase	*Sanduku*
Ticket	*Tikiti*
Passport	*Pasi*

At the hotel

To sleep	*Kulala*
To stay	*Kukaa*
I want to stay one/two/three night(s)	*Nataka kaa siku moja/mbili/tatu*
Bath	*Bafu*
Bed	*Kitanda*
Breakfast	*Chakula cha asubuhi*
What time will it be ready?	*Chakula tayari saa ngapi?*
Key	*Kifunguo*
Room	*Chumba*
Water	*Maji*
Hot/cold	*Moto/baridi*
Clean	*Safi*
Dirty	*Chafu*
Can you wake me up at . . .?	*Unaweza kuamkia mimi saa . . .?*

Food and drink

To eat	*Kukula*
To drink	*Kukunywa*
I'm hungry	*Nina njaa*
I'm thirsty	*Nina kiu*
I'd like	*Nataka*
Food	*Chakula*
Could you give/bring me . . .?	*Unaweza nipe/lete . . .?*
More	*Ingine*
A lot	*Mingi*
A little	*Kidogo*
Enough, thank you	*Basi/Imetosha, asante*
Banana	*Ndizi*
Beans	*Maharagwe*
Beef	*Ngombe*
Beer	*Bia/pombe*
Bread	*Mkate*
Butter	*Siagi*
Cake	*Keki*
Carrot	*Karoti*
Cheese	*Jibini*
Chicken	*Kuku*
Coconut	*Nazi*
Coconut milk	*Dafu*
Cod	*Tewa*
Coffee	*Kahawa*
Crab	*Kaa*
Dessert	*Chakula mwisho*
Duck	*Bata*
Eggs	*Mayai*
Fish	*Samaki*
Fried	*Kaanga*
Fruit	*Matunda*
Goat	*Mbuzi*
Grilled	*Choma*
Guinea fowl	*Kanga*
Jam	*Mraba*
Juice	*Maji ya matunda*
Lemon	*Ndimu*
Lime	*Limau*
Lobster	*Kamba*
Maize (corn)	*Mahindi*
Mango	*Embe*
Meat	*Nyama*

Milk	*Maziwa*
Mutton/Lamb	*Kondoo*
Onions	*Vitunguu*
Orange	*Muchungwa*
Pawpaw	*Papai*
Peas	*Mbaazi*
Pepper	*Piripiri*
Pineapple	*Nanasi*
Pork	*Nguruwe*
Potatoes	*Viazi*
Raw	*Mbichi*
Rice	*Mchele/Wali*
Roast	*Choma*
Salt	*Chumvi*
Shrimp	*Kamba kamba*
Soda	*Soda*
Soup	*Mchuzi*
Steak	*Steki*
Sugar	*Sukari*
Sweet	*Tamu*
Tea	*Chai*
Tomatoes	*Nyanya*
Vegetables	*Mboga*
Water	*Maji*

At the restaurant

Bill	*Hesabu*
Bottle	*Chupa*
Chair	*Kiti*
Cup	*Kikombe*
Fork	*Uma*
Glass	*Bilauri*
Knife	*Kisu*
Plate	*Sahani*
Spoon	*Kijiko*
Table	*Mesa*

Sightseeing

Can I take a photo?	*Nawesa kupiga picha?*
Where (is) . . .?	*Wapi . . .?*
Near/Far	*Karibu/Mbali*
Right/Left	*Kulia/Kushoto*
Street/Road	*Barabara*
Church	*Kanisa*
Market	*Soko*
Mosque	*Jaamati*
Forest	*Mwitu*
Hill/Mountain	*Mlima*
River	*Mto*
Tree	*Mti*
Baboon	*Nyani*
Antelope	*Swara*
Buffalo	*Nyati*
Cheetah	*Duma*
Elephant	*Tembo*
Giraffe	*Twiga*
Hippo	*Kiboko*
Hyena	*Fisi*
Leopard	*Chui*
Lion	*Simba*
Rhino	*Kifaru*
Zebra	*Punda milia*

SUGGESTED READING

Adamson, George. *A Lifetime with Lions* (Doubleday, 1968).

Adamson, Joy. *Born Free* (Doubleday, 1960).

— *Joy Adamson's Africa* (Harcourt Brace Jovanovich, 1972).

— *Peoples of Kenya* (Bantam, 1060).

Beard, Peter. *The End of the Game* (Doubleday, 1963).

Dinesen, Isak. *Out of Africa* (Modern Library, 1987).

Eldon, K. (compiled by). *Safari Diary, Kenya* (Kenway, 1986).

Farson, Negley. *Behind God's Back* (Harcourt Brace Jovanovich, 1985).

Fedder, A. and Salvadori, C. *Peoples and Cultures of Kenya* (KTDC, 1979).

Gellhorn, Martha. *The Weather in Africa* (Avon, 1981).

Grant, Nellie and Huxley, Elspeth. *Nellie's Story* (Morrow, 1980).

Huxley, Elspeth. *The Flame Trees of Thika* (Penguin, 1982).

— *Settlers of Kenya* (Greenwood, 1975).

Kenyatta, Jomo. *Facing Mount Kenya* (Heinemann, 1978).

Markham, Beryl. *West with the Night* (North Point Press, 1983).

Martin, Esmond, and Martin, Chrysee Bradley. *Run Rhino Run* (Chatto & Windus, 1983).

Matthiessen, Peter. *The Tree Where Man was Born* (Dutton, 1972).

Mbiti, J. *African Religions and Philosophy* (Doubleday, 1969).

Mboya, Tom. *Freedom and After* (Little, Brown and Co., 1963).

Miller, Charles. *The Lunatic Express* (MacMillan, 1971).

Moorehead, Alan. *The Blue Nile* (Random House, 1960).

— *The White Nile* (Dell, 1962).

Moss, C.J. *Portraits in the Wild* (Houghton Mifflin, 1975).

Mountains of Kenya (Mountain Club of Kenya, 1969).

Ogot, Methwell A. *Historical Dictionary of Kenya* (Scarecrow Press, 1981).

Ricciardi, Mirella. *Vanishing Africa* (Holt Rinehart & Winston, 1977).

Saitoti, Tepilit Ole, and Beckwith, Carol. *Maasai* (Abrams, 1988).

Schmid, John. *The Kenya Magic* (Beachwood Publications, 1983).

Thurman, Judith. *Isak Dinesen: The Life of a Storyteller* (St. Martins Press, 1985).

Trzebinski, Errol. *The Kenya Pioneers* (Norton, 1986).

Waugh, Evelyn. *A Tourist in Africa* (Little, Brown and Co., 1977).

Williams, J.G. *A Field Guide to the National Parks of East Africa* (Collins, 1967).

KENYA'S ANIMAL SPECIES

MAMMALS: CARNIVORES

Aard-wolf *(Proteles cristatus)*,
African wild cat *(Felis lybica)*,
Caracal *(Felis caracal)*,
Cheetah *(Acinonyx jubatus)*,
Civit *(Viverridae)*,
Genet *(Viverridae)*,
Hyena
> spotted hyena *(Crocuta crocuta)*,
> striped hyena *(hyaena hyaena)*,

Jackal
> golden jackal *(canis aureus)*,
> black-blacked or silver-backed jackal *(Canis mesomelas)*,

Leopard *(Panthera pardus)*,
Lion *(Panthera leo)*,
Mangoose *(Viverridae)*,
Serval *(Felis serval)*,
Wild dog *(Lycaon pictus)*,

MAMMALS: INSECTIVORES AND RODENTS

Striped ground squirrel *(Funisciurus lemniscatus)*,
Yellow-rumped elephant shrew *(Rhyncocyon chrysopagus)*,

MAMMALS: PRIMATES

Baboon *(Papio paio)*,
Tana mangabey *(Cercocebus galeritus)*,
Brazza monkey *(Cercopithecus neglectus)*,
Colobus
> black and white colobus *(Colobus angolensis)*,
> red colobus *(Colobus badius)*,

Galago *(Galago senegalensis)*,
Black-faced vervet *(Cercopithecus aethiops)*,

MAMMALS: HERBIVORES

Bongo *(Boocercus eurycerus)*,
Buffalo, African *(Syncerus caffer)*,
Derby eland *(Taurotragus derbianus)*,
Hartebeest *(Alcelaphus sp.)*,
Hippopotamus *(Hippopotamus amphibius)*,
Hunter's hartebeest or Hirola *(Damaliscus hunteri)*,
Elephant *(Loxondota africana)*,
Gazelles
> Grant's gazelle *(Gazella granti)*,
> Thomson's gazelle *(Gazella thomsoni)*,

Gerenuk *(Litocranius walleri)*,
Giraffes
> Rothschild's giraffe *(Giraffa camelopardalis rothschildii)*,
> reticulated giraffe *(Giraffa reticulata)*,

Impala *(Aepyceros melampus)*,
Klipspringer *(Oreotragus oreotragus)*,
Kudu
> lesser kudu *(Tragelaphus imberbi)*,
> greater kudu *(Tragelaphus strepsiceros)*,

Oribi *(Ourebia ourebi)*,
Oryx *(Oryx sp.)*,
Rhinoceros
> Black rhinoceros *(Diceros bicornis)*,
> White, or square-lipped, rhinoceros *(Ceratotherium simum)*,

Roan antelope *(Hippotragus equinus)*,
Sable antelope *(Hippotragus niger)*,
Sitatunga *(Tragelaphus spekei)*,

Tiang *(Damaliscus korrigum tiang),*
Topi (Damaliscus korrigum topi),
Waterbuck
    common waterbuck *(Kobus ellipsiprymmus),*
    Defassa waterbuck *(Kobus defassa),*
Wildebeest or **gnu** *(Connochaetes taurinus),*
Zebra
    Burchell's zebra *(Equus burchelli),*
    Grevy's zebra *(Equus grevyi),*

REPTILES

Crocodiles
    American crocodile *(Crocodylus acutus),*
    Nile crocodile *(Crocodylus niloticus),*
Gila monster *(Heloderma suspectum),*
Monitor lizard *(Varanidae),*
Snakes
    Aesculapian snake *(Elaphe longissima),*
    boomslang *(Dispholidus typus),*
    cobra *(Naja sp.),*
    mamba *(Dendroapsis sp.),*
    puff adder *(Bitis arietans),*
    rock python *(Pytho sebae),*
Tortoises
    giant land tortoise *(Testudo elephantopus),*
    side-necked turtles *(Pelomedusa subrufa* and *Pelusios castaneus),*
    soft shelled turtle *(Trionyx triunguis),*
Turtles, Marine
    green turtle *(Chelonia mydas),*
    hawksbill turtle *(Eretmochelys imbricata),*
    loggerhead *(Caretta caretta),*

BIRDS

Avocet *(Recurvirostra avosetta),*
Cormorant or **shag** *(Phalacrocoracidae),*
Egret *(Egretta),*
Flamingo *(Phoenicopteridae),*
Guinea-fowl *(Numida meleagris),*
Hemprich's hornbill *(Tockus hemprichii),*
Heron *(Ardeidae),*
Ibis *(Plataleidae),*
Kingfisher *(Alcedinidae),*
Lammergeier or **Bearded vulture** *(Gypaetus barbatus),*
Marabou *(Leptoptilos crumeniferus),*
Martins *(Hirundinidae),*
Ostrich *(Struthiornidae),*
Owl *(Stigidae),*
Plover *(Charadriidae),*
Pratincole *(Glareola pratincola),*
Saddle-billed stork *(Ephippiorhynchus senegalensis),*
Secretary bird *(Sagittarius serpentarius),*
Starling *(Sturnidae),*
Stork *(Ciconiidae),*
Sunbird *(Nectariniidae),*
Swallows *(Hirundinidae),*
Turaco *(Tauraco sp.),*
    Schalow's turaco *(Tauraco schalowi),*
Vulture *(Accipitcidae),*
Wading birds *(Ardeinae),*
Weaver *(Ploceidae),*

▬ INDEX